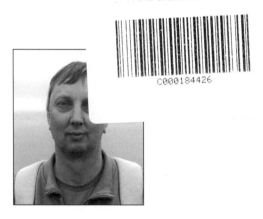

Peter Caton was born in 1960 and has always lived in Upminster, Essex. He is married with two children. After training as a polymer chemist, he set up his own business testing and manufacturing adhesives. He has a keen interest in walking, the countryside and conservation and is a member of many environmental organisations. His other interests include travelling and football (he is a West Ham season ticket holder) and he is a member of Upminster Methodist Church.

More photographs of the islands and travels, and information on the author's other books can be seen at:

**www.petercatonbooks.co.uk**

# NO BOAT REQUIRED

EXPLORING TIDAL ISLANDS

PETER CATON

Matador
5 Weir Road
Kibworth Beauchamp
Leicester LE8 0LQ, UK
Tel: (+44) 116 279 2299
Fax: (+44) 116 279 2277
Email: books@troubador.co.uk
Web: www.troubador.co.uk/matador

ISBN 978 1848767 010

British Library Cataloguing in Publication Data.
A catalogue record for this book is available from the British Library.

Typeset in Sabon MT by Troubador Publishing Ltd, Leicester, UK
Printed and bound in the UK by TJ International, Padstow, Cornwall

**Matador** is an imprint of Troubador Publishing Ltd

*To Debbie*

# CONTENTS

# INTRODUCTION

Picture the scene: It's August 1974. A small boat is heading to the Farne Islands off the Northumbrian coast. Seventy or so passengers are enjoying views of rocky islands with spectacular cliffs and watching the huge numbers of puffins, guillemot and fulmar. One more, a long haired and slightly lanky teenage lad, has his head in a bucket. OK you might want to stop picturing it too vividly now. The boat lands on Outer Farne. The lad almost steps on an eider duck camouflaged in the grass and finds three eggs in a rough nest on the rocks. Little else does he see but the inside of a bucket as the boat tosses and turns its way back to Seahouses. Perhaps his parents shouldn't have been surprised; he had once been sick in a rowing boat in Torquay Harbour. Perhaps the lad shouldn't have refused a Kwell.

And picture the scene thirty four years later as the lad with the bucket, now middle aged, of wider girth and shorter hair, walks the length of the Essex coast. He rediscovers the beauty of the sort of places his parents took him to as a child and writes a book describing the walk, the coast, its history and its wildlife. As he walks he passes many islands, which to him, like most of our island nation, hold a special appeal. Then he realises that many of these islands can be walked to when the tide is low. An idea starts to brew. We've all heard of St Michael's Mount and Holy Island, but how many other islands can be walked to? As the last stretches of the Essex coast are completed plans are mulled over and a decision made.

I would visit all the islands which could be walked to from the UK mainland - islands for which 'no boat is required'. No one else had written a book about tidal islands, or as far as I knew visited them all. Like *Essex Coast Walk*, it would be a first, an opportunity to travel to most parts of our coast, to share this with readers and to document hitherto unpublished information on tidal islands.

First I needed a way to select and define a tidal island, but just defining an island isn't as straightforward as it sounds. The 1861 census classified an island as *'any piece of solid land surrounded by water which affords sufficient vegetation to support one or two sheep, or is inhabited by man'*. It would have been perhaps a little too time consuming to carry a sheep or two around the coast with me to check if each potential island had adequate supplies of grass, but size would obviously be a factor, although not the sole criteria. Some quite small islands are of particular interest, but they would have to be named. The island would have to support vegetation (just rocks wouldn't count) and show some evidence of human activity past or present. I would exclude islands that can be reached by bridge, but the definition of what constitutes a tidal island is more difficult.

The common definition that *'a tidal island is a piece of land that is connected to the mainland by a natural or man-made causeway that is exposed at low tide and submerged at high tide'* was not sufficient. Many don't have defined causeways and some are cut off only a few times a year, whilst others only walkable very occasionally. A reasonable limit seemed to be that it was both cut off and accessible on foot at least once a month. But what does walkable mean? I decided that it would have to be reachable with dry feet, although on a couple of occasions that was stretched to dry whilst wearing wellingtons. In order to limit numbers and prevent the necessity for travel by boat, islands were to be restricted to those that can be walked to from the UK mainland, hence excluding Northern Ireland and the considerable number of islands off other islands.

A final, but overriding factor was safety. Many people have been drowned crossing to tidal islands and I didn't wish to add to the toll. Nor did I wish to encourage others to take risks, hence you will read plenty of warnings in the book. If an island could be walked to provided one uses common sense, has knowledge of tides and safe routes and takes suitable advice, including using a local guide where necessary, I would include it. I would not take undue risks, but neither would I allow the current trend for overbearing 'Health & Safety' to curtail travels which armed with adequate information I did not consider dangerous.

For the purposes of this book my definition of a tidal island was thus:

*A named area of land of significant size, which supports vegetation, shows signs of human activity, can be safely walked to with dry feet at least once a month from the UK mainland, is totally surrounded by water on a minimum of one tide each month, but never totally submerged.*

Initial investigation suggested about 20 islands met this definition. Had I known the final number would be 43 perhaps I'd have reconsidered the whole plan. Added to this I have written a little about, and visited a few of what I've called 'nearly tidal islands'. These are islands which for reasons such as size, bridges, unsafe access, or tides, fail to meet my definition, although some may class them as tidal.

With two sons and a wife to keep happy, plus a business to run, (a glue factory in Purfleet), and the constraints of tides, my initial thought of a single clockwise trip around the coast proved hopelessly impossible. Eventually I made 30 trips, sometimes to just one island and sometimes to several in an area. Depending on the significance of each island, it may have a chapter to itself, or the chapter may cover all those visited in one trip.

I've also written a little about the journeys that took me to most parts of our country's beautiful coastline and which for environmental reasons wherever possible I made using public transport, with usually a walk from the train or bus. The crossings to the islands were of course made on foot – some easy, others less so, but each is described and may assist or perhaps deter others who may wish to follow in my footsteps.

Most importantly I have written about the islands in what I hope is an accessible style and without becoming a guidebook, as *No Boat Required* is intended as a narrative to be read from start to end. For each one I've aimed to include information on its history and wildlife, to share interesting and amusing stories and to describe the island as I saw it.

Often I've spoken to those living on or responsible for managing the islands, gaining an insight into the unique nature of these special islands.

Sometimes there was little information to be discovered about an island so I've included almost all that I found, but for a few islands there is already far more published than I could find space for. For the former this book may provide perhaps the only written record about the island, and for the latter it aims to summarise what is of most interest, written from my own perspective as a visitor. In these cases I have noted other sources of information which the reader may wish to use should they wish to learn more.

Information was obtained from numerous sources, too many to mention, although I've often put the acknowledgement in the text. I've researched information as much as reasonably possible and made every effort to ensure that all facts are accurate, but will be happy to be corrected if otherwise. Where sources gave conflicting information and unless one is overwhelmingly in a minority, I've either stated this or been less than definite in my wording. In Upminster we are fortunate to have an excellent independent book shop and I'm grateful to Jeremy Scott from Swan Books (www.swanbooks.co.uk) for his help in tracking down various elusive island books. A list of the main books from which I have obtained information is shown in Appendix Three.

As well as historical facts, I've included some stories which whilst interesting, cannot always be verified. My observations and experiences of journeys and islands are recorded as they happened. Many travel writers make up or exaggerate incidents to add interest or humour. When done well this often adds to the enjoyment, but it can have the opposite result. With a scientific rather than journalistic training, I have kept to the truth, resisting the temptation to embellish.

I make no apologies for using mixed imperial and metric units, as this is one of the idiosyncrasies of the current English language. Like most people I say miles, so that's what I've written. Being of the generation who were bought up on yards, it feels right to use these rather than metres, but in most contexts 'a few yards' or 'a few metres' is pretty much the same. Conversion results in either loss of accuracy if staying with round numbers, or what can be worse, a precise conversion of a rounded number (say 100 yards to 91 metres), implying a greater degree of accuracy than may be correct. Generally I've stayed with whatever units the source quoted, but for area I've used square miles or acres, as I've yet to meet anyone who has any idea how big a hectare is.

You will read of the challenges of my journeys, whether they be from lost bus drivers, disappearing footpaths, precipitous cliffs, glutinous mud, hostile island owners, or the sea and its tides. I have retold many tales of people being stranded, rescued and occasionally drowned when visiting our tidal islands. There is a potential risk involved in walking to the islands, but with care and adequate planning this is generally minimal. As with climbing mountains, to reach some of the islands requires effort and occasionally things can go wrong. My goal was not to reach summits, but to visit all of our 43 tidal islands and probably be the first person to have done so. Attaining each goal was however as rewarding as reaching mountain tops and the views, although very different, often as spectacular.

I hope that I have been able to portray the beauty, charm and history of these often little known islands, and perhaps inspire others to seek them out.

# WARNING

Many people have been drowned in attempting to walk to and from tidal islands, and many more lives have been saved by emergency services. Whilst with suitable care all the islands described can be safely visited, it is essential that one has information on tide times, safe crossing periods and routes. The only safe way to visit a few of the islands is with a qualified local guide. Tide times can be found locally or through www.easytide.com and information on routes and safety hazards from tourist information centres.

Visits to a number of the islands are only permitted by arrangement with the owner and some are restricted for part or all of the year to avoid disturbing nesting birds. For the sake of our wildlife please observe such restrictions and above all do not take unnecessary risks. The author accepts no liability for any harm that should befall any person visiting tidal islands.

Remember that the islands are beautiful places, but the sea, mud and cliffs are all potential killers.

Be prepared and take care!

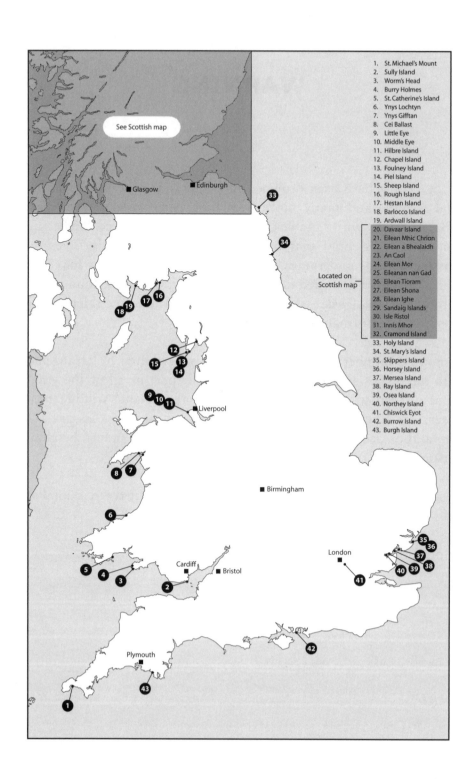

See Scottish map

■ Glasgow    ■ Edinburgh

Located on
Scottish map

1.  St. Michael's Mount
2.  Sully Island
3.  Worm's Head
4.  Burry Holmes
5.  St. Catherine's Island
6.  Ynys Lochtyn
7.  Ynys Gifftan
8.  Cei Ballast
9.  Little Eye
10. Middle Eye
11. Hilbre Island
12. Chapel Island
13. Foulney Island
14. Piel Island
15. Sheep Island
16. Rough Island
17. Hestan Island
18. Barlocco Island
19. Ardwall Island
20. Davaar Island
21. Eilean Mhic Chrion
22. Eilean a Bhealaidh
23. An Caol
24. Eilean Mor
25. Eileanan nan Gad
26. Eilean Tioram
27. Eilean Shona
28. Eilean Ighe
29. Sandaig Islands
30. Isle Ristol
31. Innis Mhor
32. Cramond Island
33. Holy Island
34. St. Mary's Island
35. Skippers Island
36. Horsey Island
37. Mersea Island
38. Ray Island
39. Osea Island
40. Northey Island
41. Chiswick Eyot
42. Burrow Island
43. Burgh Island

■ Liverpool

■ Birmingham

■ Cardiff    ■ Bristol

London
■

Plymouth

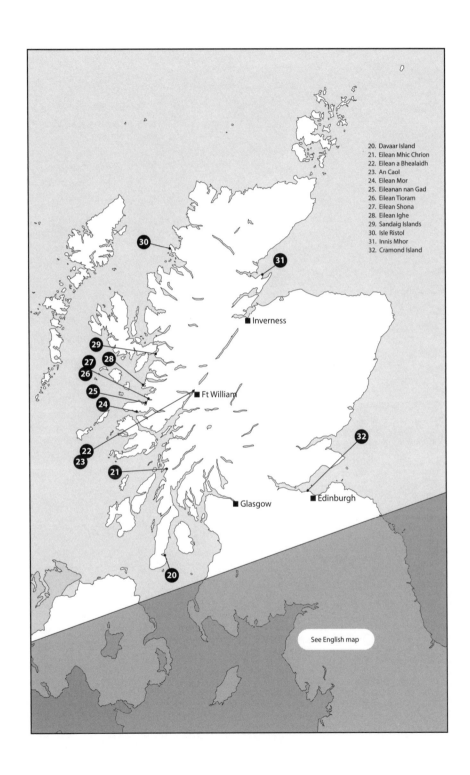

20. Davaar Island
21. Eilean Mhic Chrion
22. Eilean a Bhealaidh
23. An Caol
24. Eilean Mor
25. Eileanan nan Gad
26. Eilean Tioram
27. Eilean Shona
28. Eilean Ighe
29. Sandaig Islands
30. Isle Ristol
31. Innis Mhor
32. Cramond Island

Inverness

Ft William

Glasgow

Edinburgh

See English map

# CHAPTER ONE

# ST MICHAEL'S MOUNT

What better way to travel can there be than the Night Riviera to Penzance? Board the train late evening in London and wake up next morning in Cornwall, refreshed and ready for a day by the sea. Arriving early at Paddington, I found the purple and red coaches already waiting at Platform Three, a big green diesel engine gently ticking over at the front, ready to haul sleeping passengers 300 miles to the far west of England. At the appointed hour of ten thirty the doors were opened and passengers welcomed on board. My fellow travellers (and travellers we were, not merely passengers or customers) a mixture of holiday makers, business people and West Country folk returning home from the Capital. Friendly stewards showed us to our cabins, checking names against lists, taking orders for breakfast and times for wake up calls. Settling down in my little cabin (air conditioned with hot & cold water, wash kit and even a television screen), I was tucked up in bed by the time we pulled out of Paddington. Asleep before midnight, I was to wake up in Cornwall. Why would anyone want to fly?

St Michael's Mount is just off the village of Marazion, near Penzance. As probably the best known of Britain's tidal islands and situated almost at the tip of the country, it seemed an appropriate starting point for my travels. A picturesque rocky island, topped with a castle that was built on the remains of a monastery, St Michael's Mount is one of Cornwall's most popular tourist sites, a place of pilgrimage and not least, a home. Around 35 people live here. The island is managed by the St Aubyn family, who have lived in the castle since the mid 17th century, but is now mostly owned by the National Trust, into whose capable hands the family donated it in 1954, ensuring the preservation and conservation of the monument.

I awoke to find the train stationary. Pulling up the blind, I looked out the window to see another train alongside and a passenger staring in at me as I stood bleary eyed in my pyjamas. Needless to say I quickly replaced the blind, waiting until we were drawing out of the station to look out once more and to find that we were in Truro. As I started to dress there was a knock on the cabin door – the steward bringing my breakfast. In my state of semi-nakedness I asked her to wait a moment as I struggled to pull up my underpants, an operation which invariably takes at least twice as long when performed with urgency. There was immediately another knock and once again I asked her to wait, but this time the door opened – then rapidly shut with much apology. Nothing was said of the incident when she returned a few minutes later with my croissant and jam.

Approaching Penzance I caught my first sight of St Michael's Mount in the early morning sunshine, rising majestically 230 feet out of the sea and dominating the bay. Visible from miles around and near the south westerly tip of England, it was the first in the line of beacons lit to warn of the arrival of the Spanish Armada. The railway runs right by the sea and must be one of the most picturesque coastal sections of track in England. As we pulled into the station the steward told me she was born in Marazion, had been doing this job for ten years and never got tired of the views. I assumed she meant the sea and not gentlemen's bottoms!

It's an easy three mile walk around the gentle curve of Mounts Bay to Marazion. A cycle route starts from the bus station by the harbour and a path runs on the sea wall all the way. You can hardly go wrong, or so I thought. Two parallel concrete paths run between walls and not noticing the sign, I took the outer, but after a few hundred yards this came to an abrupt stop at a locked gate. I clambered down to the beach and continued here. Walking was easy on the hard sand until I reached two small rivers. The first I crossed by hopping from stone to stone. The second was wider and would have required removal of shoes and rolling up of trousers if I was not to get wet. I took what seemed the simpler option of climbing over the sea defence rocks onto the sea wall. Unfortunately as I clambered there were several ominous ripping sounds and a look downwards showed a large and rather indecent tear in the front of my trousers.

Anxious to reach the Mount before the tide covered the causeway, I made rapid progress along the sea wall. The occasional train passed by on the tracks to my left and from the heliport a helicopter took off noisily on its short trip to the Scilly Isles. Unlike the paths of Essex, this one was quite busy and I bode good morning to a succession of elderly ladies walking their dogs and nodded at younger ladies taking their early morning jog. Each time I ensured that my hand and water bottle were strategically placed to cover any embarrassment beneath the ripped trousers. A handy toilet provided the opportunity to change into shorts. It was still a bit cool, but whilst my legs may not be the most pleasant sight, revealing them was at least unlikely to have me arrested.

I'd emailed the island's office to get tide times and Clare Sandry advised that it would probably be possible to walk across until 10.30, but this would depend on the weather. Looking towards the distant island it seemed there was nothing but water between it and the shore, and I feared I may be too late. Seeing what looked like a boat leaving the island appeared to confirm my doubts, but then I realised it was a small van. Vehicles can drive across to service the Mount, and although from afar the van seemed to be driving through the sea, the raised causeway was clear.

The walk from Penzance took exactly an hour and at 9.00 I joined what was already a trickle of visitors on the cobbled stone causeway. Without crossing over water it didn't quite seem that I was going to an island, but as soon as I'd gone up the gentle slope to the Mount's tiny 18th century village I could sense a real atmosphere. Staff were pottering about getting ready for the day's influx of tourists and the few visitors already here wandered respectfully around the harbour, cottages and old buildings that were once the pubs, stables and net lofts of a small community. Everyone spoke quietly, almost with reverence for the island. This must be the best time to experience St Michael's Mount – early morning when the sun is out, but before the masses arrive.

To many it is a spiritual place. Pilgrims have been coming here since the 5th century when some local fishermen saw a vision of St Michael over the Mount. It was visited by the Welsh Saint Cadoc and there is some evidence that a religious community lived here before the Norman invasion. A Benedictine Priory was built in 1135 under the authority of the Abbot of Mont St. Michel, a similar tidal island in France. Despite the number of monks dwindling to just two when the Black Death swept through England in the 14th century, the monastery survived until the dissolution by Henry VIII, whose commissioners took all the valuable items from the church.

One of the relics that attracted pilgrims was the jaw bone of St. Appollonia of Alexandria, who for refusing to worship the city's idol had her teeth pulled out one by one, and after electing to be burned to death rather than renounce Christ, became the patron saint of toothache.

By the harbour was the *St Michael*, a boat with wheels. With a number plate allowing use on the roads, but the hull and superstructure of a boat, this is a lifeline for the islanders when winter storms cover the causeway and prevent small boats leaving the harbour. The castle and gardens don't open until 10.30, but the café was doing good business as we all waited. I sat outside with a drink, watching a long snake of German tourists head across the sand from the coach park to join what was now a steady stream of visitors crossing the causeway.

The island shop was open and I bought a copy of John St. Aubyn's *St Michael's Mount Illustrated Historical Guide*, to which I am indebted for much information on the Mount's history. The queue for castle tickets started just after 10.00, but as a National Trust member I simply had to show my card. More and more people arrived, some sitting on the harbour wall and others milling about, as we waited for the castle to open. I sat for a while by the harbour on one of the bollards which date back to the days that tall sailing ships moored here. Some were constructed from the barrels of old guns that were no longer required to defend the castle after the end of the Napoleonic Wars.

A set of railway tracks ran from the harbour wall, disappearing under a blue gate. A little girl asked her mother what they were and at that instant a man appeared through the gate. He explained that there's a little train that runs up to the castle. It was built in 1905 and is still used every day to carry the family's shopping through a tunnel, saving the steep walk up the hill that was once done by pack horses. He told her that you can see the train if you look over the wall. After glancing over a number of walls, interested to see it, but not wishing to appear too keen, I found it. Not quite a train in the common sense of the word, but more a long box on wheels that's pulled by a rope, the 'railway' is 200 metres long. Originally powered by water, it is now electric

It's a steep and winding path to the castle. Part way up is a well, which according to the island's most famous legend, was once used to catch a giant. Many years ago a giant named Cormoran lived on the Mount. He used to wade ashore and steal cows and sheep from the villagers to feed his gargantuan appetite. One night, Jack, a local Cornish boy, rowed out to the Mount while the giant was asleep. All night long he dug a deep pit, then as the sun rose blew a horn to wake him. Angrily Cormoran rushed down the Mount, but with the rising sun in his eyes, couldn't see Jack. The giant fell into the pit and died and the boy was given the rather unimaginative title of 'Jack the Giant-Killer' by the grateful villagers.

The path comes out on a terrace just below the castle entrance. Here cannons and battlements face west across Mounts Bay. The castle was built with heavy fortifications and over the centuries has seen many battles and sieges. In 1193, when King Richard the First was being held prisoner in Austria on his way back from the third crusade to the Holy Land, the Mount was captured by Henry de la Pomeray in the name of the King's brother John, who was attempting to seize the throne. Pomeray had fled to Cornwall from Devon after stabbing in the heart a Sergeant-at-Arms, who had been sent to arrest him for failing to pay taxes and murdering a tax collector. Clearly not the nicest of men, Pomeray refused to surrender the Mount when King Richard returned and pardoned his brother (who later became King John). An army was sent to besiege the castle, upon sight of which Pomeray was so frightened that he apparently surrendered without resistance. According to some accounts he died of fright. Others say that he bequeathed part of his land to the island's monks and part to the Knights of St John of Jerusalem, requesting that they pray for his soul, and having done so caused himself to bleed to death. They do say that bullies are the biggest cowards. After Pomeray's death King Richard gave full possession of the Mount to the monks and placed a small garrison of soldiers in the fort.

In 1473 St Michael's Mount was captured once more. This time by the Earl of Oxford, who entered the Mount with his men disguised as pilgrims, but then produced weapons from under their cloaks and forced the monks and military garrison to hand over the island.

Four years later Perkin Warbeck arrived in Cornwall from Ireland, claiming to be Richard Duke of York, the younger of the two princes who had disappeared from the Tower of London, having almost certainly been murdered by their uncle, Richard III. A well educated young man of great charm, Warbeck made a very credible imposter and fooled many, including King James IV of Scotland who allowed him to marry his beautiful daughter Lady Katherine Gordon. Warbeck was warmly welcomed in Cornwall and captured St Michael's Mount, where he left his wife and young son as he marched eastwards. At Bodmin he was proclaimed to be King Richard IV and joined by 3,000 followers, however a siege of Exeter was less successful. Warbeck was captured and taken as prisoner to the real king – Henry VII. The King's cavalry continued to St Michael's Mount, where they found Katherine and took her prisoner. Henry was said to have marvelled at her charm and sent her to the Queen in London with an escort of honourable matrons. Perkin Warbeck was hanged two years later after being accused of involvement in another conspiracy, but Katherine remained faithful until his death. Even when he was forced to confess to her that he was an imposter, she is reputed to have said that it was the man and not the king that she loved.

I have to admit that whilst I like a quick look round stately homes, it's generally the exterior, grounds and gardens that I find of most interest. And so it was with the castle. While some visitors will stop to read every information board and scrutinise every picture (I once had an aunt who took an excruciating amount of time looking for family likenesses in each portrait), I'm generally content with a wander through, pausing only at rooms of particular interest or beauty. Hence I stopped at the Chevy Chase room. This was originally the monks' refectory and the walls were probably built by Abbot Bernard in the 12th century. With its wood beamed roof, royal coat of arms over the fireplace, plasterwork hunting frieze, Cromwellian armour and centrepiece of an early 17th century oak table, the room has much character.

Visitors emerge onto a terrace, with views out to sea and down the steep hillside to the gardens, which were designed to be viewed from above. The chapel entrance is from the terrace and this is another building of great history and atmosphere. Much of the architecture is 14th century, as the original chapel had to be largely rebuilt after an earthquake in 1275, however the base is almost certainly that of the first church which was consecrated in 1135. The sun shone in through the beautiful east stained glass rose window, giving a quality of light often lacking in old churches.

During building work in the late 19th century a low doorway was discovered on the right of the altar, with steps leading down to an underground chamber. In this dungeon was found the body of a man over seven feet tall. Who he was and why he was imprisoned here, has never been discovered. A stairway from the chapel leads up the tower, from which lamps used to guide fishing boats home. On the top of the tower is a chair projecting over a precipitous drop to the sea. It's said that the first of a newly wed couple to win a race to the top and sit on the chair will rule the household. If only I'd known that 28 years ago!

Services are still held regularly in the chapel, which was originally part of the priory. In 1977 it took on a new role when H.R.H. the Duke of Gloucester, Grand Prior of the Order of St John, attended a service of investiture of the order. The church is now recognised as a place of prayer and pilgrimage for members of this Christian order, which helps people across the world and is best known for its work with St. John Ambulance.

The tour route enters the castle living areas once more. The blue drawing rooms, which were converted from a ruined Lady Chapel and contain Chippendale chairs and fine Rococo Gothic plasterwork, held my attention for a few minutes. Visitors then walk through a tunnel which was cut by miners during a time of recession in the tin industry. It is likely that the St Aubyn family had the tunnel made more out of kindness to provide work for the unemployed miners, than for the need of another passageway in the castle.

On the path back down from the castle is a sentry box that had been built to help with defence of the island during the Civil War. In 1640 the Mount had been sold by the Earl of Salisbury to Francis Basset, a Cornish landowner, who became a leading Royalist military commander when the war broke out in 1642. He increased the garrison of soldiers and strengthened defences, the island being of great importance to the King as ammunition from France was imported to the harbour in exchange for Cornish tin. Francis Basset took a leading role in the fighting, leaving his wife Anne in change of the Mount. In 1644 he was knighted by the King, but died a year later, with his brother Sir Arthur Basset succeeding him as Governor of the Mount. By now the Royalists were facing defeat and the Parliamentary army under General Fairfax advanced across Cornwall. On 12th March the Royalist army in the county surrendered, but the garrisons at St Michaels' Mount and at Pendennis Castle near Falmouth, held out. The Parliamentarians began a siege of the Mount and after mounting an honourable defence Basset took the advice of the Duke of Hamilton, who was being kept prisoner in the castle, and surrendered. Grateful that they had avoided a long and expensive siege, the Parliamentary leaders allowed Basset and his officers to sail with their arms to the Isles of Scilly, which were still loyal to the King.

The castle gardens are open to the public less often than the castle, but were the highlight of my visit. Buffeted by gales and continually drenched with salt spray in winter, in summer they become a tranquil oasis, warmed by the Gulf Stream and heat retentive granite cliffs. The warmth and shelter of the south facing cliff allows a wide variety of tender and exotic sub-tropical plants to be grown here. Early May was a good time to visit, with many plants in flower and the steeply tiered terraces awash with colour.

Visitors first walk through a grassy area with shrubs and in spring, a mass of bluebells. The large number of bluebells on the island is thought to date back to prehistoric times, when a forest grew in the bay before incursion of the sea, which was thought to have occurred in Roman times. By the shore is one of the three Second World War blockhouses which were built around the base of the island to defend against possible attack from German submarines. A platoon of infantry was stationed here, in what must have been one of the army's more pleasant postings, although on one occasion the village was machine-gunned by enemy aircraft.

Beneath the castle walls a maze of paths and steps criss-cross the steep cliffs. Above, the castle stands majestically, the view from beneath showing how well the new Victorian wing which was built under the flat terrace roof, had been blended into the original buildings. Below the steepest cliffs (so steep that gardeners have to abseil to tend parts of them), are the walled gardens. These were built in the 1780s having been designed by two daughters of the fourth St Aubyn Baronet. Cultivation of the gardens would have taken place much earlier though, with monks growing herbs and vegetables. The borage and soapwort that grow wild on the island probably descend from plants tended by medieval monks.

Many of the garden's plants originate from the southern hemisphere.

Some remain from experiments by Reverend Boscawen of Ludgaven, a noted plant collector with contacts in Australia, New Zealand and South Africa, and a good friend of Lord St Levan, baron of the Mount. Trials were carried out to see which plants would survive in the Mount's salt laden winds and despite the harsh conditions, many thrived here. Amongst the more exotic plants in the garden are sparmania africana, giant agave, aloes, yuccas and strelitzia.

There are two places to eat on the Mount: The Island Café near the garden entrance, which was once the castle laundry and the more upmarket National Trust Sail Loft Restaurant behind the harbour. I chose the former and enjoyed an excellent Cornish pasty (made in St Ives) sitting outside in the sunshine, watching over the causeway. This was now under water, but the last few intrepid visitors were paddling across, saving the £1.50 fare for the ferry boats which had just started running. Although only covered to a depth of around five feet, currents are often strong and it can be extremely risky to try to wade to the island.

I spent a while wandering around the village once more. St Michael's Mount is thought to have been the site of a tin port in the late Iron Age and trading was carried out here until the 19th century. Tin and copper were exported and in 1727 the harbour expanded to promote this trade and the import of timber from Norway. By 1811 it supported a population of three hundred, with fifty three houses, three schools, a Wesleyan Chapel and three public houses. The last of these, The St Aubyn Arms, still stands. It's now a private house, the pub being shut in 1902 after it is said that some of the islanders, having had too much to drink, were disrespectful to King Edward VII as he arrived to visit the Mount.

Although there were now more visitors on the island, with the castle and garden open, they were well spread out. Whilst only 27 acres, the Mount seemed able to absorb a large number of people without losing the serenity that I'd experienced in the early morning. St Michael's Mount is our second most popular tidal island, 211,000 people visiting the castle in 2010 and many more making the crossing but not the climb. With the harbour now full of water and the causeway covered, it was now truly an island, but even when joined to the mainland had seemed very much a special place – a small community and not a part of Marazion 450 yards across the sands.

I wandered around the harbour, reluctant to leave, but knowing I had a train to catch back to London. At the top of the steps where I boarded a little boat back to the mainland, is an imprint of Queen Victoria's foot, made when she landed here from her royal barge in 1846. Her diary records that the housekeeper was 'a nice tidy old woman' and that the church organ which Prince Albert played 'sounded very fine'. Half a dozen boats were running to and fro, dropping and collecting visitors at Chapel Rock on the sands. There was once a chapel here dedicated to the Virgin Mary, where pilgrims may have prayed while waiting for the tide to fall and allow them to complete the final stretch of their journeys. When the tide is higher the ferries run to Marazion harbour or Gwelva by the sea wall.

There was time for a quick look around Marazion, a pleasant little town with some nice pubs and restaurants looking out on the island. It has a long history, being Cornwall's oldest chartered town and for many centuries was more important than Penzance, but is now mainly known as the setting off point for St Michael's Mount. I considered catching a bus back to Penzance, but instead chose to walk, stopping every so often to look back on the Mount, which was by now very much an island, with no indication that one can walk to it for several hours each day.

Before catching the 16.00 train back to London I'd allowed a little time for a necessary bit of shopping – a trip to Millets for a new pair of trousers, providing warmth and more importantly preserving my decency on the long journey home.

# CHAPTER TWO

# SULLY ISLAND

---

**FOR SALE £1,250,000**

Island 14.55 Acres
Causeway Access
Panoramic Views, Severn Estuary
Rare Flora and Fauna
Commission Your Own Stamps

SULLY ISLAND!!!! Available for the first time in nearly 30 years! A rare and unique opportunity to acquire a Welsh landmark. Sully Island is located 450 metres off the South Wales coast in close proximity to Cardiff and Penarth. Sully Island covers 14½ acres with outstanding views over the Severn estuary, home to rare flora and fauna with a dinosaur footprint from the Triassic period found nearby. The owner of the island can even commission their own stamps.

Unaccompanied viewings can be undertaken but extreme care must be exercised.

**Chris John + Partners – Cardiff**

---

How could I turn down an opportunity that was both rare and unique? So once again here I was at Paddington station, this time for the 9.45 to Swansea, en route to an unaccompanied viewing of an island that had just been put up for sale. Two hours and an excellent breakfast later, we pulled into Cardiff, a city I hadn't visited since three consecutive end of season Millennium Stadium finals with West Ham. With a tidal deadline there was no time to linger though, so after grabbing an M&S sandwich for lunch, I jumped on the little train for the 15 minute ride to Penarth.

Sully Island is opposite the village of Swanbridge and roughly equidistant from three stations; Penarth, Dinas Powis and Cadoxton. I chose the first of these as the map promised a pleasant walk along the coast. Walking down through Alexandra Park and past Penarth's impressively restored Victorian pier, with views across the Bristol Channel, it indeed started well. Today was one of those days where there's no blue sky, but milky sunshine penetrates patches of thin cloud, and I was soon quite hot. Stopping at a viewpoint to put on a cap (sadly not my favourite well worn West Ham hat, that had been round the Essex coast with me, but had recently been left in a Romford cinema), I traced the indicator arrows out to sea. Opposite was Weston-super-Mare and just down the coast the islands of Flat Holm and Steep Holm, whose names aptly describe their shapes.

After the last houses of Penarth a path continued along the cliffs, marked Llwybr Cyhoeddw, although I couldn't find this anywhere on the map. Disappointingly, with tall hedges either side there were no views to enjoy. It came out at Lavernock Point, where in 1897 Marconi sent the first radio signal over open sea, to Flat Holm. Missing the opportunity for wise words to go down in history, his very first message, transmitted in Morse code was 'ARE YOU READY', followed by 'CAN YOU HEAR ME', to which he received the reply 'YES LOUD AND CLEAR'. With no path on the cliff beyond here, I had to take the road inland around Marconi Holiday Village. It was from here that things started to go wrong.

The map showed a footpath on the left a short distance after the holiday park, but there was a Public Footpath signpost immediately after the entrance. It wasn't shown on the map and again I couldn't see Llwybr Cyhoeddw, which was marked on the signpost. It wasn't until much later in the day that it dawned on me – it's Welsh for public footpath! The bilingual signs and announcements in Wales remind me of the weekend sailor who dutifully uses all the correct nautical terminology, until times of crisis when he shouts 'For God's sake turn right'!

(For those who may have been offended by my perhaps inappropriate comments with regard to Welsh language, the apology can be found in chapter six).

The path was heading back towards the coast, so off I went. Taking the opportunity of a secluded small wood to change into shorts, and ignoring another path to the right, I continued towards the sea. Passing the remains of Lavernock Fort, I came out on the cliff where an observation post overlooks St Mary's Well Bay and beyond it my first view of Sully Island. Here the path ended. The map showed it running along the shoreline, but didn't show another caravan park, this one surrounded by a barbed wire fence. With the tide low it may have been possible to clamber over rocks along the bay and round the headland to Swanbridge, but there was no way of knowing if I could get round. I might have been able to walk along the grass in front of the fence and through the trees on the cliff the other side, but with no footpath or signpost, this too could well have been impassable. The easiest way seemed to be through the Bay Caravan Park, but a locked gate barred my way. Instead I tried working my way round the edge, hoping to come out on the road to Swanbridge. It was a nice walk through Lavernock Point nature reserve, but all paths headed east. Eventually I came out back at the small wood where I'd changed into shorts, on the path that I'd ignored earlier, having completed a full circle, but no nearer to Sully Island. I was hot and frustrated.

Back at the road I continued to the path that was marked on the map. This was quite overgrown and it wasn't long before I found out perhaps why few people choose to use it. At Sutton Farm there was a sign warning of guard dogs loose. The path runs adjacent to the farm's lawns and within seconds this evil looking canine monster bounded across the lawn barking and growling at me. Just a worryingly low fence, topped with a single strand of barbed wire kept the snarling brute from the public footpath. Raising up on hind legs, he bared his teeth, as if to let me know he was perfectly capable of jumping the fence. Now I'm not an expert at translating doggy language, but I'm pretty sure he was saying that should I choose to continue on the path he would have no hesitation in sinking those fangs into my backside. Commonsense said that he couldn't get out. Instinct for self preservation and a desire to retain full buttock integrity suggested that I should leg it. Faced with a killer dog and a path overgrown with nettles that may not even have led to the sea, I turned back.

Just as I'd found in parts of the Essex, poor signposting and people keeping their own bit of coast to themselves, were conspiring to frustrate the coastal walker. So now it was road walking all the way to Swanbridge and a far from direct route. I thought of cutting a corner by climbing up to the old Taff Vale Railway, which used to run to the village of Sully just west of the island, but decided it looked too overgrown. After the caravan park entrance there was a path coming up through trees on the cliff. This may have been the way through from St Mary's Well Bay, but on the other hand it may not. My decision to take the road was quite possibly correct, as since visiting I read David Cotton's account of his British coast walk, where he described the path by the bay having a 12 foot gap due to erosion and the only way through being over slippery rocks, tide permitting.

I'd expected to take an hour from Penarth. Two and a quarter hours after getting off the train I walked into the little village of Swanbridge. Then I realised I hadn't got my hat. Retracing steps I found it back at the top of the hill. Back down to Swanbridge and at last, Sully Island.

There was no For Sale sign, but a large notice warned that many people had been drowned attempting to visit or return from Sully Island. The fast rising tides and strong currents have caught out many a person and great care must be taken to allow adequate time for crossing before the tide covers the causeway. In May 1949 a group of Scouts were visiting the island and after misjudging the tide, became trapped. Rather than wait for help, they attempted to cross, but two boys were swept away by the current. The group leader tried to rescue them, but he too was swept off. Margaret Vaughan, a 14 year old girl, was with the party and she bravely swam 30 yards against the current and managed to help the leader drag one of the boys towards the shore. A lifebelt was then thrown to them and all were helped from the water. For her bravery Margaret Vaughan was awarded the Albert Medal, which was exchanged for the George Cross when this award was introduced in 1971. Her original medal is now in the care of Cardiff Museum.

When I arrived the tide was still well down and a wide expanse of rock separated Sully Island from the mainland. There's no man-made causeway and visitors pick their way across the mostly flat rocks, although with care needed on patches of slippery seaweed. Climbing up onto the island, my first impression was that it didn't look anything special. Not worth over a million pounds anyway. There are a few paths, but a fair proportion of the area is covered with impenetrable scrub, a result of the lack of animals and human intervention. Rabbits used to live here in huge numbers, but died out with myxomatosis in the 1950s. Apparently every so often new colonies set up here, although I hope they heed the warning notice before setting off across the rocks. Crossing to the western end, I found a sheltered spot looking out to sea to eat my long overdue lunch.

A Bronze Age burial barrow at the eastern end of the island tells us that prehistoric man came here and archaeological finds have shown that the Romans visited. In 1899 a group of workmen digging a trench unearthed the body of a Roman citizen, along with a brass vase containing a hoard of treasure. This they decided to share amongst themselves and promptly scarpered. When the authorities found out they went in pursuit and recovered the find, part of the haul having found its way as far as Liverpool. The coins included Golden Auries of Diocletian, dated AD 300, giving a clue as to the age of the body. Also in the treasure trove were three rings; one with a massive octagonal sapphire-lapis lazuli (found only in South America and Afghanistan), one with a fighting cock cut deeply into it suggesting that it was a seal and one a cameo set in gold depicting the head of Medusa.

Norsemen were known to have used the bay to anchor their longboats between trips to raid, rape and pillage, as was their wont. At the south eastern headland are the remains of a Saxon fort or fortified homestead, although these are being gradually eroded away.

During the 13th century the island was used as a base by Alfredo de Marisco, a Norman pirate known as The Nighthawk. With his gang of ruffians and deserters, Marisco terrorised the locals with brutal atrocities and raided vessels as they passed the island. Becoming bolder, he would lie in wait by Sully Island until a prize vessel was spotted entering Cardiff Bay, which would then be attacked, robbed and its crew murdered without mercy. However on 14th July 1242 his reign of terror came to an end. After sighting a vessel apparently in trouble and drifting helplessly towards Lundy, he ordered his men to attack, but as they approached the vessel it came alive with the King's men. A battle ensued and the pirates were slaughtered without mercy. Having fallen for the King's trap, Marisco was captured and publicly hanged, much to the pleasure of the local people.

In later years the island was well known for involvement in the local smuggling trade and it is said, although seems rather unlikely, that a storage tunnel runs to Sully House on the mainland. More latterly there was for many years a family living on the island, believed to be amongst the last of the beach cave dwellers who eked out a meagre living along the shores of Britain. The island has however been uninhabited for many years and will remain this way even if a new owner should wish to construct their dream house here, as building is not permitted.

Sully Island had made the news (well the South Wales Echo and the Penarth Times) only a month before my visit. A rusty unexploded Second World War bomb was found by walkers and army bomb disposal experts were called from Hereford. In true unflappable local Bobby style, Inspector Paul McCarthy of South Wales Police told the reporter, 'It seems as if we have a World War Two bomb, but it shouldn't be any risk to the public. It is out of the way on Sully Island and since the Germans dropped it, it hasn't blown up for 65 years or thereabouts'. In true local paper style, the Penarth Times headed the story 'Island Costs a Bomb' and speculated that its discovery may put off potential buyers for Sully.

By now the sun had gone and I needed all my layers of jacket, trousers and waterproof to keep out the strong sea breeze. With lunch eaten and extra clothes on, at least my bag was now nice and light. Exploring the seaward side of the island I found its hidden beauty. Remarkable rock formations, eroded by the sea and enormous boulders thrown up by the waves. Cliffs with huge overhangs and layers of red and cream marls and sandstone. Beautiful rock pools, almost at cliff height, the rise and fall of the tide being so great here – second only to that at the Bay of Fundy in Nova Scotia in the whole world. I clambered around on the rocks, looking up at the cliffs with their folds of colour, the gentle undulations formed by differential squeezing of periglacial ice.

It's only a small island and doesn't take long to explore. I followed the grassy footpath that goes to the highest point – the bronze age barrow. This is a good place from which to survey Sully, with views to Barry on the mainland and looking back out to sea, the islands of the Bristol Channel, with the coast of Somerset and hills of Exmoor beyond. The seaward side of the island is the more dramatic, with its cliffs and rocks, and with less scrub is more easily accessed. Beneath the cliff two lads were fishing from the rocks. This is apparently a good spot, with bass, whiting, cod, dogfish and conger eel often caught around the island. I went back to have another look at the rock formations and noticed the fisherman packing up. Soon they were gone and I was alone on the island. Even without the £1.25 million, for a few minutes I could call it mine.

As at St Michael's Mount, I lingered a while, reluctant to leave this little island that I'd travelled 200 miles to see. Eventually I headed towards the mainland, passing through the marshy area on the landward side where grasses grew taller than me. Perhaps as a result of the lack of grazing animals, a number of plants can be found on Sully that do not generally grow in the area. These include marine spleenwort, adders tongue fern and the rare bee orchid, and are presumably the 'rare flora' referred to by the Estate Agent.

Before setting off back across the rocky causeway I went to inspect an old wreck lying on the shingle. Its origin is unknown, but it has clearly lain here for many years and is now just a skeleton of a boat. It has been suggested that it is the SY Scotia, a famous Antarctic survey vessel, which came to grief close to Sully in January 1916, however this had a longer keel.

Although the expanse of rock was smaller than when I'd arrived, there was still a wide strip leading back to the mainland. Amongst the rocks were tiny pools, many ringed with purple sea anemones, ready to open their faces once the sea returned. Between the pools were little patches of minute shells, mostly complete and many having been brought here on the currents from far off places.

Back at Swanbridge I stopped for a drink at the Captain's Wife, which looks out across the sea to the island. The pub was originally Sully House and incorporates a row of cottages that were the homes of local fishermen, whose small fleet of vessels used the now ruined Swanbridge harbour. Sully House was owned by a ship's captain and legend has it that his wife accompanied him on one of his voyages, but unfortunately died at sea. Sailors are superstitious about having a corpse on board, so the captain hid the body, doubled-up in a lead-lined box. On returning to port he found that the box and body had disappeared, presumably taken by a member of crew who thought it contained treasure. The wife's ghost was said to roam the area, seeking her resting place. However, during a more recent renovation the doubled-up body of a woman was found under flagstones in the stable and the skeleton reburied. After this the ghost of the Captain's Wife was never seen again.

When I emerged from the pub half an hour later the tide had risen considerably. The causeway was still passable, but it was approaching the time when to do so would be foolhardy. Deciding against repeating my unsatisfactory journey from Penarth, I walked the mile west towards the village of Sully. Every few minutes I looked back to see that the water had risen further and after a while stopped to watch Sully become an island. The tide was certainly rising at a tremendous rate and I could see how people might misjudge it and get trapped. With the rocks covered and water on all sides, Sully looked a very different place. A real island rising out of the water, remote and deserted, until once more the rocks are revealed.

I'd intended to walk to Cadoxton, a suburb of Barry, but at Sully found a bus stop. The prospect of a ride back to Penarth appealed more than a walk along main roads, but without a timetable I had no idea as to whether the wait would be five minutes or five hours. With good fortune however a bus came along after just a couple of minutes and the return to Penarth was somewhat more straightforward than my walk this morning.

So should I make an offer for Sully Island? It has interesting history, geology and good views. The rock formations on the south side are well worth visiting, but other than these I didn't really feel that Sully was exceptionally beautiful and nor did I sense that special island atmosphere. Yes I liked it and maybe if the sun had been out it would have seemed more special, but I have the feeling that to really appreciate Sully Island you'd need to stay until the sea has covered the rocks and it has become a true island. So I shall turn down the opportunity to commission my own stamps and keep that £1.25 million in my pocket.

# CHAPTER THREE

# WORM'S HEAD & BURRY HOLMS

A trip to South Wales for sun, wind, rain and three tidal islands.

The Travelling Chef – what a wonderful concept. While passengers sit back and enjoy views of the Thames Valley, the Severn Bridge, then the Welsh hills, a chef works away in a tiny galley, producing superb breakfasts, snacks and lunches. A triple decker club sandwich with bacon, sausage, tomato, mushroom, omelette and a backdrop of the green English countryside, made for my perfect breakfast as we sped towards Swansea. And people wonder why I choose to travel by train.

Multimap shows the nearest railway station to Rhossili as Pembrey and Burry Port, which indeed it is if you don't mind swimming 3 ½ miles across the Loughor estuary. I preferred to take to train to Gowerton, one station beyond Swansea, and continue by bus. And these were proper rural buses; the sort where drivers go out of the way to help, not the city ones who wait until a running passenger almost reaches the door before driving off. Changing at Killay, we headed out onto the Gower Peninsular, crossing moorland with occasional glimpses of high cliffs and the sea, showing why this was the first place in Britain to be designated as an 'Area of Outstanding Natural Beauty'. Twice we stopped for sheep and ponies who preferred to eat in the road rather than graze the miles of heath on either side. A commendable network of buses run across the Gower, with visitors encouraged to leave their cars behind and at one crossroads the driver called out that a connecting bus hadn't arrived. No problem though – a quick phone call to its driver and a rendezvous was arranged in the next village.

Arriving at Rhossili, I checked into the Worm's Head Hotel situated right on the cliff edge looking across the bay. All bedrooms have sea views and I could see both Worm's Head and Burry Holms from my window – the ideal place to stay for a tidal island visitor. The view was voted 11<sup>th</sup> best in the world in a poll run by Jacobs Creek and I wouldn't argue.

When visiting St Michael's Mount and Sully Island I'd had to choose dates when the tide was low in the daytime, but to visit three islands in one short trip required more careful planning. The best solution seemed to be to find a time when the tide was low at Rhossili in the evening and hence again the following morning, then move on to Tenby in time for the next low at St Catherine's Island. Planning ahead was hampered when the only tide tables I could find were for just for the following 28 days and estimating beyond this based on advancing by 45 minutes per day proved incorrect. I hadn't realised that the time by which each day's high tide moves forward varies and it was only when I found the Easytide website that I realised the error and had to change my hotel booking.

With both islands still surrounded by water there was plenty of time for a late lunch in the hotel bar (the only 'pub' in the village), looking out across the beautiful bay. I fancied the chicken with red wine sauce, but my request to swap the type of potato was declined – 'The kitchen won't allow it'. I had scampi instead. Rain had been forecast to start during the afternoon and continue for 24 hours, so I set off along the cliffs to take photos while it was still dry. Burry Holms could be clearly seen three miles away at the far end of the sands and at the southern tip of the bay Worm's Head stretched out into the sea. A peninsular when the tide is down, but now an island with waves crashing over its rocky causeway. Far below people walking on the 3 miles of beach were just tiny specks on the sand, while others surfed, resembling seals clad in their black wetsuits.

A man let me through the gate at the top of the path and spotting the West Ham badge on my jacket commented that us Hammers fans get everywhere. Indeed we do as not 30 seconds later a man sitting on a wall greeted me with 'Up the Hammers'. We chatted for a while, unusually for walkers, not about the weather or scenery, but our football club's failure to sign a striker for the new season.

By now the rain had started and not wishing to have to wait in the wet while the sea retreated at Burry Holms, I spent a while wandering round the village, starting at the National Trust shop and Information Centre.

Much of the Gower, including 24 miles of coastline, is owned and managed by the National Trust, who have to balance the varying demands of farming, wildlife, tourism and local people. As well as the hotel, Rhossili has a couple of cafes and just three other shops. One of these sold high quality local crafts and the other two general holiday bits and pieces, with a small food selection. I bought a cheese sandwich, not knowing if I'd be back from the island before the bar stopped serving food. After returning to the hotel to pack a rucksack and put on waterproof clothing, I was ready to go.

## Burry Holms

So after a ten minute delay for a lost sandwich (I'd put it in the wardrobe to stay cool), I set off in the rain. There are three routes to the end of the bay; over Rhossili Downs, a path at the foot of the Downs, or along the beach. I chose the first of these; the most strenuous but the most rewarding. The path leaves Rhossili from just behind the church and almost immediately starts to climb the steep cliffs. More used to the flat coast of Essex, I stopped several times to admire the view before reaching the top. From here it was two miles of most enjoyable ridge walking. Despite the rain there were splendid views to the left along the bay to both islands and the Pembrokeshire Coast far beyond, and to the right almost the whole Gower Peninsular. With large expanses of heather, grazing sheep and ponies, the terrain reminded me of Dartmoor, although here the roaring sea could be heard from far below.

A Trig Point at 193 metres (627 feet to those of us more used to understanding elevation in traditional units), marked the highest summit, although the path continued to gently rise and fall as I headed due north. A young foal with its parents stood on the path, watching me closely as I passed, but with friendly horsey eyes. Unlike cows, horses usually look pleased to see walkers and don't have that threatening 'about to stampede' stare. The way down was steeper than the Rhossili end and from the top looked almost vertical. It was hard to keep my feet on the slippery grass, especially where the path resembled more of a stream and I was glad to have new boots with good grip (although less happy with the blister they gave me later). Even so I had to zig zag across the cliff, but managed to avoid a fall or more likely a roll to the bottom.

Walking through the campsite at the appropriately named Hill End, I followed the path onto the beach, passing windsurfers returning for their tea. It was a further mile to Burry Holms, easy walking on firm sand with the strong wind behind me. The prospect of the return into wind and driving rain was less inviting. The island is less than 100 yards from the shore, separated by rocks with a strip of sand between them. These are known as Spaniard Rocks and the tiny picturesque sandy beach just beyond the island is notable for the large number of Spanish gold coins found here, washed up from some unknown shipwreck. Climbing up onto the island I headed for the obligatory sign warning of the dangers of attempting to cross when the tide is high. This I noted was in English only.

Before water levels rose with the retreat of the last Ice Age, Burry Holms was an inland hill overlooking a large plain. Now a small tidal island it is less well known than its partner at the southern end of the bay. Admittedly its outline is less dramatic, a gentle mound shape, but its greater remoteness limits visitor numbers, adding to its appeal to me. I was not just the only person on the island, but probably the only person anywhere within the best part of a mile.

A number of archaeological studies have shown that Burry Holms was used by Mesolithic (Middle Stone Age) hunters. Flints were found in 1923 and a more detailed survey undertaken by the National Museum of Wales in the late 1990s. Over eighty microliths, (sharp shards of flint, which would have been embedded into bone, antlers or wood to make a spear effective for both hunting and fishing) have been discovered on the island. One had an impact fracture on its tip, suggesting that its Mesolithic owner took the broken spear to Burry Holms, where he discarded it before making a new spear to resume hunting. The ample supply of stone and flint, and variety of objects discovered, suggest that stone tools were made here. Due to the acidic soil bones and wooden tools would not have survived, but it is thought that with its prominent position overlooking the plains and close to the River Loughor, the island may well have been the location of a Stone Age settlement. There is however clear evidence that Burry Holmes was inhabited by Iron Age people, both from dating of yellow glass beads found in the sand and the impressive earthworks of their fort on the northern side of the island.

A rough narrow path runs round the island's perimeter, but great care was necessary close to the cliff edge, with the wind strong and surface slippery. A fall onto the rocks below would have undoubtedly been fatal. With the island so exposed there are no trees or shrubs, just grass, flowers and tiny blackberry plants with fruit growing inches above the ground. At the seaward end of the island was a circle of concrete about a yard in diameter, with a disc of metal running inside it. This I assumed was the remains of some kind of lookout or gun, which might be as old as the Napoleonic Wars, or as comparatively recent as World War Two.

I climbed up to the earth ramparts of the fort, then down to the remains of two stone cottages. Both had just one wall still standing and can just be seen from Rhossili. From afar I'd first thought they were people but then realised they never moved. Sheltered behind one of the walls I sat down to eat my sandwich, glad to be out of the wind. On this side of the island vegetation grew a little higher, with nettles and a few patches of bracken, but even these hardy plants are unable to survive on the exposed south.

On the eastern side there was once a chapel, which legend says was built by St Cenydd, one of God's holiest messengers, who as a baby was rescued from a storm by a flock of seagulls and carried to safety on the cliff tops of Worm's Head. King Arthur was then ruler of the land, based nearby at Loughor, and the infant Cenydd was brought before him. The child was crippled by a deformed leg, said to be the result of an incestuous relationship by his mother and Arthur's courtiers advised that the baby was evil so should be executed. The King however felt that God alone should determine the infant's fate, so he was placed in a wicker basket and cast adrift on the River Loughor. Cenydd was carried out to sea where during the night a terrible gale blew up, tossing the basket towards the jagged rocks of Worm's Head. Just as it was about to be dashed against the rocks the seagulls picked it up, flying to the top of the cliff, where they laid the child on a bed of soft feathers.

For eight long days and nights the gulls shielded Cenydd from the cold and wind, then on the ninth day an angel visited the baby, leaving him a brass bell to suckle for nourishment. Later a deer provided milk for the growing child, then when he was a small boy the angel returned again, telling him to eat a diet of five kinds of herbs. The angel instructed Cenydd in what was good and holy and he remained on Worm's Head until the age of 18, when God told him to travel north to another headland. Despite much pain from his leg Cenydd completed the journey, stopping at Burry Holms, where he built a chapel and lived for many years, passing on the word of the Lord to those who visited him.

Nothing remains of Cenydd's chapel, but when the island was excavated in the 1960s evidence was found of timber dwellings which it was thought may have been the work of Caradoc of Rhos, a 12th century holy man. Ruins of a much larger stone church or monastery, with a semi-circular chancel, were also found and it is thought that by the 14th century a large hall, school room and living enclosures had been added, with the stone chancel replaced by a larger square structure.

Although excavation has uncovered many secrets of Burry Holms, there are still mysteries. Not least is why the site declined, from what appeared to be a thriving place of worship visited by pilgrims, to become one of Wales's lost churches. It may be that after the Reformation pilgrims stopped coming and no one contributed to the upkeep, but with little evidence of its spiritual past, one has to imagine how it was and rely on the island's remoteness and on nature for inspiration. There is still an annual pilgrimage to Burry Holms, with a simple but moving service held by the ruins, looking over the ocean as a summer's day draws to a close.

Unlike my first two island visits, today I didn't feel a reluctance to leave Burry Holms. In wind and rain it certainly had wildness appeal, but an hour was ample for me to soak up the island's atmosphere and my trousers to soak up a good proportion of its water. Like many wild places, it is probably at its best in sunshine, but still has a certain raw beauty whatever the weather. However, there seemed little point in staying to get even wetter, so I made my way back across the rocks. What I hadn't realised is that the easiest crossing point is a narrow sandy strip, which looking from the mainland runs immediately to the right of the tallest line of rocks. Returning from the island however I climbed over the slippery rocks, twice slipping and almost falling. With still no one else around this wouldn't be the best place to break an ankle. My wife was convinced that I'd return from one of the islands in a rescue helicopter, but eventually remembering the sandy strip I found the easy route and arrived back on the beach with all limbs intact.

The three mile walk back along the sand was what you might call bracing

– headlong into the wind with rain beating down on my face. I halted frequently, turning to look back at the gentle hump of Burry Holms, a little smaller at each stop. What a strange name for an island I thought. It sounded more like a third division footballer. It is derived from the Viking word 'holmr', and seems to be spelt Holmes as often as it is Holms. I have followed the Ordnance Survey and left out the E. The word Holm (as in Flat Holm and Steep Holm in the Severn Estuary) is of Norse derivation, meaning island in a river. My first four tidal island visits would include just one calling itself an island, the other three being a Mount, a Head and a Holm.

Walking right by the sea the occasional large wave caught me out, covering my feet before I could escape, although they could hardly get much wetter. The rain at last relented, although it was hard to tell what was rain and what was sea spray. Further out on the breakers a few hardy surfers enjoyed some evening sport, while a lone kite surfer sped along parallel to the beach. I'd promised my wife a shell from each island and pleased to spot one still intact, picked it up, but dropped it quickly on realising its owner was still at home. I chose another one!

Almost back at Rhossili I paused at the wreck of the Helvetia, a Norwegian oak-built sailing barque, which came to grief here in 1887. She was one of two such ships lying off Mumbles Head in a south-easterly gale, that on the morning of 1st November were driven from their anchors in increasing wind. One was able to make it to the safety of Lundy, but the Helvetia was swept around Worm's Head into the shallow waters of Rhossili Bay. Initially the crew stayed aboard, the captain worried that someone might steal the ship, but as a change in the wind caused her to drag her anchor and with nightfall approaching, the decision was taken to abandon the vessel. The wreck of the Helvetia was discovered on the beach the next morning, surrounded by her cargo of 500 tonnes of wood. In a massive salvage operation over the next few weeks the timber was systematically collected and auctioned, South Wales timber merchants obtaining it at bargain prices. The wreck of the ship itself was sold to a local man, Jack Bevan, but before he had a chance to strip the valuable copper keel, she had started to settle in the sand. Nevertheless he made good use of the Helvetia's deck boards as flooring for his kitchen. Just the boat's skeleton can now been seen protruding from the sand, a well known Rhossili landmark and with Worm's Head behind it, the subject of many a photo.

Dusk was falling as I climbed the steep slope back to the village. The weather had denied me a Rhossili Bay sunset, said to be one of the best in the world, but it had shown me cliffs, beach and tidal island in a less than gentle mood. It had been a wonderful walk and no less enjoyable for lack of sunshine. I hoped however that tomorrow would at least be dry.

## Worm's Head

Opening my curtains the weather was only marginally improved, but the deserted sweep of golden sands just as spectacular. There cannot be many better views from a hotel bedroom than from the Worm's Head Hotel. The view from the dining room too is superb – the whole span of Rhossili Bay, with the Downs behind and tidal island at either end. The toast machine was less spectacular with the instructions a twee little rhyme ending *'If you follow these words you'll be sure to combine, crispy brown toast, every time.'* Indeed this was perfectly correct – if you put the bread through twice!

It took 15 minutes to walk along a wide gravel path to the headland opposite Worm's Head, passing several fishermen returning from the island. A Japanese couple wandered about on the cliff, the lady dressed in pristine white hat and coat, with multicoloured umbrella. A handful of British hikers were setting out for walks, conventionally dressed in shorts and cagoules. To add to the stereotypes, the two American families at breakfast had decided just to view the island from the warmth of the hotel.

Like Sully Island, there's no man-made causeway to Worm's Head and it's a walk or scramble across rocks, depending on the route you take. The hardest part was the jagged rocks closest to the mainland, after which it was a case of picking a way between pools over mussel encrusted rocks, and with much care needed so as not to slip into the water. The rock pools were quite beautiful, but with limited time before the tide was in, I decided to leave exploring them until the return crossing.

Climbing up onto the Head, I immediately spotted a seal below the cliff. Walking over for a closer look I found there were seven in total, just bobbing about in the water, their big round eyes looking up at me, almost as if asking to be thrown a fish. Grey seals are often seen around Rhossili

Bay and basking sharks are regular visitors, as is the occasional pod of dolphins.

A mile long, Worm's Head is made up of three parts, its distinctive shape being the origin of its name. From the bay it has the shape of a giant sea serpent and when Viking marauders first arrived here the twisted land mass must have seemed like some huge majestic creature. Hence they called it 'The Wurm', meaning dragon, later corrupted to Worm. The large flat topped 150 foot high 'Inner Head' is the dragon's body, the rocky 'Low Neck' leading out to the strikingly shaped 'Outer Head'. The outline is very different from that of a traditional island or peninsular, and it's easy to see how the invaders named it. Maybe if the local Welsh people had been a bit imaginative with some pots of paint, the dragon could have been made to look even more real and the Vikings scared away.

I walked round the narrow footpath at the top of the cliff on the southern side of the Inner Head, a view opening up of the Outer Head and a natural stone arch, Devil's Bridge, a collapsed cave. The rocks linking the sections of the head are even more jagged than those by the shore and are only crossed by the most agile visitors, with much scrambling and care required. They aren't covered at high tide, but waves often splash over them. Before setting out I'd thought there would be plenty of time to explore the island and was surprised to find that the sea was quite close to both sides of the causeway. Consulting the tide table I realised I'd made an error of an hour, forgetting to adjust for British Summer Time. The expected causeway closing time was 11.50, so there was no way I could risk climbing further onto the Worm. The route is only passable for roughly 2½ hours either side of low tide and it's easy for the careless or reckless visitors to get stranded. Even the young Dylan Thomas had got himself trapped here, falling asleep on the Inner Head and missing the tide. He wrote of his experience;

'I stayed on that Worm from dusk to midnight, sitting on that top grass, frightened to go further in because of the rats and because of things I am ashamed to be frightened of. Then the tips of the reef began to poke out of the water and, perilously, I climbed along them to the shore.'

Before climbing to the top of the Inner Head I spent a few minutes looking across the rocks to the impressive Devil's Bridge, the route to the Outer

Head. Access to this is however prohibited between 1st March and 31st August to protect nesting birds. It is a notable landfall for migrating birds and home to colonies of seabirds. Kittiwake, fulmar, shag, razorbill and guillemot nest here, as do small numbers of peregrines and red-billed chough, who have recently returned to the area after a long absence. Beyond the bridge the rocks have been flattened by the sea, forming what vies with the hanging valley and oxbow lake to be geography teachers' favourite feature, a wave cut platform. Occasionally an octopus can be spotted here, hiding in one of the water filled joints.

On the Outer Head is a water spout, which in very rough weather can rise as high as the crest of the Head. When the sea is calmer water rushing into the cave forces air out through fissures in the rock, with a hissing or booming sound. Apparently if an unsuspecting person wearing waterproofs can be persuaded to sit over it, as the hole blows they will inflate like a Michelin Man.

A number of caves run under the Worm, but most are at least partly water filled, requiring diving gear to enter and great care. The best known can be accessed by climbing down the cliff at the far end of the peninsular and entered from a ledge. With the entrance 5 yards above the high water mark, it is dry other than in stormy seas, however both climbing skills and caving experience are necessary to explore it safely. Archaeological excavation has uncovered the bones of prehistoric man, mammoth, bear, reindeer and rhinoceros, plus flints and sling-stone, proving that the cave was once easier to access. Henry VIII's official antiquarian John Leland was intrigued with the cave and wrote;

*'There is a wonderfull Hole at the poyany of Worme Heade, but few dare entre it and Men fable that a Dore within the spatius Hole hathe be sene with great Nayles on it'.*

He was referring to a local legend that behind a nailed door in the cave is an underground passage leading to other caves near Llandybie and Cerreg Cennen Castle in Carmarthenshire. As these are both over 25 miles away, it is hardly surprising that archaeologists found no evidence of the passage.

The Inner Head is grassy and was once used for grazing sheep, the salty grass said to give particularly tasty meat. The sheep too apparently enjoyed the seclusion of the Worm and were said to be most reluctant to return to mainland pastures. In 1932 Wilfred Benyon, a Rhossili farmer, reported that his whole flock escaped from their field and attempted to cross the causeway to the island, but were caught by the rising tide and all seventy drowned. The land is very fertile and another Rhossili man once decided to plant potatoes on the southern side of the Worm. They grew most successfully, being ready before any in the village, but others were deterred from following his example by the difficulty in getting the crop back over the razor-like rocks.

Reaching the top of the Inner Head I could see that the tide had come in some distance since I'd crossed and there was now only what looked like a narrow strip remaining of the bed of mussel shells that cover the centre and lowest part of the causeway. A little concerned that I had stayed too long, I hurried down the hillside. Coming up was a young lady, followed by two lads and on greeting her it was clear they were not British. With limited English she was however able to tell me that they were Polish and I was able to explain the need to return to the mainland soon.

Once back on the causeway I realised there was not quite so much need for haste, the dry strip that had seemed just feet wide from afar, still maybe 10 yards across. There was time for a quick look into the magnificent rock pools, once featured in the BBC Coast programme. The hundreds of pools of as many shapes and sizes teemed with life. Ringed with anemones and with seaweed a thousand shades of green, yellow and brown, they are some of the most beautiful that I've seen anywhere. Hermit crabs disturbed by my approach tiptoed from one crevice to another and in every pool tiny fish darted about. Soon the sea would arrive and their little homes would once more become part of an ocean.

Crunching across the barnacle encrusted mussels I made my way between the approaching waves, scrambled across the rocks and up the steep mainland cliff. Stopping part way to survey the scene I was pleased to see the three Polish people returning, leaving the Worm deserted until the tide fell again. Although it hadn't been possible to explore the whole of the island, I had seen that it is not only beautiful, but a most unusual and mysterious place. Worm's Head had been my fourth tidal island and whilst all had their own beauty, this had a ruggedness not quite seen in the other three.

At the top of the cliff, looking out across the causeway and to Worm's Head, is a small white building. Once a coastguard station, this is now the National Coastwatch Institution (NCI) Worms Head Station, helping to ensure the safety of the 300,000 people who visit the area every year. I wandered inside and chatted to the two watchkeepers on duty; David Evans from Swansea, a retired Royal Navy Lt Commander, and Audrey Frank the Deputy Station Manager, a Rhossili resident and former managing agent for classical musicians. Both exuded enthusiasm about the area, with obvious pride in the job they were doing and were very happy to talk to me about the station's work.

The NCI states its purpose as 'To act as the eyes and ears of the Emergency Services' and David explained that their main task is to watch out for potential problems, giving advice or warnings as necessary, but that if people are in difficulties they immediately call HM Coastguard. It is not their duty to effect rescue, but to alert the appropriate service. Most incidents involve people being stranded or potentially stranded on Worm's Head, but there are also medical emergencies, usually slips and falls on the rocks or narrow cliff paths. With powerful binoculars they watch the island, keeping a close eye for anyone who may be unaware of the rising tide, or those who deliberately delay their return to the last minute. David said that they had seen me (a man in a blue coat) on top of the cliff and had watched me return. Whilst it's a slightly strange feeling to be in the view of powerful lenses, it is comforting to know that in this potentially dangerous place there are dedicated volunteers keeping an eye out for problems. If necessary they use a loud hailer siren to attract attention, then signal for the people to either return or wait as appropriate. It's extremely dangerous to try to cross the causeway once covered and there had been a number of fatalities before the station opened in 2007.

I was surprised that Audrey said that they're not allowed to leave anyone on Worm's Head over high tide unless they've advised that they wish to stay (sometimes fishermen choose to remain for what is at least a 7 hour wait). NCI have to consider that people may not be suitably clothed for a long wait on the exposed Head and that the weather could change, or that they might try to wade and get into difficulties. If anyone is stranded they alert the Coastguard Control Centre in Mumbles, who will usually call out the Horton Inshore Lifeboat (IRB), or if necessary a helicopter. The local helicopter ambulance can land on the island, but the Navy Search &

Rescue has to use a winch to recover casualties. The IRB takes 20 minutes to arrive and drops its charges at the foot of a cliff on the mainland, from where the Rhossili Cliff Rescue team bring them to safety. In the first two years after opening the NCI station was involved with 30 rescues from Worm's Head, dealt with 7 injured persons, 6 missing persons and prevented 34 accidents.

As we chatted I got to see the NCI in action. A lady came into the lookout saying that she was in charge of a group of students and one had strayed over the rocks towards the island. The tide was coming in fast and he was at risk of being stranded. As David watched through his binoculars, Audrey went outside to sound the siren. The lad however took no notice, waving back to his friends, but either oblivious to the warning, or too 'cool' to show any reaction. The leader said that he was a Saudi student and the clown of the group. The tide was due to cover the causeway at 11.50, but by 11.30 the two edges of sea had met, partly explaining why I had thought there was so little time left when looking down from the hilltop. Advertised crossing times are only a guideline and wind or atmospheric pressure can cause it to be impassable earlier. It was clear that the student was at least going to get his feet wet, but that if he didn't turn back soon the lifeboat would have to be summoned. David said that the lifeboatmen don't mind being called out as they get expenses for each launch and they jokingly complain that since the NCI station opened they get less beer money. Eventually our Saudi friend decided to come back, splashing through the shallow water to safety and probably a lecture from his group leader. There was now no one on the Worm until early evening when once more the sea would reveal the rocks.

As I walked back up the path to Rhossili the sun poked its head out from behind the cloud, the first I'd seen of it in my 24 hours on the Gower. I'd been fortunate to go on the Worm when it was dry and reasonably clear, and although it would have been nice to have the light and clarity of bright sunlight, yesterday's wild weather seemed in keeping with the mysterious aura of Rhossili Bay's two tidal islands.

After picking up my bag from the hotel, a quick chat with the receptionist who like everyone I'd spoken to on my travels so far was most interested to hear I was writing a book on tidal islands (I hope they'll all buy it) and a last look along the bay's golden sands, I made my way to the bus stop, joining the only other waiting passengers, a retired couple. Almost immediately the bus arrived, several passengers alighting, the last of them a lady with a walking frame, helped down by the driver. Telling us that she was from Swindon and travelling around South Wales, she said how much she loved the friendly Welsh people. So much so that she insisted on hugging the driver, the other two passengers and me. I didn't like to admit that I hailed from the wrong side of the Severn Bridge.

As the bus turned round the waiting couple and I exchanged polite pleasantries, 'as you do'. However, not 'as you do', when I sat down in the bus, selecting a seat with a good view forward, the couple ignored all the other empty seats, choosing to sit immediately in front of me. Not only was my view obscured, but the lady spent the whole journey turning round and asking me questions – What was I doing here? Where did I live? Where do I work? How old are my children? Generally one of the pluses of travelling by public transport is meeting interesting people and chatting on the way. Unfortunately every so often you encounter someone who doesn't read the increasingly short replies, the obvious staring out of the window and the lack of any return conversation. Today I had found such a lady. Of course I could have moved, but how rude that would have been. I was however glad to be getting off at Killay, to change for Gowerton and my journey on to Tenby and St Catherine's Island.

# CHAPTER FOUR
# ST CATHERINE'S ISLAND

*'Good morning. I am sorry but a visit to the island is not possible.'*

Standing on Tenby's South Beach, St Catherine's Island is probably the easiest of our tidal islands to reach, but one of the few to which the public are denied access. It is privately owned and said to be unsafe for visitors. Enquiries at the Tourist Information Centre confirmed that it's closed, but led me to the owner, a Mr Graham Fry, proprietor of the Royal Lion Hotel. The short email above was his response to my request to arrange a visit.

Now I know that a few people have gained access to the island, as they've posted accounts and photos on the internet. They have however remained anonymous and even blacked out their faces. The intrepid explorers, or trespassers, depending on your point of view, had required climbing skills and to keep a beady eye out for the local constabulary.

So should I accept the word of the Tourist Information and content myself with viewing the island from the beach, or should I attempt illicit entry? Only a few weeks before I visited, the police, with Tenby's inshore lifeboat standing by, had removed three youths from the island. All three were taken into custody and arrested. Two were issued with fixed penalty notices and the other released with no further action. Does that suggest I'd have a one in three chance of getting off scot free even if caught, or as a wilful trespasser of more mature years, would they throw the proverbial book at me? Others have gone onto the island without being apprehended, but I could hardly publish a book advertising my misdemeanours and expect no one to notice. I decided to leave it until I got there and see how the land lay.

It was a most pleasant train ride along the Loughor estuary, then on the banks of the River Tywi to Carmarthen and through countryside to Tenby. Checking in at my hotel I asked about St Catherine's Island, explaining that I'd hoped to be able to visit. The most friendly hotelier was not slow to mention Mr Fry, saying that he had 'a reputation in the town'. He was surprised that I'd even received a reply to my email and thought there was little point in pursuing an authorised visit. Apparently he owned property all over the town, much of which like the island, was 'left to rot'. I had considered staying at his Royal Lion Hotel, in the hope of a meeting, but after reading some rather uncomplimentary internet reviews, decided it wasn't worth double what I was paying here. My parents once stayed at his Grade 2 listed Royal Gatehouse Hotel, which used to be next to the Royal Lion, and found the service so poor that they refused to pay the full amount of the bill. They received a rather snooty letter saying that the hotel would not pursue them for the balance. This hotel, a famous Tenby landmark and one of the most sought after places to stay during the town's Victorian heyday, was destroyed by fire in March 2008. It had been empty for some years and there were apparently rumours in the town of foul play. Plans have since been submitted for a multi-million pound development on the site of the Royal Gatehouse, incorporating the Royal Lion, plus the listed 1913 Gatehouse Cinema which Mr Fry also owns.

St Catherine's doesn't have a causeway, however, formed from a huge mass of limestone, it stands on the sand, aloof from the town and when the tide is high is most definitely an island. I'd visited it once before, in 1968 when we had a family holiday in Tenby. Aged 7, all I recall is looking at the island as we played on the beach and visiting a zoo on it. I remember more of the boat trip to Caldey Island and its monastery, three miles further out off the Pembrokeshire coast.

My first sight of the island was from the pathway running from the bottom of the town to the beach. Most impressive it looked, topped with a Napoleonic fort and standing on the golden sand with water surrounding all but the very front. I walked across the sand already feeling a little conspicuous, a lone male with a camera on a beach crowded with families and young children. At least I was wearing shorts and T-shirt, not the shirt and tie that my father considered appropriate seaside attire for our early childhood holidays. I think he became slightly more relaxed as we got older, possibly even loosening a top button if he thought no one was looking.

Stone steps run up the cliff face to the island, but after the nineteenth step a padlocked iron gate bars the way. A notice on the top of the gate announced – NO ADMITTANCE PRIVATE PROPERTY – and another below warned of unsafe structure, falling rocks, cross currents and danger of being cut off by the tide. Visitors were not welcome. With the beach crowded and children playing all around I decided to find some dinner, returning for further investigation when it was less busy.

Tenby with its beautiful setting, sandy beaches, interesting shops and good food, offers all that is best about British holiday resorts and generally attracts the nicest type of family visitor. I went into Tenby Bookshop and the Tourist Information Centre to see if they had any books about St Catherine's Island. Neither however could offer anything other than showing me a paragraph in an old holiday guide which I already had, so I have compiled information on the island's history from a variety of sources. Where they conflicted I've taken what seemed to be the majority view.

Not a great deal is known about the island's early history. It was probably once a place for religious meditation and solitude, with a small chapel on the summit being one of a number dotted along the South Pembrokeshire coastline. Dedicated to St Catherine, the patron saint of spinners and weavers, this gave the island its name. However it is likely that people lived here long before the chapel was built, as Roman coins, a human skeleton and an Egyptian effigy have all been uncovered. Also what appeared to be a large kitchen midden, with bones of domestic animals – sheep, ox and pig. Two stone hermit cells were also thought to have been sited on the island.

During the Napoleonic Wars and with concern that the French may try to invade, a chain of coastal fortifications was built around the UK, at the recommendation of a Royal Commission instigated by Lord Palmerston. It was intended that there would be batteries at Tenby, Caldy Island, Lydstep, Freshwater East and Freshwater West, but the fort at St Catherine's Island was the only one of the five to be built. Its purpose was to protect the newly constructed Admiralty Ship Building Yard at Pembroke Dock and to prevent a landing at Tenby, which could have served as a bridgehead for an overland attack on the port of Milford Haven.

The building contract was secured by a George Thomas of Pembroke Dock and work began in July 1867, under the direction of Colonel W. Llewellyn Morgan of the Royal Engineers. Construction took three years and cost £40,000, considerably exceeding the original estimate of £16,620. To enable workmen to pass to and from the rock at high tide, a temporary narrow wooden trestle footbridge was built linking the island to Castle Hill. Materials were brought onto the island by boat and taken up to the fort with ropes and pulleys. During construction one of the workers fell to his death from the cliffs and his funeral is thought to have been the largest in Tenby's history. Every household was said to have closed its doors and a member from each attended the funeral.

The fort was of a simple rectangular construction, with a series of gun casements facing north to cover Tenby harbour and the beach towards Saundersfoot, and south along the South Beach towards Penally and Manorbier. Each held three 7 inch RML (rifled muzzle loader) guns firing through iron shields. The roof was fitted with three gun platforms for 9 inch RMLs. Two small rifle galleries protected the west face and entrance, which was approached over a drawbridge. The basement held an armoury which could store up to 555 barrels of gunpowder. Like all of Palmerston's forts, St Catherine's never fired a shot in anger and hence they were often referred to as 'Palmerston's Follies', although this was probably a little harsh, as the key purpose of any fortification is deterrent. However artillerymen used to fire the fort's guns annually, when householders of Tenby were warned to open their windows as the shells roared out to sea.

Returning from the town with a tray of cod and chips, I sat looking out towards the island, accompanied by a large and noisy seagull who clearly expected me to share my tea. Not a chance! The early evening sun was shining brightly and little boats were bringing day trippers back over the blue sea from Caldey Island. A few children still played on the beach, while a steady stream of families made their way up the slope heading for cars, train, or Tenby's many hotels, guesthouses and holiday flats. I didn't envy the parents, the long walk up from the beach with hot and tired children often being the least enjoyable part of a seaside holiday. Chips consumed and gull disappointed, I made my way across the beach for a closer investigation of the possibility of being able to get onto the island.

St Catherine's Island is actually in two parts, a large rock at the front, linked to the main island behind by a natural arch. The tide was just low enough for me to walk under the arch and take some photos using it as a natural frame. These 'artistic' shots with such a contrast in light rarely seem to come out as well as you'd expect, although I used to be able to achieve good results with a 35mm SLR film camera. I still haven't got the hang of using digital, which is now necessary for publication, tending to fall into the common trap of taking many mediocre shots in the hope of getting a few good ones, rather than carefully choosing settings and composing just a few. What I won't do with digital pictures however is cheat. Some of my photos have been cropped a little, but none have been manipulated or had colours changed. Whilst often the weather wasn't ideal for photography, the pictures in the book reflect each island as I saw it.

There was no way that anyone other than a skilled climber could have ascended the cliff from either side of the arch. Parts of the island were less steep with grassy slopes running up to the fort from above the rocks, however these areas were well below the low tide mark. The sea would have been too deep to wade so swimming required to reach them. Only the correct, but barred route of steps and path could be potentially feasible. Returning here I decided that it might be possible to climb around the gate, albeit with a degree of risk and to follow the path to the top of the rock. However, beyond this a metal bridge links the two parts of the island, running over the top of the stone arch and an older but broken wooden bridge. At the start of the bridge was a metal gate, not merely the width of the walkway, but extending out either side. Adorned with more Keep Out warnings, to reach the fort I would have had to climb either over or round the gate, neither of which looked to be safe manoeuvres. Of course there was also the chance of being arrested, but by now I'd decided that I was prepared to take that risk. It was however my personal safety that was more concerning. As a man of almost 50 I was undoubtedly less agile and probably more risk aware than the youngsters who'd posted accounts of their trespassing exploits on the internet.

As I stood by the gate once more, considering whether to take the risks, I noticed a gull squawking at me from the rock above. Was he saying 'go for it' or 'don't be so silly'? The whole situation reminded me of Monty Python and the Holy Grail – a dodgy bridge over a drop to certain death, guarded by a strange animal, with a mysterious fort beyond. Would I be asked a question about the air speed velocity of a swallow? At Burry Holmes I'd been concerned about slipping on rocks and my wife's worry that I'd be brought back from one of the islands in a helicopter. With 38 islands yet to visit it seemed too soon to take the risk. One helicopter could be put down to bad luck, but two could be judged as positively reckless. So with two dangerous climbs and unknown hazards within the derelict fort, I very reluctantly decided that as Mr Fry had told me – a visit to the island is not possible.

It was therefore with much disappointment that I walked back down the 19 steps. I had been onto only the very edge of St Catherine's Island and unable to get inside the fort which holds much history within its walls, having become more than just a military establishment. With it no longer required to defend us from the French, in 1907 the island was sold privately for £500, then quickly re-sold, this time to the wealthy Windsor-Richard family, who were extensively involved in the South Wales iron, steel and coal industries. They turned the fort into a luxurious summer residence, with the principle rooms furnished in period styles. The main hall was carpeted with the skins of animals from Asia and Africa and decorated with glass cabinets, hunting trophies and stag heads. The family were actively involved in the town's social life and with its huge open fireplace the hall was a focal point for many lavish celebrations, including the Tenby Hunt Ball. They travelled widely and on their return from hunting trips abroad, local boatmen would transfer the Windsor-Richards' luggage and trophies to the landing stage, from where they would be winched up the cliffs by servants from above.

When the Windsor-Richards sold the island and left Tenby in 1940, much of the décor and furniture from the fort was sold in the town. Some can still be found in local homes. The island was then virtually abandoned for many years, until it was purchased for £10,000 in 1962 by a Tenby businessman. He spent a great deal of money repairing the damage of years of neglect, then opened it to the public. In June 1968 the small zoo which I had visited as a child was opened in the old fort, but the venture was short lived, and despite a change of operator closed in 1979. Since then various plans have been proposed for the fort, but none have come to fruition and it has stood empty, gradually decaying and closed to the public.

St Catherine's Island is probably one of our more interesting tidal islands, and on the beach of a popular holiday resort, one of the most accessible. It is a great shame that it appears abandoned with the public forbidden to visit. Hence I contacted Welsh Heritage, suggesting that this is something which should be put right before the fort deteriorates beyond repair. Some grounds for optimism were provided by the reply from Richard Kevern from Ancient Monuments Administration of Cadw, the Welsh Assembly Government's historic environment division (Cadw is a Welsh word meaning 'to keep'). He agreed that the fort is an important structure and advised that for this reason it has been protected as an ancient monument. However, although this protects it from unauthorised works, the scheduling legislation does not include powers to make an owner maintain or repair a monument. He confirmed what I had been told in Tenby, that the private owner has not carried out any works for some time.

Unfortunately Mr Kevern explained that it is not feasible for the Welsh Assembly Government to take all such sites into state care and they would generally only do this where there was no other way forward. They have therefore looked to Pembrokeshire County Council to take the lead on finding a locally appropriate solution, with Cadw providing advice and financial assistance. In 2006 the Council submitted a lottery funding bid for £20 million to repair and re-use the fort, a scheme which would have been preceded by Compulsory Purchase. Unfortunately the application failed to make the final shortlist and since then the Council has decided that in view of the costs, an incremental approach is required. Access is one of the key and most expensive elements of any proposal for opening of the fort and the Council is looking to commission designs for a low water landing stage and bridge.

Melissa Howells, Projects Coordinator for the Quality Regeneration & Tourism of Pembrokeshire District Council confirmed to me that they have been trying for many years to work with the island's owner to bring a solution for its future, but so far have been unsuccessful. Apparently he has very unrealistic ideas about the value of the property and is unwilling to sell for less than what he feels is the right price. My email to Mr Fry asking what his plans are for St Catherine's Island elicited no reply.

It was reassuring to learn that whilst there is no solution yet in place for the fort, it has not been forgotten and that a lot of work is being invested in trying to develop a scheme for its conservation and re-use. I hope it will not be too many years before St Catherine's Island is once again open for all to enjoy.

# CHAPTER FIVE
# YNYS LOCHTYN

*'It is very difficult to approach, the only pedestrian access would be a very steep scramble down a cliff, before a further scramble across rocks and then it is only accessible at very low tide. It would not give you very much time, to get there and back, I haven't tried it and I wouldn't recommend it either!'*

These were the words of National Trust warden David Jones who is responsible for Ynys Lochtyn, a small island near Llangrannog in Cardigan Bay. After travelling to the beautiful West Wales coast I can fully concur with David's comments. My warning might have been even stronger.

It was an early start from Essex to allow plenty of time to connect with the 10.54 from Cardiff to Fishguard. Had I missed it there would have been a 12 hour wait in the Welsh capital, as just two trains a day run on the line that connects with boats to Rosslare. Arriving at Fishguard Harbour, of the hundred or so passengers I was one of less than ten not catching the Irish ferry, and the only one walking towards the town not the car park. However before I'd gone a hundred yards a car pulled up, the heavily tanned driver calling 'Peter'. Rapid scanning of brain failed to recognise the face, or to think why anyone I knew would be hailing me so far from home. Then he enlightened me – he was from Hertz car hire and guessing that my 13.15 pick up time meant I was arriving by train, had kindly come to collect me.

The very limited train service meant that although it would have been possible to travel onwards by bus, it would have required an extra night's stay. Hence, for the first time I was reluctantly hiring a car. It was a pleasant drive to Cardigan where I was to stay the night, but before checking into my hotel a little investigation was required.

Whilst looking at the map on the train I'd noticed what might be a tidal island on the eastern shore of the Teifi Estuary, a couple of miles from Cardigan. I therefore took the road along the estuary, parked near the hamlet of Gwbert and set out to explore. The path passes Cliff Hotel and skirts Cardigan Golf Club. From here Crain y Gwbert appeared to be separated from the mainland, but also to be part of the golf course. Players could be in for a long wait if it was indeed a tidal island. I soon found however that this was not an island that I'd missed, but is joined by a narrow strip of land, either side of which there are steep drops to rocks below. There was once an Iron Age fort here and now two holes of the golf course cover the headland. What a lovely place to play the game, although knowing how golf balls are mysteriously attracted to water, I suspect that there are quite a few lost in the rocks below. A mile north is Cardigan Island, only 200 metres from the mainland, but definitely not tidal. A nature reserve, with no public access, the island is an important nesting site for seabirds.

After a quick walk into Cardigan for chips, I set off for Llangrannog, 12 miles from Cardigan and roughly half way between Fishguard and Aberystwyth. There are very few buses to the village, so without a car I'd have had to get off the Aberystwyth bus at Brynhoffnant and walk 2½ miles along the hilly lanes. It would have been possible, but not with the evening visit required to do the trip with just one night away.

I was one of the few visitors who chose to park for free in the field at the top of the village and walk half a mile to the sea. Most preferred to pay £3.50 and contribute to the congestion and sea front car parks that detract from the beauty of many seaside villages. Llangrannog itself is not unattractive, but its real beauty is a sandy beach hemmed in either side by steep dark cliffs. Once a small commercial port, it's now a popular surfing beach, with RNLI lifeguards. To maximise balance if scrambling were to be required I wasn't taking a rucksack with me, so on a warm early evening a pre-walk drink in The Ship was, I felt, fully justified. Similarly sustenance from a particularly large ice cream seemed excusable as I started to climb up from the little bay.

For a mile I followed the Ceredigion Coast Path, a 60 mile route along this beautiful coastline that opened in 2008. I saw no one walking and could hear just the sound of birds in the sky and waves crashing onto rocks far below. At Pendinas Lochtyn, a hill and Iron Age fort, I left the main path, walking downhill along the green headland towards the little island of Ynys Lochtyn, one of the most spectacular spots in West Wales. (Incidentally why do we say North of Scotland, South of England, but leaving out the 'of', always South, North or West Wales?).

Sheep grazed on the headland which was once ploughed by a German of the name of Bill Baumer who owned Lochtyn Farm. He used a Fordson Caterpillar track tractor on the steep gradients. As I walked down the grassy slope I couldn't see whether it would be possible to safely cross the gap between mainland and island. Arriving at the point of the headland I still couldn't tell.

There was a path of sorts disappearing over the edge of the cliff, but David Jones was right; it would be a very steep scramble. Although two hours before low tide, the sea had retreated from the narrow gap to the island, revealing rocks below the cliff. These were where I would land should I slip. If I were lucky enough not to die instantly the sea would be back in a few hours to finish me off. There was no one around to hear a shout for help, or perhaps more realistically, a splat as I landed on the rocks. Should I be fortunate enough to remain conscious there was no mobile signal to summon help. If I were to make it to the bottom, there was another cliff to climb onto the island and more rocks beneath. All in all I either had to stay on the mainland or make sure that I didn't slip. Oh and I forgot to mention – I'm not very fond of heights!

However, the fact that there is a narrow path suggests that people do make the journey and I'd been told that anglers fish from the tip of the island. It is though a dangerous descent and I would be increasing the risk by going alone. I walked around the cliff surveying the situation and finding a spot with mobile reception phoned my wife. Having left instructions for her to alert the coastguard if I didn't call again in two hours, gingerly I set off down the cliff.

The first section over loose stones was the steepest. To keep centre of gravity low I slowly lowered myself down on my bottom. Not the most dignified descent but no one was there to see. Twice stones rolled from beneath me, landing on the rocks below, but soon I'd managed the first section. The next was less steep but more slippery, the path now of mud that was soft after heavy rain the previous day. Again I descended crab like, bottom resting firmly on the mud every few feet. The final section was almost sheer over rocks, but with plenty of foot holds, and the drop now of just broken leg not fatal height, it was soon completed. Crossing the rocks was no problem and brought me out onto a large flat rock wave-cut platform. From here began the ascent of Ynys Lochtyn.

Although not quite as high as the mainland cliff, the climb is just as steep, starting with rocks then a very narrow path. Climbing was easier than descending, but the muddy path above a sheer drop to the rocks required great care. I leaned to the left and held on to clumps of grass, although they would surely have come away should I have slipped, leaving the coastguard to wonder why the dead man on the rocks was carrying vegetation to the island. Soon however I was safely on the Ynys Lochtyn, with time to explore before the not so simple matter of getting back.

The steep cliffs around the island have claimed a number of lives over the years and there have been other fortunate escapes. In February 1997 a coastguard Nissan Terrano lost traction on the wet grass above Ynys Lochtyn. The driver managed to jump out just in time but the vehicle fell over the cliff, landing on the rocks below. Coastguards removed the radio but had to leave the vehicle for several days before it could be recovered, by which time it had been further damaged by waves bashing it against the rocks.

In another incident a local farmer sadly lost his life when his vehicle went over the cliff south of Llangrannog while he was checking his animals. In May 2010 the New Quay lifeboat were called out to rescue a dog that had fallen over the cliffs by Ynys Lochtyn. A crew member was put ashore and located the dog who was lucky to have suffered just a broken leg after his 200 foot fall. Others have been less fortunate and RNLI records show a number of calls to rescue much loved pets who've fallen from the cliffs between the island and Llangrannog, but failed to survive the drop.

There is little information published on Ynys Lochtyn and I'm grateful to both the warden David Jones and Bryan Davies who runs the community website for Llangrannog, for their assistance. Even the name is a mystery. Ynys is of course Welsh for island and Lochtyn may have Viking connections or is perhaps a Celtic word. Whilst Iron Age and Roman people had settlements on Pendinas Lochtyn it's not known if they used the island. There are remains of a rectangular structure on the west facing slope of the island and possibly a similar feature to the south, but not a great deal is known of them. The building is characteristic of medieval times, but may have been occupied far longer.

Ynys Lochtyn has two summits, the smaller and lower section closest to the mainland being joined to a higher hill on the seaward side. In all it is about 300 metres long, 50 metres wide and rises to 29 metres. On the southern side is a striking vein of white quartz which runs from the top of the island down the cliff. The island is grassy, kept short presumably by rabbits, although the occasional intrepid (or stupid) stray sheep apparently find their way over here, but don't stay long as there's no fresh water.

Cardigan Bay has resident populations of bottle nosed dolphins and harbour porpoises, both of which can often be seen from Ynys Lochtyn and the surrounding cliffs, however none were visible as I scanned the sea. I had to wait until the next morning when I drove to the beautiful little beach of Mwnt a few miles from Cardigan. Here several porpoises were swimming no more than 80 yards from the beach where they come in to catch fish. Nor did I see red legged choughs who occasionally fly past the island. Apparently concrete puffins were once placed on Ynys Lochtyn to try to attract the real birds. Herds of cows never migrated to Milton Keynes to interact with their concrete bovines and nor did puffins fall for this little deception.

On a landward side of the island is an impressive archway and several caves run into the jagged cliffs. It is said that falling rock alters the caves and can change the approach to the island from year to year. Unlike some of the islands which I was to visit later, the hard rock is slow to erode and Ynys Lochtyn has not changed greatly from the days when Lloyd George walked here from Llangrannog, finding it 'a very relaxing place'.

Also inspired by the island was Edward Elgar, who exhausted by the completion of his hugely successful *Pomp and Circumstance* orchestral marches, travelled to Wales for rest and recuperation. No sooner had he breathed the sea air than his impulse to compose returned. Whilst sitting on Ynys Lochtyn he heard the faint melody of a folk song floating on the breeze and was inspired to create *Works for a String Orchestra*. Once back in London his new piece for strings was quickly sidelined by larger projects, but four years later he received a letter from his close friend August Jaeger. She was putting together a programme for the newly formed London Symphony Orchestra and wanted a new work by Elgar as its centrepiece. Jaeger suggested that something for strings only would 'sell like hot cakes' and from his earlier Ynys Lochtyn work Elgar composed the brilliant *Introduction and Allegro for Strings*.

Even though it was not yet low tide, with another tricky descent and climb to get back to the mainland, I couldn't sit down and relax. Once more I gently lowered myself over the cliff edge, soon finding that as on the outward journey, descending was harder than climbing. It's not so much the steepness, but knowing what is below. A small drop onto soft sand and I'd have been scampering. A big drop onto rocks that are soon to be covered by sea and I was inching my way down. At one point on the muddy path I stopped, looked down at the rocks below and momentarily decided that I didn't want to go on. It took however just a few seconds to realise that the alternative was a night on an island without food or shelter, so downwards I continued. Eventually back on the rocky platform I was in no mans land. Hidden from the world but with the sea to return in a couple of hours. The climb back up the cliff was perhaps the easiest of all and soon I was back on mainland Wales.

Perhaps I should have taken David Jones' advice, but another tidal island had been ticked off the list. A beautiful island on a lovely coastline, but one of the hardest to reach. St Catherine's Island could easily be accessed if Mr Fry would allow the gates to be opened, but I'd had to make do with stepping on just the very edge. Ynys Lochtyn has no compromise; either you view it from the mainland or you scramble down and up the cliffs.

I must therefore end this chapter with a warning. I was perhaps a little foolhardy to make the journey alone onto Ynys Lochtyn. With great care I survived to tell the tale as of course others have done. However it would have taken just one slip for me to end up on the rocks, perhaps dead or perhaps injured, lying there as the tide came in. It is not for me to say whether or not others too should climb to the island, but it would be irresponsible not to warn of the risks.

# CHAPTER SIX

# YNYS GIFFTAN & CEI BALLAST

The Cambrian Coast, a remote and beautiful coastline running northwards from Aberystwyth, holds many memories from childhood holidays. I'd hoped to find a tidal island here but was disappointed on learning that although the road is covered at high tide, Shell Island near Harlech can always be walked to over sand dunes. It seemed I wouldn't be revisiting old holiday haunts, but then had a phone call from my father. My parents still come to the area regularly, and on a trip to Aberdovey he'd noticed Ynys Gifftan described in an Arriva Trains leaflet as an island you can walk to at low tide – a tidal island! Close examination of the map showed another, Cei Ballast off Porthmadog, with added interest that this is a man-made island.

Two weeks later I was at Marylebone station setting off for North Wales, travelling with the best train operator in Britain – Wrexham & Shropshire Railway. This little company offers all that is best about rail travel; a smooth and comfortable ride, quiet trains with locomotives not under floor engines, every seat at a table and lining up with large windows, cheap fares even if bought on the train, friendly staff who are only too pleased to help, and perhaps best of all, superb catering with a chef on every train. My lamb shank would have graced a top restaurant. They are not always the quickest trains, but if I have time to spare I'll go out of my way to use them. This was to be a trip where the travel and scenery were as enjoyable as the islands.

My brother in Shrewsbury provided a convenient overnight stop and opportunity to see nieces and nephew. It was interesting to observe another family's morning routine and stresses, and comforting to know that our teenager isn't the only one who has to be almost dragged from his bed.

My first morning stress was at Shrewsbury station. Here a long queue of customers, each ordering a different one of the seemingly infinite coffee options, threatened to prevent me buying a sandwich before the 9.27 left for Aberystwyth. Just in time someone else decided to help serve, and I was duly on the way to the Welsh coast. It's a nice ride through Welshpool, Newtown, Caersws and on to Machnylleth, where a change of train was required.

The train ride along the Cambrian Coast is a journey that everyone should do once in their lifetime. A spectacular ride through beautiful scenery that few seem to know is there. Leaving the Aberystwyth line at the isolated Dovey Junction (one of the very few British stations with no road access), we snaked alongside the beautiful Dyfi estuary, running through a series of tunnels and on a ledge cut into the rock. I'd found a copy of the Arriva Trains guide, which told us to look out for oyster catchers and egrets, both of which were duly present in good numbers. At Penhelig a large party of teenagers with back packs joined us, increasing the noise level from the quiet chatter of tourists, walkers and locals already aboard.

Heading north after Aberdovey, we continued to hug the coast, looking out on the Irish Sea, alternating between the sea wall and a ledge high above it, slowing occasionally where there are risks of rock falls and shelters protect the train. At Morfa Mawddach the teenagers, who I'd established were from Wakefield and on an Outward Bound Trust expedition, left us to start their walk along the Mawddach estuary, one of the most beautiful in Wales. Man's hand has enriched the view, providing the focal point of Barmouth Bridge, a half mile long wooden viaduct from where we used to fish for crabs on our holidays. After crawling over the bridge, we stopped in Barmouth, once a shipbuilding town, but now a busy holiday resort.

The line continues by the sea, sometimes right by the beach and sometimes behind a patchwork of fields and dry stone walls. Moving slightly inland we passed Dyffryn where my father's family holidayed during the war, the coastguard instructing them on pacing a safe distance from a mine before they could play on the beach. Later the owner of the holiday bungalow where they stayed sent a postcard advising that 'the risk of hospital was gone', his cryptic message letting them know that the beach was now safe, but without risking the Germans finding out.

Soon then there were glimpses of the almost tidal Shell Island, with its 300 acre campsite, the largest in Europe. A short while after Harlech, where the castle perches on near vertical cliffs above the station, I was to have my first view of Ynys Gifftan, its gently rounded shape rising above the Dwyryd estuary. Beyond the island could be glimpsed the white domes and towers of Portmeirion, the Italianate village. A popular tourist destination, it has been the setting for many TV programmes and films, including most famously *The Prisoner*.

At Talsarnau station I noted a path heading towards the island, but already had my doubts it would continue over the mud that was now under water. After crossing another wooden trestle bridge we stopped at Penrhyndeudraeth, where there was once an explosives factory, and where two girls who'd joined at Harlech with large art portfolios alighted. I assumed they were returning from college and it was good to see that this railway is still well used by locals as well as visitors. A few minutes later I too was leaving the train, having enjoyed the hugely scenic and interesting ride.

Once the main port for exporting Welsh slate, Porthmadog is now a bustling tourist town and even in March the little cafes and shops were busy with visitors, many of them having arrived on coach trips. It is perhaps now best known as the terminus for two narrow gauge steam railways that run through the Snowdonian mountains, the Welsh Highland to Caernarfon and the Ffestiniog to Blaenau Ffestiniog. There's actually a third little line, the Welsh Highland Heritage Railway, but at just a mile long this is more of the grown men playing trains type of attraction.

This was a rare occasion when I aimed to visit two non-adjacent islands on the same tide. Hence I was on a tight timetable. Cei Ballast is only a couple of hundred yards from Porthmadog harbour, but the map showed a permanent channel between them. My plan was to cross to the other side of the Glaslyn estuary, walk through the woods to the headland at Trwynypenryn, then back to Cei Ballast across a mile of sands that according to the map appeared to be dry at low tide. The Cobb, a man-made stone causeway, runs across the estuary carrying a road, footpath and the Ffestiniog Railway. With a train due I saved myself the mile walk, getting off at Boston Lodge Halt, and suspecting that the other passengers considered I was too tight to pay the not inconsiderable fare for a longer ride.

Looking over the sands as we crossed the estuary it was hard to see if my intended route was walkable, but it seemed that there might be a way through the channels and marshes closer to the Cobb. Hence rather than take the footpath to the headland I set off back along the Cobb, looking for a dry route to the island. First I tried the salt marsh but the channels were too wide and the mud too soft. Continuing on the causeway until about halfway back to Porthmadog, once again I climbed down over the sea defences and sought a way across. Again soft mud and wide channels thwarted progress. It was not yet low tide, but with a train to catch to Ynys Gifftan, Cei Ballast had to be visited before the waters were at their lowest. Returning to the Cobb I sat on the rocks to consider options.

Porthmadog Harbour Master had told me that Cei Ballast can be walked to 1½ hours either side of low tide, and perhaps more on a big tide as it was today, although on neap tides it's not dry. However low tide times aren't published for Porthmadog (they can be estimated from Criccieth times) as fresh water from the Glaslyn river means they wouldn't be accurate, so caution is needed. The Harbour Master said he walks to the island from South Snowdon Wharf, a not very attractive 1970s estate on a promontory just south of the harbour. Perhaps the estate featuring in the December 1974 edition of Concrete Quarterly, the magazine of the Cement and Concrete Association, could give a clue as to why it isn't particularly pleasing on the eye. However although I was now within the 1½ hour time window, there was still a wide strip of water beneath the wharf wall and a maze of channels between the Cobb and the island. As I'd already found, unless suitably attired much of the mud was too soft to walk on, and even in wellies care would have been needed. Perhaps I should have tried to cross from further down the estuary as originally planned. I was beginning to think that Cei Ballast would be a tidal island I couldn't visit, but also to doubt that it would qualify anyway.

Then I made a decision. I hadn't travelled 260 miles to give up 200 yards from an island. I would bend my rules and get wet! Trousers rolled up I splashed through channels, which with careful choice of crossing point were not much more than 6 inches deep. Soggy boots showed that Cei Ballast was failing the 'can be walked to with dry feet' definition, although the tide still had a little to fall.

Arriving on the island I found I wasn't alone. Moored on the beach was a yacht, *The Ravan*, and as I approached a couple appeared from inside. They'd been keeping it here for several months while doing it up, and it was nearly seaworthy again. The lady said that I could have walked from the headland, but the distance is further than it looks and the soft sand hard going.

Cei Ballast was once just a sandbank and although it looks natural, was entirely man-made. When Porthmadog harbour was built in the early 19th century ships came from all over the world to collect Welsh slate. The ships, many of which were made locally, were designed for sailing with heavy loads and with little call for imports to Porthmadog, they carried stone ballast for stability. At the end of the voyage the ballast had to be dumped and the sandbank outside the harbour was a convenient point to leave it. Gradually the stone built up until an island was formed. Once the pile had grown sufficiently a steam crane was positioned on top of it, enabling unloading to be carried out more efficiently. The crane took a couple of hours to build up steam, so as the driver had to start work early a house was built for him on the island. His name was Lewis and for many years the island was known locally as Lewis's Island.

Being formed of stones from all parts of the world Cei Ballast forms a unique geological site, now rising to a height of 6 metres. Over time the island became vegetated and now is mostly covered with thick scrub. This was pretty much impenetrable from the northern side, but the yacht couple suggested I walked around the beach. At the southern end there's less vegetation and I was able to explore some grassy glades. The house is long gone, although there is some evidence of buildings, presumably either Lewis's home or the base for his crane. At the edge of the beach and running all along the eastern side of the island are the remains of wooden jetties, where the ships would moor while their ballast was unloaded.

Now the island is quiet with few visitors. It has a thriving wildlife population and attracts just the occasional visitor, either by boat or like me, across the mud. Like most of our tidal islands there are occasional strandings here and the lifeboat is called out every so often to rescue those who fail to respect the tides. The couple on the yacht told me that they were involved in one stranding, when two lads stole the small dinghy they use to get to the island at high tide. Not understanding boats, they managed to burn out the engine and became trapped on Cei Ballast. The police were called but although by now the tide was low, they refused to pursue the miscreants due to 'health and safety'. They were however apprehended later, but the couple felt (perhaps with justification) that the lenient sentences received didn't reflect the loss of their expensive engine.

I returned to Porthmadog the quick way, splashing through the channel by South Snowdon Wharf, the route that the couple with the boat use. The water was a few inches deep and even at low tide does not completely dry. However I had shown that Cei Ballast is accessible on foot and confirmed that it be reached with dry feet from the headland, even if this is not an easy walk. Despite my doubts Cei Ballast qualifies as a tidal island.

Climbing up the metal ladder to the wharf, I walked back into the town, stopping briefly at the Tourist Information Centre. The lady was very helpful, but had little information on the island, although was able to confirm that the correct pronunciation is 'Kay' Ballast. It is sometimes called Ballast Island. She did have one book which mentioned it, but that was in Welsh. Indeed I was having to change my view on Welsh signage and offer humble apologies to anyone who may have been offended by my comment in chapter two. Whilst Welsh isn't widely used in the south of the country, I'd heard it used in Cardigan and in this area it is often the first language. People were speaking it on the train and in shops. The Harbour Master had answered his phone in Welsh and for the tourist information lady English was clearly a second language. As in the south, signs were bilingual, but here with Welsh widely used, duplication was necessary.

The tide was turning as I took the train three stops back to the little village of Talsarnau. It was going to be tight to visit two islands on one tide, but the map showed a nice easy path straight from station to island. For a few hundred yards there was indeed an easy path, running between fields where newborn lambs frolicked, capered and generally did what little lambs do. One family came running up to greet me, perhaps hoping I'd provide a little snack, but with food reserves now dwindled to just a kit kat, I decided my need was the greater. Mummy sheep could eat grass and her two lambs soon decided that milk would suffice.

The OS map shows a dotted green line to the island but warns that 'Public Rights of Way to Ynys Gifftan can be dangerous under tidal conditions'. Just over the sea wall was an old signpost, but blank with no warning or directions. What neither the map or sign said, was that there's quite clearly no path. First there is half a mile of the Glastraeth (green beach) marsh to cross, where the grass is cropped short by sheep. Meat from salt marsh sheep commands a premium price and Wild Meat, a company based in Somerset, and one of the UK's specialists in salt marsh lamb, source from Glastraeth. I didn't let on to those sweet little lambs where they'll be ending up.

The marsh is interspersed with a mass of deep channels and although with the tide low most had only a few inches of water, the sides are steep and muddy, so it took me some time to find a way across. There was no path and no way of reaching the sea without jumping or splashing through channels.

My considerable doubts of the existence of the path shown on the map crossing the sands to Ynys Gifftan were proved to be correct. There was no path, but worse, just beyond the rapidly eroding edge of the marsh was a channel, roughly 15 yards wide and couple of feet deep. Turning to the right I found the end of the channel by a little inlet, and from here it was mostly dry sand to the island. However, there were waves on the channel and the tide appeared to be coming in. The Harbour Master had said it was safe to cross for an hour either side of low tide, so in theory I still had at least 30 minutes. Weather conditions however can affect the times. I had no desire to spend a cold night on an island, with inadequate clothing and just that Kit Kat for dinner. People have been caught out on the mud here and last year someone had to be plucked from the sea by a helicopter, the water being too shallow for the lifeboat. Although they now have a surf rescue boat with low draught, I didn't fancy trying it out. The delay crossing the marsh and talking to sheep had jeopardised my visit to Ynys Gifftan. A decision had to be made, and quickly.

Just like Cei Ballast, I was reluctant to give up so close to an island, although preferred to be neither stranded nor drowned. Deciding that it would be OK if I was quick and turning to check on the channel at least once a minute, I set off at pace across the sands. There were a few patches of water and the sand soft in places, but I was soon on a little beach on Ynys Gifftan. The island is mound shaped, rising to a height of 39 metres and with a track around the southern edge. I would like to have explored but that would surely have meant spending the night here, so with a quick look at the cottage, returned across the sands, following my outward footprints to avoid the soft areas.

Back on the mainland the channel didn't seem to have grown. Waves were still slopping onto the sand, but it seemed neither deeper nor longer. I watched it for a while then I twigged. It wasn't the tide coming in but wind making the waves. The channel wasn't growing and the island was not going to be cut off for a while. I could have stayed there longer. Slightly annoyed with myself I considered going back, but by now the safe hour was past. Safety had to prevail. Many people have been drowned visiting tidal islands and it would be a shame if the book was to be incomplete due to recklessness by the author.

Ynys Gifftan, which is owned by Lord Harlech, has probably been uninhabited since the mid 1960s and the cottage is now in poor condition. It was however once the centre of the island's farm and Celt Roberts from Talsarnau kindly provided me with information on its tenants. Hugh and Mary Williams started farming here around the turn of the 20th century, Hugh working both on the farm and in the slate quarries at Blaenau Ffestiniog. It is thought that he had an accident at the quarry, either breaking or losing a leg, and with no compensation forthcoming Mary had to work the farm as well as bringing up their four children. The difficulty of life on a tidal island was illustrated on one occasion when Hugh suffered severe stomach pains in the middle of the night and Dr Pritchard had to be called from Penrhyndeudraeth. The doctor never relished being called from his bed at the best of times, but a night time call to Ynys Gifftan was something else. He was however persuaded to attend, but whether he returned with wet feet is not known.

Sir Ifor Williams, an expert on Welsh place names, once said that only fools try to explain their origin. Nevertheless I shall give you two possible explanations for the unusual name of Ynys Gifftan. The first is that the island was a gift to Lord Harlech from Queen Anne – hence Gift Ann. The second is that there is a farm on the other side of the river called Abergafran, gafran being the Welsh word for goat. A young goat would be a gidan and perhaps goats were once plentiful on the island. Maybe it was called Gafran or Gidan Island, which over time became corrupted to Gifftan. OK so neither explanation sounds particularly convincing, but they are the best I can offer.

With time to spare I walked along the sea wall to the next station, Llandecwyn, a tiny halt right on the shore. Trains only call on request and as dusk fell I put out my arm as if to hail a bus. After a moment of slight panic when it appeared not to be stopping, the rear of the train pulled up at the short platform and I was soon back in Porthmadog and ready for dinner.

I'd selected the Royal Sportsman Hotel, a 19th century coaching inn made from local slate, as it's mentioned in Bill Bryson's *Notes from a Small Island,* probably my favourite travel book. The hotel website quotes prominently from his book: '*I examined the meagre stock of hotels with some care – I felt entitled to a spell of comfort and luxury after my night in a cheerless Llandudno guesthouse – and I chose an inn called the Royal Sportsman*'.

If you judge a hotel by the number of times you are called sir during the checking in process, then the Royal Sportsman is indeed a fine inn. If however you judge by its definition of a steak pie (a small disk of puff pastry perched in the middle of a dish of meat doesn't comply with mine), then it does not excel. The hotel chose not to display Bryson's next sentence, '*My room was adequate and clean, if not exactly outstanding, and suited my purposes*'. Nor did it advertise the presence of a small step into the bathroom, cunningly designed to trip the semi-conscious guest on a nocturnal trip for a pee, and as memory function disappears at 3am, to trip them again as they return to the bedroom 60 seconds later.

Next morning the sun shone as once again I crossed the Cobb. The tide was high, Cei Ballast very much an island, and the mud which I'd struggled to cross now rather prettier blue sea. I was on the Ffestiniog Railway once more, travelling back not by the quickest route, but a scenic ride through Welsh mountains. Where once slate trains ran by gravity to the docks at Porthmadog, now tourists are pulled by steam engines, most of which used to drag the empty trucks back up the line. Running through forests and along mountain sides, by fast flowing streams and serene lakes, in tunnels and around horseshoe bends, and climbing over 700 feet on a 13½ mile journey, it is a spectacular ride.

With the emphasis on scenery rather than engine numbers, tourists easily outnumber railway enthusiasts (they don't like being called spotters by the way and contrary to popular belief some of them don't even wear anoraks), but I was pleased to find that the staff complied with the usual preserved railway stereotypes. A young work experience girl in the shop at Porthmadog who sold me a postcard of my train's engine (David Lloyd George, the most powerful on the line no less) complete with special railway stamp, but neglected to say that the only box I could post it in was on the station platform. An elderly but kindly gentleman for guard, who explained the posting procedure, but declined to take the card lest he should leave it in his pocket for weeks. Instead he directed me to a jolly lady in the station shop at Blaenau who would happily have posted it, but was beaten to the job by the obligatory over-keen railway teenager. The type with almost certainly more badges than friends, but on whom the future of the railway will one day depend. My young nephew received the card a few days later, delighted with the engine's resemblance to 'Mighty Mack', a Thomas character with faces at each end. (Perhaps I should tell you that according to the company's website, it's a double fairlie locomotive built to the design of Robert Francis Fairlie using two articulated power bogies at either end of the engine with an 0-4-4-0 wheel arrangement. Or perhaps I shouldn't?).

At Blaenau Ffestiniog I changed to the Conwy Valley line, the single coach train carrying a handful of locals contrasting with the nine carriages on the steam train mostly filled with tourists on coach holidays. I don't know if I should, but I find the spectacle of disembarking coach passengers mildly amusing, and the hundred or so who tottered their way across the station platforms didn't let me down.

Hemmed in by mountains and huge piles of slate, Blaenau Ffestiniog is a grey and often depressing place. Like Princetown in the middle of Dartmoor and Buxton in the Peak District, it seems to rain here more days than not. In fact with an annual rainfall of 79 inches it is Britain's second wettest town (Fort William is the wettest). Today however was probably the first time I'd visited and seen a speck of blue sky. Enough maybe to make a shirt for only a particularly diminutive sailor, but having never been here in anything but dismal weather I almost expected to see residents coming out of their houses to stare at the strange bright light in the sky. The 20 minute wait proved ample to explore the town, sort out the postcard problem and leave time to spare for coach passenger watching.

Leaving the grey slate of Blaenau and passing through the longest tunnel in Wales, the Llandudno train came out in the rugged Lledr Valley with mountains close by either side. After Betws-y-Coed the scenery softened as we ran alongside the very full Conwy river. With snow melt from the mountains, the water almost overtopped the bank. The line often floods here and a few years ago had to be closed for several months. Two ladies sitting opposite commented that millions had been spent on the road but locals wanted the railway sorted. This line was just as scenic as the Ffestiniog, but with people getting on and off at most little stations, slightly more fulfilling in that it provided a true service for all its passengers, not just a ride, and at a considerably cheaper price too.

From Llandudno Junction the journey home illustrated more contrasts of rail travel. The train to Shrewsbury was so packed it wasn't a case of would I get a seat, but could I find a few square inches to stand. It had connected with the Irish ferry at Holyhead and at each station some of those standing in the vestibules had to get out with their luggage to enable others to move in and out the train. The sausage bap I'd bought in the station buffet had to be eaten standing in the aisle, trying not to drop crumbs on the heads of passengers seated either side.

There hadn't been room for the refreshment trolley to get on at Llandudno Junction, but at Chester things improved. A good proportion of the passengers got off, allowing me to sit, and Britain's most amusing refreshment trolley man boarded. I'd encountered him once before and as soon as the trolley appeared with the announcement 'Ice creams – tootie fruitie', I knew we were in for a treat. 'Alligator sandwich – make it snappy' – Down the carriage he went asking everyone if they wanted anything from the 'lucky trolley', – 'Cup of tea, 150 lucky pennies – I'm not mean, the company mighty be'. 'Viper's noses, Squirrels on sticks', all with a dead pan face. 'Albatross – sea bird flavour'; the journey to Shrewsbury was greatly enlivened. With 50 minutes to wait there was time for a quick cake with my brother, then back on the Wrexham & Shropshire to London. With the menu lacking albatross, sea bird flavour or otherwise, I rounded off a most enjoyable couple of days by treating myself to the lamb shank once again.

## Post Script:

Sadly the Wrexham and Shropshire Railway has ceased operating, a victim of the recession and restrictions on competition which prevented it from picking up passengers at major West Midlands stations.

# CHAPTER SEVEN

# LITTLE EYE & MIDDLE EYE & HILBRE ISLAND

With mainland Wales having no tidal islands north of Porthmadog (there are however several off Anglesey), my next trip was to the Dee Estuary. Here three islands, Little Eye, Middle Eye and Hilbre Island, lie off the Wirral Peninsular and are accessible on foot from the coastal town of West Kirby.

Hilbre (generally pronounced 'Hilbray') is one of the minority of tidal islands to be the subject of a book, and although long out of print, Swan Books were able find a copy of *Hilbre – The Cheshire Island*. Edited by J.D. Craggs of Liverpool University and including an account of a year on Hilbre by Ann, wife of Tim, the island's warden in 1977, the book gives a real insight into the life on a tidal island and great detail of its natural history. Although written almost 30 years ago, J.D. Craggs has provided me with much useful information on the history and wildlife of these islands, which along with more recent locally published material, made Hilbre one of the easiest to research. It is however interesting that whilst the islands are well known and treasured by many locally, and have featured on the BBC Coast programme, I found hardly anyone outside the locality who had even heard of them.

My journey here was far from direct, starting with a meeting of the Football Supporters' Federation in Walsall, going on to a night with my parents in Ledbury, then thanks to engineering works on the Birmingham line, a lift to Hereford and train to Liverpool. After a distinctly mediocre but quick lunch in a Chinese buffet restaurant, Merseyrail took me out to the Wirral. More of a day trip than holiday destination, West Kirby has a limited choice of accommodation, however a bed & breakfast in Hoylake, two miles east, took my fancy. And what a good choice it was.

At the outset I decided that unless of specific interest, I'd only write about accommodation if it was particularly good or bad. Firkin House was most definitely the former. Two thirds the cost of local hotels, but beautifully decorated, with all the room facilities you could want, freshly cooked breakfast and a view of the sea from my window. Plus, what is often the main benefit of a small establishment, friendly proprietors who are interested in their guests and genuinely keen to please. Linda and Richard had been running the B&B for ten years and catered for a wide range of customers, including Ron Frewin, the British sand yachting champion who comes here three times a year for events on the vast sands of the Dee Estuary. Linda told me that I was sleeping in his room, a tenuous claim to fame, but one I shall note nevertheless.

The information pack in my room gave details of several local walks, including the route along the coast to West Kirby and advice on getting to the islands. I felt that this was perhaps a little too detailed, but then realised that the 'i' was a misprint and it was your wellies that it was advising to take with you!

Before checking in I'd gone down to the sea for a quick look at Hilbre Island surrounded by water with the tide still high. By the time I returned to the seafront, having chatted with Linda and got myself sorted, the water had receded. There was just sand and mud between me and the island, but I'd read many warnings that it isn't safe to walk from Hoylake. The mud is too soft and the tide comes in very fast. However it was a most pleasant two mile walk to West Kirby, starting along the beach, then on a path running between the sea and Hoylake Golf Club, home of the 2006 Open Championship won by Tiger Woods.

Approaching West Kirby I passed a lone and very drunk Scouser, singing on the beach. Was he put there by the Tourist Board to perpetuate the stereotype I wondered? Fortified by an extremely jammy doughnut from Morrisons' café, I set out across the sand from the corner of West Kirby's large marine boating lake, where colourful sails darted across the water. A notice board on the shore displays a map showing the recommended route – directly to Little Eye, to the east of or over Middle Eye and straight on to Hilbre. Any other routes, including the most obvious way of a straight line from West Kirby, are potentially dangerous. I'd already seen how deceptive the estuary can be, finding myself sinking in a patch of mud on the otherwise sandy beach close to the shore at Hoylake. Here the mud covered just my boots, but much care is needed and like most tidal islands, Hilbre has its tales of travellers getting into difficulties.

Ann Cleeves writes of a frightening experience getting lost walking from the island in thick fog and eventually realising that the footprints she was following were her own, leading in a circle. On another occasion of poor visibility two officials from the Mersey Dock and Harbour Board were being driven across the sands by her husband, who lost his bearings and driving too far south of Little Eye, found the Land Rover stuck fast in a patch of soft sand. The warden was well equipped with waterproofs and wellingtons, but the officials dressed in office clothes were somewhat less prepared for a walk through rain and mud to fetch help.

It took me 15 minutes to reach Little Eye, having splashed through a number of channels several inches deep, which tested the waterproof properties of my walking boots. They failed the examination so maybe I should have followed the mis-spelt footwear advice from Firkin House. Several birders who'd stayed out on Hilbre over high tide passed me on the sands and a handful of other people were walking out to the islands, mostly accompanied by their dogs. At the last channel a rather boisterous canine bounded up to me and in turning to avoid the worst of his splashing I managed to drop my notebook into the water. As usual in these situations, the owners didn't apologise, anything short of biting an arm off generally excused as 'just being friendly'.

Little Eye, sometimes called The Eye, is a tiny island, with less than half an acre exposed at high tide. J.D. Craggs notes that constant erosion was causing the island to reduce in size with 'disturbing rapidity' and thirty years on the effect of climate change can only be accelerating such loss. Hence Little Eye may be one of the first of our tidal islands to disappear. There are no buildings, but at the south end is a stone base, the remains of a landmark built by the Dock Board to guide shipping through the sandbanks to Wales. Predominantly rocky, with little vegetation other than short grass, Little Eye provides insufficient cover to support mammals or nesting birds, although in winter the island is used as a high tide roost by large numbers of wading birds.

Walking across the island I continued over sand and rocks to Middle Eye, which is sometimes known as Little Hilbre and was once called Middle Island. On the west side of the island are rock and sand pools, but Middle Eye itself is mostly covered in grass and bracken, with no buildings. Part of the island was once cultivated and the banked outlines of three small fields are still visible. Sheep were once grazed here to keep the grass short and bracken was cut for animal bedding. In the Second World War Hilbre was occupied by the RAF and Middle Eye used as a part of a decoy system with lights lit to confuse enemy bombers attacking Liverpool. Before climbing up onto the island I explored a tiny rocky inlet, with a natural arch in one corner. A splendid little feature, seemingly almost in miniature to match the size of the island.

A path runs across the island, which with rocky cliffs on the northern side is much higher than Little Eye. I stopped for a moment to watch a heron standing motionless at the waters edge. With rocks below I was just thinking that this side is not easily accessible, when I saw a teenage lad sitting half way down the cliff. He called a greeting as I passed and to my slightly concerned enquiry confirmed that he was OK. As I looked back a few minutes later he and another lad appeared, popping up over the cliff top, so all was indeed well, although I would be more than a little unhappy if it were my children climbing unsupervised on such steep rocks.

Before moving on to Hilbre I walked off a little to the north of Middle Eye with the aim to take a photo, but soon found myself in soft mud, confirming the advice to take the path over the island or stay close to its landward shore. Rain had been forecast to start at 4pm and having commenced as light drizzle on time almost to the minute as I'd left West Kirby, had now become quite heavy. After returning to Middle Eye to don waterproofs, I headed over slippery rocks to the main island.

The main slipway onto Hilbre is on the south west corner, but not knowing this I went to the right, scrambling up a narrow path and coming out near the Bird Observatory. It had taken me 50 minutes from West Kirby, including stops for photos – less than the hour that it's advised to allow. In pouring rain I spent the next hour exploring this most interesting island. Roughly four times the size of Middle Eye, at 11 acres it is however one of the UK's smallest inhabited islands.

Hilbre is fortunate in having its own charity to help take care of the islands, the Friends of Hilbre which was formed in 2001 and has a current membership of around 150. Should, like me, you wish to join, their website is www.deeestuary.co.uk/hilbre. The Dee Estuary is a Site of Special Scientific Interest, a Ramsar Site as a wetland of international importance for wetland birds and an EU Special Area of Conservation. The three tidal islands and the surrounding foreshores are owned and managed by Wirral Council and form an official National Nature Reserve. The Friends of Hilbre aims to promote the conservation, protection and improvement of the nature reserve, assisting by providing volunteer help, funds and education.

Sue Craggs from the 'Friends' told me that there is a lot of incorrect information written about the islands and a tradition of 'homemade' Hilbre stories. For example, I had been told that the current ranger David Cavanagh had been married on the island. Then I was told from what appeared to be a reliable source that although he and his fiancée Fi who had met on Hilbre, had hoped to register for marriages one of the Victorian buildings, they found (like the Queen) that if you register a place for one wedding you have to let Joe Public be married there ever after. Hence they married in a local parish church in Wirral and held the feast at their home on the island. The third and correct version of the tale came from David himself. Whilst in principle they had no objection to people being married on the island, the problem of logistics with marquees, caterers and supplies having to be brought over by Land Rover between tides, plus other little issues such as the only toilets at that time consisting of buckets, meant that it wasn't really practical. Hence they held the wedding and reception on the mainland, but had an extra celebration on the island the next day, having great fun arriving by boat as the tide was in. So the story I'd originally been told about wedding carriages driving over the sands wasn't quite right. Taking note of Sue's warning, I've tried to corroborate information sources wherever possible, but will apologise now should I have inadvertently perpetuated any Hilbre myths.

The islands are composed of bunter sandstone, a soft rock which is also present on the Wirral and it's thought that they were connected to the mainland until the end of the last ice age, around 10,000 years ago. Increased water levels from melting glaciers then cut a channel north of West Kirby. There appears to be some disagreement amongst experts as to whether the higher areas of land formed separate islands, or if they were initially one and became separated by wave action, an erosion process that continues to this day.

From finds of flint arrowheads and scrapers we know that Neolithic man visited, whilst a bronze axe head and burial urn indicate that Bronze Age people came or lived here. Romans inhabited Hilbre, which would have been an important signalling position and defensive outpost for the city of Chester, although they left little sign of their presence, just the occasional coin, buckle or brooch having been uncovered.

Fragments of jewellery and pottery from the 3rd, 4th and 7th centuries suggest continuing occupation, and major relics dating from just before the Norman conquest have been found. A cross head carved from a piece of red sandstone and thought to have been made around 1000 AD by masons from Chester was discovered in 1862. Two years later a keeper unearthed a stone slab, and on hearing of this a local antiquarian Ecroyn Smith rushed to the island. He discovered four skeletons beneath the stone, but finding it too heavy to lift, grubbed about among the bones, ruining the chance to undertake a proper excavation. Smith commented that such an excavation would take several men and weeks, but after his act of archaeological vandalism the bones eventually disappeared. More recent investigation suggests that they probably dated from around 1050.

Like many of our tidal islands Hilbre has spiritual connections. Monks probably lived here from around 1080 and certainly from 1140, the islands belonging to the Norman Lord Robert of Rhuddlan who gave them to Saint-Evroul-sur-Ouche Abbey in Normandy, who in turn passed responsibility to St. Werburgh Abbey in Chester. No physical signs of their presence remain, although it is said that a monastic ghost by the name of Jack still inhabits Hilbre. The monks are however involved in two legends of the island.

The first concerns the discovery of a dying girl on Hilbre. The daughter of the Governor of Shotwick Castle, she fell in love with a young man who she wished to marry against her father's wishes. He however arranged a marriage with a suitor of his choice and during the voyage to Wales, where the ceremony was to take place, told his daughter that he had ordered the death of her lover. On hearing this she threw herself overboard and was washed up in a cave on Hilbre, where she was found by a monk. Known as the Lady's Cave, this can still be seen on the south west corner of the island.

The second legend, known as the Story of the Sands, took place in the 12th century. Richard, Earl of Chester had been attacked and cut off from his city by the Welsh while on a pilgrimage to St. Winifred at Holywell. He managed to get a message to his Constable, William Fritz-Nigel of Halton, who raised an army and rode fast to Hilbre, hoping to find boats to carry them to Wales. However there were no boats and William sought the help of a monk who advised him to pray to St. Werburgh for aid. Immediately the waters of the Dee divided just as the Red Sea had done for Moses, and the Constable's army was able to ride over dry sands to Wales and rescue Richard. The grateful Constable William, fulfilling a promise which he had made on the island, gave to St. Werburgh the village of Newton-by-Chester. It would seem that there is at least some truth in the story, which was translated from Latin by the Chester monk Henry Bradshaw in around 1500, as the gift of Newton-by-Chester is recorded in a charter of 1119. Bradshaw however ends his tale by saying that the sands over which the army passed have 'To this day been called the Constable's Sondes', however if this was true in 1500 it no longer applies, although there is a 'Constable Bank' further down the Welsh coast near Colwyn Bay.

It could of course have just been exceptional conditions of tide and wind that made the waters part, but the 'miracle' may have been partly responsible for Hilbre becoming a minor place of pilgrimage in the 13th and 14th centuries. However once it became a busy trading port and centre for commerce, the island was no longer considered a sanctuary, the last monks leaving in 1538 after the Dissolution.

The island continued to be inhabited through the centuries, although today just the ranger and his wife live here, sometimes assisted by students spending summer months on Hilbre. This year Alison, Kathryn and Ciaran were staying in the Buoymaster's Complex, their work including bracken cleaning, gate hanging, exploring two Victorian wells, and the less enviable tasks of dealing with litter and the composting toilets. The existing buildings and many relics from the past tell us much about the island's history and give it very much the look of an outpost. It is more what you'd expect of a remote Scottish island or Scandinavian village than a settlement a few miles from Liverpool.

At the far end of the island are the ruins of a lifeboat station, which was built in 1849 and used for 90 years until the Hoylake station gained a tractor, allowing the boat to be launched at all tides. The Hilbre boat was required only at low tide and the crew reached it by running across the sands, or riding on horseback or in wagons. The sturdily built walls and slipway make for an atmospheric ruin, especially in the rain and with no one else around. Inside the bricked off part of the ruin is a Victorian tide gauge, powered by clockwork and still used to plot the height of tides. One year the gauge kept failing and after several visits by Dock Company officials, engineers and even divers, the problem was eventually found to be caused by a crab sitting on the float!

As I climbed over the rocks to the waters edge I spotted a lone grey seal poking its head out of the water. I'd expected to see more as hundreds are known to live here and as I stood scanning the sea a couple of other visitors joined me. Responding to my enquiry as to whether they had seen seals, the gentleman told me they were 'keeping away from people like us' and pointed to West Hoyle sandbank a mile or so north. Here we could just see the black bodies of maybe fifty seals pulled up on the sand. I later read that numbers peak in August, but that they only use the estuary to haul-out, feed and moult and many disappear in autumn to breed. Most are thought to originate from around Ramsey Island in West Wales, but in recent years tagging has suggested that they may also travel here from the Isle of Man, Ireland and Scotland. One seal tagged at Colonsay in the Hebrides was tracked by satellite to the Dee Estuary, making the journey in just four days.

As it was mid September perhaps some had already swum off in search of mates. The number of seals using the bank is increasing, with around 150 in 1982, 600 in 2005 and a record count of 825 in June 2010. It is at high tide when the seals can generally be seen swimming around Hilbre or lying on its rocks, making them a well known and much loved feature of the island. This however wasn't always the case, as J.H. Ingram's 1952 book *The Islands of England* describes seals making a nuisance of themselves and a shoot being organised by the Fishery Board to prevent the creatures spoiling salmon fishing.

The other couple soon left, leaving me as the only remaining visitor as I explored the rest of Hilbre. The path crosses two bridges which were put up in the 1970s using stone from Birkenhead demolition sites and passes eight distinctive rectangular holes in the rock. These are often mistaken for graves or even baths belonging to the monks, but in fact are the footings of a wooden landmark beacon which was shown on maps here until around 1830.

By the northern cliff is a white solar powered beacon, a relatively recent navigation aid erected by Trinity House. Beyond this the distinctive Telegraph Station looks out across the estuary. This unusual building, white with a pointed tiled roof and large semi-circular window, fits well with the hotch potch of little structures across the island. It was built in 1841 by the Trustees of Liverpool Docks and formed part of a chain of signal stations running from Holyhead to Liverpool. At that time an optical telegraph system was an essential means of communication between ship and shore, providing a means of transmission by semaphore between a port and its approaches. In the case of Liverpool there were nine stations and the Hilbre Keeper would train his telescopes on the neighbouring stations at Foel Nant (above Prestatyn) and Biston Hill. The round holes in the windows through which the telescopes were mounted can still be seen. Semaphore arms on three masts north of the building were controlled from inside, with the various positions used to convey messages according a set code. It was claimed that the record time to send a message from Liverpool and receive a reply back from Holyhead was 23 seconds, although this seems hardly believably. Perhaps more likely is the story of the insubordinate Holyhead telegraphist, who irate at being asked to repeat a message, sent 'You are stupid' and within a few minutes was reading the reply from Liverpool, 'You are dismissed'!

Behind the Telegraph Station is a tall mast, once used as a giant theodolite to measure the height of sandbanks, but now redundant with the advent of satellite surveying and depth sounding. On the eastern side of the island is a small complex of buildings, little altered from Victorian times. A white building with tall chimney stack is the Telegraph House, which once housed the telegraph keeper and his family and around this are several outbuildings, formerly a stable, pigsty and goat shed.

Amongst the buildings was once the Seagull Inn, the island's public house. J.H. Ingram comments that there must be some doubt as to whether there was enough trade to support such an establishment on a small island, although apparently people from West Kirby used to walk out there in the evening. He suggests that the pub was probably built to excuse the comings and goings of smugglers, who stored contraband in underground chambers on the island. Ingram names Laurie Higgins as the landlord in the mid 19th century, an Irishman who lived here in poverty until suddenly coming into money by dubious means. The traveller Richard Ayton wrote in 1813 that according to local gossip the innkeeper and his wife had obtained their riches by wrecking.

I thought no more of Mr Higgins until visiting Ardwall Isle and reading in *The Solway Firth* by Brian Blake, what appeared to be exactly the same story about an Irishman who around 1850 ran a pub on the island with doubt as to whether there was sufficient trade to support it and suggestion that it was used to cover the activities of smugglers. This Irishman also lived in poverty and came into money allegedly related to a wrecked ship. His name too was Laurie (or Larry) Higgins and as a result Ardwall was often known locally as Larry's Isle.

So where did Laurie Higgins run his pub and is this another incorrect Hilbre story? I turned to Dave Cavanagh and Sue Craggs for help. Dave told me that he too had heard the story and always thought it was true, although now I had told him about Ardwall he wasn't sure. He could imagine a true story being wrongly attributed to different tidal islands due to the vagaries of well meaning people's memory. He was however able to tell me why there was a pub on the island. The shore to the east of Hilbre was once very different, with a lake (channel) between Hoyle sand bank and the shore, from which Hoylake got its name. The lake was a sheltered anchorage, which could accommodate up to 400 tall ships and it was from here that King William of Orange left for his battles in Ireland. These ships together with the smaller coastal traffic and crews of the 'Mersey Flats', which used to transport cargo to the mainland, would have provided plenty of custom for the pub on Hilbre. He didn't think that it was built to hide the activities of smugglers, but suggested that if anything 'naughty' was going on Hilbre was probably a good place to do it.

Sue was able to add to this that the Seagull was the popular local name for the former pub on Hilbre, which appeared in licensing records between about 1790 and 1823, but under the name of 'The Boat'. The licence was said to have been transferred to the Dee Inn in West Kirby, which has long since closed. J.D. Craggs says that the public house was first recorded on

Hilbre in 1793 and that the story goes that its licence was transferred to the Dee Inn, which was recorded in 1844 and the 1850s, but later became a private house and was eventually demolished. Sue said there were allegations of the pub being used for smuggling, but thought that 'wrecking' probably meant looting wrecks rather than luring ships to their doom. In a maritime area like the Dee and Wirral there were many families of sailors, so deliberately causing deaths was not considered acceptable, however any ship breaking up on the sand banks was considered fair game.

So did Mr Higgins run the pub on Hilbre or Ardwall? The stories are identical, but there seems no firm evidence either way. Both islands may well have been involved in smuggling, but with greater shipping activity and less remote population, Hilbre probably had more trade for a pub and so it less likely to have been purely cover for illegal trade. The dates suggest that Hilbre is less likely to have been home to Higgins, as both books indicated the mid 19th century, but Hilbre's licence appears to have ended in 1823, although to further complicate matters Richard Ayton mentions the story in 1813. Perhaps most telling however is that Ardwall was known as Larry's Isle. There seems no way to verify the tales, but on balance I tend to believe that it's more likely to have been in the Solway Firth that Laurie Higgins ran his pub, and that connection to Hilbre is perhaps another of the island's myths.

Like most islands, Hilbre's population was once higher and at one point it even had regular postal deliveries. Keeper Lewis Jones had heard of the Postmaster General's boast that there was not a hamlet in the country which didn't receive the penny post, so wrote to enquire as to whether there had been some mistake in omitting Hilbre. True to his word, deliveries were started in 1898, with a postman calling at the island on Tuesdays and Fridays.

The rain had relented for a while, but soon returned harder than ever, so to put waterproofs back on I sought shelter from the wind behind a large mound in the middle of the island. Unfortunately my leggings couldn't be found when packing, so I'd borrowed my wife's rather gaudy purple pair, last aired on a very wet day on the Essex coast. Luckily there were few people around to see my strange attire. We'd once been shown how to don waterproofs in a storm by a Norwegian mountain guide, but I didn't really get the hang of it and with much flapping of plastic there always seems a possibility of clothing, rucksack or me sailing away in the wind. Beneath the mound is an air raid shelter and the generator room from World War Two which powered the lights on Middle Eye. Next to the mound was a small enclosure holding Hilbre's two very wet Manx Loghtan sheep, who seemed quite unconcerned by the rain, making no effort to shelter. You can never tell what a sheep is thinking. As they watched me walk by they could have been wistfully eyeing up my waterproof clothing, or they might have been secretly laughing at a man wearing bright purple.

Three bungalows towards the end of the island were built by local families between 1890 and 1920, one originally being a navvies' hut on the Manchester Ship Canal and brought to Hilbre on a barge. The most southerly building on the island is the Hilbre Bird Observatory, from which birds are continuously monitored in connection with a national network of observatories and ringing stations. It is manned about 240 days a year, with full lists recorded of species seen and their numbers. Birds are trapped, measured, weighed and ringed before being released, providing much information on populations and migratory patterns.

The Dee Estuary is one of the ten most important in Europe for over-wintering of wildfowl and waders, many of whom roost on the three islands at high tide. As I walked towards the islands a large flock of dunlin flew low over the sands and oystercatchers poked about, their orange beaks probing for food. Even with my limited recognition skills I could see that there are a good variety of birds on and around the islands, but couldn't have guessed that in excess of 230 species have been recorded here. It is one of the best sites to see leach's storm petrel, a small ocean going bird, which during its southward migration can get blown off course, sometimes ending up in the mouth of the River Mersey. The birds are most often spotted off Hilbre after westerly autumn gales, as they battle back out to sea.

Numbers of several species of waders have recently reduced due to disturbance of their roosts and a volunteer wardening service now operates during winter months to explain the effect that people walking, bird watching, horse riding and sailing can have on the birds. Being largely free of ground predators the islands make good nesting sites, with breeding populations denser than similar mainland habitats. Typically about ten species breed here, with linnets, shelduck and meadow pipits the most common. Rare birds are spotted from time to time, the list including some interesting names – laughing gull, bee-eater, surf scoter, red-rumped swallow and pallas's warbler.

Kestrels are often seen on Hilbre, sometimes teaching their youngsters to hunt, the island's population of field voles providing ideal food. The voles are probably the only mammal indigenous to the island and it's thought that they may be forming their own Hilbre sub-species. Island populations of wild mammals make an interesting study, with there often being less diversity of food and habitat, and fewer competitors than on mainland, plus potential effects of small gene pools and of man's hand in introducing or eradicating species. Of course for tidal islands there is the additional factor of whether animals are able to make their way across the sands or causeway.

A.A. Bell reports on a number of mammals that have been recorded on Hilbre and considers whether permanent populations could be maintained. Hedgehogs make an interesting example, with groups of regular sightings, then many years without. Although the hedgehog is capable of a surprising turn of speed and can roam up to two miles in a night in search of food, it seems unlikely that they could negotiate the sand and shallow channels from the mainland. The pattern of sightings suggest more than an odd specimen that may have accidentally been brought to the island and it appears that hedgehogs have been deliberately introduced on a number of occasions. However each time they have died out within a few years, probably because there is insufficient food to allow them to establish a permanent population.

Rabbits were recorded in 1540, possibly survivors from a warren maintained by the monks, and again at various dates until the mid 20th century when they died out. Burrows were present on both Hilbre and Middle Eye, and for a while these were used for nesting by the occasional shelduck. No evidence remains of the burrows, or to suggest that rabbits were able to make their own way to Hilbre, so it is assumed that those that lived here were introduced, probably originally for food.

Common rats and house mice once lived here, probably introduced by man, whose hand was also present in their demise, populations rapidly declining after the arrival of the new keeper's cat in 1977. A more surprising inhabitant of both Hilbre and Middle Eye was the water vole, with good sized colonies here in the late 1960s. How they arrived is a mystery, but the most likely explanation seems to be that some were deliberately introduced into the island's small pond. With little aquatic vegetation and trapped on an island, the voles were forced to adapt to a terrestrial existence, where they were able to take advantage of a greatly improved food supply and breed rapidly.

Foxes are occasionally seen walking across the sands and it is likely that the odd one may lie up on the islands for a few days, but there is no evidence of any having been resident for a longer period. Both stoats and weasels have also been seen crossing to the islands, but although they appear to have stayed for weeks or even months, their failure to colonise suggests there is inadequate prey for breeding. Possibly the most unexpected mammal sighting was a fallow dear spotted on the sands between West Kirby and Little Eye one October morning in 1971. It eventually set off down the estuary, taking to the sea and was rescued by a boat put out from Hilbre. With no known deer herds in Wirral and the creature's readiness to take to the water, it's likely that it had already crossed the river from North Wales. It was thought impractical to allow so large an animal to remain free in the area and it was later accommodated in Chester Zoo.

Studies have shown at least 75 species of spider on the islands, with the population on Middle Eye similar to that in wet heathlands of Wirral. As they are unlikely to have walked across the sands and it would seem improbable that occasional accidental introductions would give the same species composition, it is believed that the spiders present now are descended from those living here when the islands were part of the mainland. On Hilbre, where there has been greater human interference, the spider composition is similar to Middle Eye, but with the addition of a number of species usually associated with buildings, such as house spiders, which it is assumed have been brought over accidentally in straw or building materials.

With its importance for shipping, from 1828 Hilbre was leased and later purchased by the Trustees of Liverpool Docks, who for many years sub-let part of the land to Trinity House for use as a buoy depot. Although the Telegraph Keeper and Buoy Master were neighbours, there was some conflict between the two bodies. The Dock Board allowed their man to keep livestock, but declined to permit the Buoy Keeper to have a cow, stating that there was 'not sufficient herbage on the island to keep two cows'. Their refusal however may have had more to do with legal caution than concern of over grazing. Most of the buildings on Hilbre today were a result of the Dock Board's activities and indeed had it not been for their work in combating erosion Hilbre would be a very different place today.

In the late 19th century Hilbre's primary focus changed from concerns with shipping to becoming a popular day trip destination for visitors. Initially the visitors were mostly local and seemed to cause few problems, however with the opening of the railway to Hoylake then West Kirby, their numbers grew. There was great controversy in 1888 when Nicholas Rundell, a tenant of Hilbre, erected a locked gate across the path. Writing to the Dock Board he expressed his concerns that 'the number of people of all classes invading the island is increasing, some of a decidedly rough and boisterous class'. A local newspaper account in 1900 spoke of 'several picnic parties 'of sorts' evidenced by the quantity of paper and bottles lying about', and litter bins made their first appearance that year. Ten years later the Dock Board declined a request by Hoylake Council for the provision of public conveniences, on the grounds that they were only necessary on Sundays and Bank Holidays. Presumably they thought that those visiting on other days, although fewer in number, were stronger in bladder. The Board added their concerns about those coming to Hilbre, saying 'a very nice class of people have been displaced by a very undesirable class of roughs both male and female. Frequently on Sundays about 300 roughs visit the island, taking with them intoxicating liquor and playing cards'.

It was reported that on the August Bank Holiday of 1911 two thousand visitors descended on Hilbre and measures were needed to control numbers. The Board had considered closing the property on Sundays and Bank Holidays, but instead decided on a ticket system. These were obtainable in advance and those arriving without permission would receive a formal warning letter from the Dock Solicitor. The system was not popular locally and the Chief Constable refused to allow his men to collect tickets, a duty which therefore became a major part of the keeper's duties. Many visitors however didn't bother to buy them and solicitor's letters went to addresses, both real and fictitious, throughout Merseyside.

With little use now for the islands, in 1945 the Dock Board sold them to Hoylake Council for the sum of £2,500, to 'use, hold and administer the property for recreational purposes to the end that the property may be preserved for the enjoyment of the public under proper regulation and for no other purpose whatsoever'. In the charge of Wirral Council, the islands continue to be preserved for the benefit of wildlife and visitors. Whilst the bye law requiring permits still exists, generally only groups of more than six are asked to obtain these, with others free to visit as they wish, subject of course to the tides. Nowadays most visitors are bird watchers, or those taking a gentle stroll across the sands to enjoy the beauty and history of the islands. The vast majority seem to be of the type that would have been approved of by the Dock Board. I can report no sign of 'roughs' and that if anyone was carrying playing cards they were keeping them well hidden.

I was the last visitor to leave Hilbre as I set out once more across the rocks and sand. By Middle Eye the rain had stopped and by Little Eye the sun was out over the Snowdonian mountains to the west. Now I had the familiar feeling of not wanting to leave. Again I had seen an island in one of its wilder moods, although the pouring rain seemed quite fitting with the remote and almost outpost nature of Hilbre. By now all the birders, dog walkers and island visitors were back on the mainland. I was alone on the expanse of sand and back on Hilbre, just the ranger, his wife and the three students would remain as the tide rose and the island became cut off until morning. I stopped frequently as I headed towards West Kirby, looking back at the islands with the distant mountains behind, and taking photos of the sands with evening light falling on its furrows, channels and worm casts.

Back on the mainland I bought fish and chips and ate them looking across to the islands as dusk fell. With autumn approaching, today time had been limited by daylight rather than tides and soon the Welsh mountains were just dark outlines on the horizon. I caught a train the one stop back to Hoylake and before returning to Firkin House walked down to the shore once more. Out to sea a red light flashed every three seconds and my eyes could just make out the shape of Hilbre, the warning light flashing above the middle of the island. Next morning I returned for a final look before catching the train home. The sun was shining and the islands looked inviting. It was tempting to return to experience them in better weather, but the tide was rising and my ticket valid only on the booked train, however one day I shall return to these islands, with their beauty, wildlife and history, yet so close to our northern cities and industry.

## CHAPTER EIGHT
# CHAPEL ISLAND

Everyone to whom I mentioned my plan to walk across the sands to an island in Morecambe Bay expressed considerable concern that I may not return to tell the tale. Such is the reputation of the sands since 23 Chinese cockle pickers tragically drowned here in February 2004. Indeed it can be highly dangerous to venture into the bay and every year lives are lost. Today however I was to be in the safe hands of Ray Porter, a local fisherman and official guide to the sands, appointed by the Duchy of Lancaster. I was joining a guided walk from Ulverston to Chapel Island.

The walk was run by Morecambe Bay Partnership, a charity who aim to improve the environment and quality of life around Morecambe Bay. Susannah Bleakley, a lovely lady who had organised the walk and enthused about the island and bay, was most interested that I was writing a book on tidal islands. She put me in touch with Jack Manning, a local fisherman, who in turn gave me the name of Jack Layfield, an authority on Chapel Island who I arranged to meet before we set off.

It took little more than two hours for Virgin Trains' Pendolino to whisk me the 209 miles from London to Preston. (Don't tell Mr Branson though, but I actually preferred the old trains. The ones which rattled rather than swayed, where all the seats lined up with windows, most had tables and there were windows you could open should you wish – speed isn't everything). Changing to the Barrow train, I got my first glimpse of the sea just before Lancaster, then at Carnforth we branched off along the picturesque Furness Line. It was good to see that the charming little stations still had their original buildings, with hardly a concrete booking office or bus shelter waiting room amongst them. Much of the ride skirted the sea or salt marshes, as we passed through the villages of Arnside,

Silverdale and the larger resort of Grange-over-Sands. I'd been advised to sit on the left and as the train passed over the 49 span Leven Viaduct, got my first view of Chapel Island, looking tiny in the wide expanse of sand and water.

It was just before one that I arrived at Ulverston, probably the prettiest station on the line and a short walk from the town centre. I'd found out the day before that the town's annual carnival parade was today and warned that it would be packed. Indeed it was busy, but a helpful policewoman directed me to my guesthouse. With the walk not until 4.30 I had time for a wander round the town and a spot of lunch.

Ulverston is very much a small country market town, rather than a Lake District resort, although some use it as a holiday base, or stay a night when walking the 75 mile Cumbria Way, a long distance footpath running from here to Carlisle. Its greatest claim to fame is being the birthplace of Stan Laurel and a statue of Laurel & Hardy stands outside the Coronation Hall.

The town is a couple of miles from the sea, linked by the Ulverston Canal, which is claimed to be the deepest, widest and straightest in the UK. It was completed in 1796 and enabled large ships to reach the port of Ulverston, where they brought goods such as timber and coal. Slate, iron, charcoal and copper were loaded here, as was gunpowder which was taken to West Africa in exchange for slaves. The canal was used commercially until the First World War and is now owned by GlaxoSmithKline, whose large pharmaceutical factory occupies much of the western side.

After seeking directions from another handy policeman and detouring via a garage for an ice cream, I set out along the towpath. With the sun shining brightly and a variety of birdlife on the water, including several families of cygnets (or signatures as my four year old nephew calls them), it was a most pleasant walk down to Canal Foot and the shore of Morecambe Bay. I was soon distinctly warm and pleased to find that there's a pub by the sea. The Bay Horse Hotel was once a staging post for coaches crossing the sands and provided a most welcome drink.

Stepping out of the pub, I was immediately approached by an elderly gentleman who said I must be Peter. This was Jack Layfield, but how he knew that I was the person to whom he'd spoken on the phone I had no idea. Whilst my teenage son had recently been stopped by the police in my parent's home town of Ledbury for 'walking with a swagger and not looking like a local', I don't think there was anything about my appearance to suggest my Essex roots (I'd left the Burberry baseball cap, hooded top and white stilettos at home).

Jack is a most charming man and was clearly delighted to be able to tell me about Chapel Island, 'his paradise'. He pointed out the channel of the River Leven, the river that drains from Lake Windermere, and told me how porpoises used to chase salmon here. He told me about the railway viaduct to our left and how it had been strengthened in World War One to carry Welsh coal round the coastal line, en route to our fleet in Scapa Flow. Looking back from the sea, he pointed out Hoad Hill and its monument based on Eddystone Lighthouse, celebrating the life of Ulverston born Sir John Barrow, whose illustrious naval career had taken him to the position of Second Secretary to the Admiralty, where he promoted many voyages of exploration and scientific discovery. As we looked across the sands to Chapel Island, Jack told me that censuses of 1851, 1861 and 1871 had all showed that it was inhabited, but that the only building now is a ruin. He wasn't sure if I'd be able to climb up to this as it was surrounded by tall nettles.

As we talked the weather rapidly changed, the sunshine being replaced by heavy rain. Jack got on his bike to cycle home before he got too wet, while the forty or so walkers milled around waiting for the off. A couple of rumbles of thunder brought doubts as to whether we'd be allowed to go out onto the exposed sands, but then Susannah, having signed us all in, introduced our guide Ray. I'd expected a long safety talk but he gave just one warning:

*'If you start to feel you're sinking don't stop. Just keep going!'*

Down the slope once used by stage coaches and out onto the sands we went. A selection of cagoules and umbrellas, of hats and walking sticks, of young and not so young, plus the obligatory dog, heading off in pouring rain to wade through rivers and dodge quicksand, to find a tiny island and return before the rising tide would drown us all. Oh how very British.

Ray had already surveyed the safest route and taken his tractor to place flags at intervals on the sand. Hence we headed east from Canal Foot, soon crossing the first channel which was only about 15 yards across and knee deep. The water was surprisingly warm. The next channel, the main River Leven was wider, faster flowing and thigh deep. I lifted the bottoms of my shorts to keep them dry, but for the two young girls on the walk it was well over waist high. Even at close to low tide I could see how people could be swept away. I thought of Edwin Waugh's account of his dramatic and very nearly fatal trip to the island, *An Adventure on Ulverston Sands*, recorded in the book *Lakes Counties of One Hundred Years Ago* by John March and John Garbutt, an extract from which I'd read on the train this morning.

Around 1854, Edwin Waugh, widely regarded as Lancashire's finest poet and writer, was staying with a friend at Bardsea, just down the coast from Ulverston. Expressing interest in Chapel Island, his friend said he would take him there. They set out with plenty of time before the tide rose, but were delayed by the friend going back for food. Returning the friend told him 'Come on. We've no time to lose now. But we can manage it'. Waugh detected a note of earnestness in his voice, but did not think much about it at the time as the sands still seemed quite dry between them and the island. He followed in silence, looking round at the beautiful scene with his mind at ease. His friend was a very good walker, in the prime of life and Waugh soon began to feel that the pace he was setting was rather too much, especially with a heavy pair of double-soled boots and a thick coat loaded with books and papers. However he laboured on, perspiring freely, but soon reached patches of wet sand where the feet sank at every step. Not seeing the need for such haste he asked his friend to slow, but pointing to where a white sail was gliding by towards Ulverston behind them, his response was urgent, 'Come along! The main channel's filling. We've a channel to cross on this side yet. D' ye see yon white line. It's the tide rushing in! Come on! We can't go back now!' It was only then that Waugh began to see the seriousness of the situation and tramped on his heels through the soft wet sand.

In a few minutes they came to a shallow channel, eight or ten yards across. The two men splashed through without speaking, the water only just above the knee, but rising rapidly. Thinking the danger was over Waugh stammered 'Stop! Slacken a bit. We're all right now', but was startled by the tone as much as the words of reply 'This is not it. This is nothing.

Come on!' Shouting 'Double!' his friend broke into a run, and Waugh, exhausted, with no breath for an answer, struggled on desperately. In three or four minutes they reached the old bed of the River Leven, fifteen to twenty yards wide, but growing at a great rate as the tide came in. Waugh stopped at the edge of the water telling his friend he could not go so fast. Turning round with a wild look, the friend almost screamed 'But you MUST. It's DEATH!'

They entered the channel without further words. Revived a little by the water, Waugh struggled forward. Soon his clothes began to grow heavy and in the powerful currents he could hardly keep his feet. Expecting to be forced over at any moment, he strove on, the water deepening at every step. A thousand thoughts crowded his mind. He recalls the terrible stillness of the scene; the frightful calm of the blue sky; the rocky island with its little grove of trees swaying gracefully in the sunshine – all so beautiful yet all looking down with such majestic indifference upon them as they wrestled for life in the rising tide. In mid-channel, where the water was up to his breast, his friend gave a wild shout for help and Waugh instinctively did the same, but although the island was just 40 yards away there was not a living soul in sight. The rocks echoed their cries; but everything was still as death, except the trees waving in the sunshine. Edwin Waugh remembers his heart sinking and feeling for an instant as if it was hardly worth struggling any longer.

Then he bears testimony to a brave act on the part of his friend. In the deepest part of the channel, with water near the top of their shoulders, he put out his stick shouting 'Get hold!' Waugh was only able to feebly grasp it, but it was enough to allow him to keep his feet and in a few yards they began to ascend the opposite bank. Soon they were on dry sands, with clothes hanging heavily and hearts beating wild with mingled emotions. The two men clambered across rocks until finding a little footpath that led through the grove and to the fisherman's cottage, the only dwelling on the tiny island. Inside they found the old fisherman's wife, who was deaf so had not heard their desperate shouts for help, although even if she had, would hardly have been able to assist. She took their sodden clothes, giving them her sons' working clothes to wear while theirs fluttered on bushes outside the cottage. Telling them to rest in bed, she soon came in with a quart pitcher full of hot tea and setting it down on a chair at the bedside told them 'Now, get that into ye; an' hev a bit ov a sleep'.

When the old fisherman returned from Ulverston a few hours later, followed soon after by his two sons, he told the men that they had chosen a route to the island as foolishly as it was possible to do. He recounted tales of many a man he'd pulled out of the channel, both dead and alive. With low water approaching and nets to tend, he said he must be off, but Waugh and his friend went with him, helping fill a great basket with flukes (flounders). Returning to the cottage, they put on their own now dry clothes and bade farewell to the fisherman and his family, taking with them two dozen of the finest flukes, strung out on a stout cord. When they drew near the friend's house the two men agreed that it would be best not to mention 'this little affair' to their people, but as he sat at supper that night Edwin Waugh could not help feeling thankful that they were eating fish, instead of being eaten by them.

I was glad that my wife hadn't seen Waugh's account before I left and decided it may be wise to keep it from her until I'd visited the other islands in Morecambe Bay.

As we got closer to Chapel Island I made my way to the front of the group to take a few photos. An oyster catcher greeted us, with its characteristic piping 'kleep kleep' call. Large numbers of these attractive wading birds, with their long bright orange-red beaks, live in Morecambe Bay, feeding on the abundant cockles and muscles. I already felt guilty that we were invading the birds' island.

Jack Manning, who visits the island regularly to tend his nets, told me that until the 1990s there were about 100 gulls nests every summer, then in 1990 half a dozen eiders nested here. Their numbers increased year on year, but the gulls decreased, until in 2006 there were none at all. That week he had however seen one tiny gull chick with its mother squawking overhead. For the last three summers there had been 200 eider nests on the island and Jack Layfield had told me that this year some had laid a second batch of eggs. He was concerned that the visitors would disturb them, as he said that when startled the birds fly upwards, crushing the eggs beneath them. I saw one nest on the island, with four speckled eggs, that I think were oystercatcher's. I hope our short visit did not bring the birds harm. Ringed plover often nest on the shingle around the island and once a pair of kestrels nested high up on the cliff, successfully rearing their brood.

*Castle, St. Michael's Mount*

*Warning - Sully
Island Causeway*

WARNING ! WARNING !
DANGEROUS TIDES
MANY PEOPLE HAVE BEEN DROWNED ATTEMPTING TO VISIT OR RETURN FROM
SULLY ISLAND.- THE CAUSEWAY IS A DEATH TRAP. PLEASE TAKE GREAT CARE.

*Worm's Head*

*St Catherine's Island*

*Ynys Lochtyn*

*Hilbre Island & Middle Eye*

*Little Eye (Hilbre)*

*Guided Walk to Chapel Island*

*Rough Island*

*Hestan Island*

*Ardwall Island*

*Davaar Island*

*Cave Painting - Davaar Island*

*Castle Stalker*

*Loch Moidart - Shona Beag from Eilean Tioram*

*Shona Beag & Tidal Islet*

*Eileanan nan Gad*

Chapel Island has rocky peninsulas at each end, with higher cliffs in the middle. We set foot on the eastern end and gingerly made our way across the slippery rocks. Footwear chosen for walking on sand and wading through water was not ideal for clambering over rocks, and much care was needed. At the foot of the cliff was the skeleton of a sheep. The unfortunate creature must have drowned elsewhere and been washed up here, as there are no large mammals on the island. James Melville wrote of Chapel Island in 1969, saying that the only mammals he had seen here were rats, no doubt descendants of some from vessels wrecked nearby when Ulverston was a flourishing port. He noted that they found ready homes in rocks, but that their numbers appear to be considerably diminishing. I saw no evidence of rats, but plenty of rabbit droppings. I wondered if they had found their own way here, or been introduced to the island.

There's no path around the island, but we were able to climb onto the cliff and with much care walk half way around the perimeter. Whilst small, once on the island I found it larger than expected, partly as its profile is smaller from the Ulverston direction. Centuries ago it was actually larger, as much limestone was taken away for building on the mainland. The bore holes for explosives are said to be still visible. In villages along the Morecambe Bay shore there is a tradition that the stone was taken to Liverpool for use in construction of Mersey Docks, but there seems to be no documentary evidence to confirm this.

With trees and impenetrable brambles to the cliff edge on the eastern side, we climbed down onto surrounding rock. From here it would have been possible to walk uninterrupted across Cartmell Sands to Flookburgh. This however hasn't always been the case, as the Leven channel sometimes moves its position in the bay. In fact locals say that it used to change from one side of the island to the other every decade, but hasn't switched since 1976, staying between Chapel Island and Ulverston.

Although Jack Layfield had doubted that we'd be able to get to the island's only building, the ruined chapel, one of the group managed to get up the steep path through the trees. Wearing shorts I was more susceptible to the nettle stings and thistle pricks, but was able to follow him and look inside without too much damage to my bare legs. The building is not quite as it seems and has an interesting history.

Originally known as Harlesdye Isle, the island lay on the ancient route across the bay and would have been a safe haven for travellers caught out by the tide on the Leven Sands, considered to be the most dangerous in Morecambe Bay. In the 14th century Cistercian monks, probably from the nearby Conishead Priory but possibly from Furness Abbey, built a small chapel here to serve the needs of travellers and fishermen. It is after this that the island was renamed. The chapel eventually fell into ruin, but was recorded by William Wordsworth in *The Prelude, Book Tenth* after he passed the island on one of his several journeys across the sands:

> *"As I advanced, all that I saw or felt*
> *Was gentleness and peace. Upon a small*
> *And rocky island near, a fragment stood*
> *(Itself like a sea rock) the low remains*
> *(With shells encrusted dark with briny weeds)*
> *Of a dilapidated structure once*
> *A Romish Chapel, where vested priests*
> *Said Matins at the hour that suited those*
> *Who crossed the sands with ebb of morning tide."*

Nothing remains of the original chapel although the building which I climbed up to is often mistaken for this. In fact this was built in the 19th century by Colonel Thomas Bradyll, the then owner of Conishead Priory, which after the Dissolution had become a private estate. It was actually constructed to resemble a ruin to enhance the view from the priory, so rather than being the remains of a holy place of worship, the building is actually a folly, although none the less atmospheric and intriguing.

Chapel Island nearly became a railway station! In 1837 George Stephenson was considering alternatives to the hilly route over Shap Fell, which the main West Coast line to Glasgow now takes. His idea was to take the railway from Lancaster to Morecambe (then know as Poulton), before proceeding across the sands to Humphrey Head on the Cartmell Peninsular and then cross the Leven Estuary to Furness. The line would have passed through Chapel Island, which he proposed as a station. Embankments would have been built on the sands, with the area inside of these reclaimed.

A year later the route across Morecambe Bay was surveyed by John Haughe, who put forward a more ambitious proposal to the Caledonian,

West Cumberland and Furness Railway. He concluded; '*Upon a careful examination and consideration of all the circumstances and localities, I am of opinion, that the object the Committee have in view is perfectly feasible, and that there is not any difficulty, in an engineering point of view, in carrying a railway across these two bays*'. Starting from each side of the bay piles would have been driven deep into the sand, using a machine constructed for the purpose, which mounted on wheels would move forward as work progressed. Haughe considered that the work could be completed in 3½ years and that the embankments would require 10,453,785 tons of material. The Leven and Crake rivers would have been diverted with tide-gates and bridges built to allow vessels to pass. He estimated that the total cost of this section of the line would be £434,131 9s 4d, but that at £23 per acre, the value of the 52,000 acres of reclaimed land would easily exceed this. However the plan was turned down by Parliament on the grounds of being too expensive and the costs underestimated. Both schemes were dropped and eventually the line built from Carnforth to Ulverston, over which I'd travelled earlier in the day. How different would the bay have been and what a sad loss of an island if the plans had gone ahead.

Close to the island were Jack Manning's fishing nets. These are 'baulk nets', which are stretched out across the sand to catch fish on the ebb tide. Today they were 'hung up' (not fishing), with the bottom cord of the net secured along with the top cord, so fish cannot get in. When set for fishing the bottom of the net lifts on the incoming tide, allowing fish to pass, but falls on the ebb forming a barrier, 'baulking' the fish by preventing them going out to sea. The nets are movable, so once stocks in one area have been caught they can be taken to another position in the bay. Jack knows that baulk nets have been used here for more than 200 years, because his family have fished in the bay since 1800 and perhaps before that. He officially retired in 1997, but in 2006 realised that this particular type of net may never be used again, as it is a labour intensive job to set it up and there are now easier ways to catch fish. So that the method could be recorded for posterity he set up a net to film it. This actually renewed his interest and now he goes out to catch fish when he feels like it. The day I spoke to him he'd caught 70 pounds of flukes, the main fish it traps, although it also produces the occasional sea bass or mullet.

In the year 2000 the shifting channels of the River Leven removed 20 feet of sand from an area close to the shore, exposing some ancient fish traps which were not known or recorded. Jack carried out much research on these and by radio carbon dating of timber found that they were put there around 1350.

Somewhere in the undergrowth on the western side of the island is a memorial stone commemorating the death of a man who died in the 1990s. He is not buried here, but the stone marks the fact that his wedding reception was held on Chapel Island. Jack Layfield had given me instructions on how to locate it and as the rest of the party started to leave, Susannah and I tried to find it. Unfortunately we didn't have time for a thorough look and not wishing to be left behind to find our own way across the channels, had to admit defeat.

I'd been first to arrive at Chapel Island and was last to leave. I had found it to be of much interest and by its location, atmosphere, bird life and history, to be a very special place.

As we walked Susannah showed me a patch of quicksand. Not the most deadly type, but enough to feel our feet sinking. I have since read of a man who spent hours stuck fast in Morecambe Bay quicksand, unable to move, even to turn and see the incoming tide. With great fortune he was rescued by the emergency services just as the waters reached him. Not so fortunate were a man and his young son, stranded on a sand bank. As the waters rose the father put his son on his shoulders so he could continue to talk on his mobile phone, but even though rescuers could hear their shouts, the pair could not be found in thick fog. The voices got weaker until all that could be heard on the phone was water, their two bodies being found later.

The Leven was still flowing out to sea as we waded back, but was now a good six inches deeper. Rain in the last couple of days was causing it to swell and even below waist depth I could feel the strength of the current and wouldn't have wanted to be here alone. It would be a foolish person who attempted the crossing without a guide. The rain had stopped while we were on the island and as we returned in the early evening sun there were good views to the low fells behind Ulverston and the southern peaks of the Lake District beyond.

Back at Canal Foot, farewells were said and the other walkers got into their cars, while I strolled back along the canal. My visit to Chapel Island had been a thoroughly enjoyable experience. Susannah had promised to let me know when there was a walk to Piel Island and I looked forward to once more venturing out onto these mysterious and strangely haunting sands.

Back in Ulverston the procession had finished but many revellers remained. Not the children and families, but drinkers, filling the pubs and spilling out onto the pavements and squares. I went back to the guesthouse to change, then set out to find food, dumping my wet trainers on the way (I'd brought my oldest pair for one last outing, now sacrificed with the waters of the River Leven). Having enjoyed an excellent kebab sitting on a seat in the town, I took another wander, ending up at the railway station. The Barrow train was due and the platform quite busy with people returning home after the festivities. Amongst them were five members of a Scottish pipe band who I'd seen in the procession earlier. As the train was announced one started to play, soon joined by another, then a drummer. They played for a couple of minutes, stopping as the train drew into the station, with a round of applause from their fellow travellers. A fitting end to a most enjoyable day.

Unfortunately, and as I'd expected with my room facing a public car park, the night was not so good, returning revellers waking me at regular intervals. I declined the cooked breakfast in the morning, preferring to walk down to Canal Head for another look across to Chapel Island. It is rare for me to refuse bacon and eggs, but the island was calling me. Three men were fishing from the end of the short jetty, but otherwise the shore was deserted. A Public Byway signpost pointed straight out into the bay, showing the ancient route, with a somewhat understated warning in small letters:

**This route has natural hazards**
**Seek local guidance**

With the fast flowing incoming tide and nothing but water between the island and shore, it was hard to imagine that yesterday forty of us had walked to what looked a small speck in the sea. I got my final glimpse of Chapel Island from the train as we crossed the Leven viaduct once more. Now surrounded by water on all sides, it looked far too small to have housed a family, to have so much history and be held in such affection by the people of South Cumbria. I would see Chapel Island again en route to Foulney and Piel Islands, but for now was to leave it to the birds, perhaps the way it should be.

# CHAPTER NINE
# FOULNEY ISLAND

It was a cold February day with snow sprinkled on the fells when I next crossed the Leven Viaduct and looked across the sands to Chapel Island. On a dull and slightly misty winter's morning the island looked even more remote and mysterious than when I'd walked to it in July. No parties of walkers would be visiting today and the birds could enjoy the island to themselves.

I was en route to Barrow-in-Furness and Foulney Island, a long spit of land protruding into Morecambe Bay, and the only one of the ten Furness Islands that can be reached on foot without crossing sands or bridges. With dangerous sands and fast rising tides, I was having to visit the Cumbrian islands out of sequence, fitting in with guided walks that are mainly run in the summer, but it was only on buying the Ordnance Survey map that I'd discovered Foulney Island. Research confirmed that this can easily be walked to, the causeway only being covered on higher tides. It's actually three small islands joined by the sea wall, but the distinction between Little Foulney, Foulney and St. Michaels Island is not particularly clear.

I'd travelled up via Stafford for a work meeting, then Manchester to watch West Ham play United. Predictably the former was the more successful, West Ham's inevitable defeat being compounded by a long wait in a snow storm for a train from Old Trafford. Severe weather had been forecast for the North West and I set off with a rucksack well stuffed with warm clothing. An out of the way corner of England, I'd only been to Barrow once before, back in 1966 when returning from a family holiday at Seascale. Aged five, one of my few clear memories of the holiday is changing trains at Barrow and being excited that the one we were boarding to Crewe had a steam engine.

With rain or snow forecast I'd decided to get the bus from Barrow and walk back from the island. The next bus wasn't for an hour and a half, so there was time for an excellent late breakfast at Tastebuds cafe and a look in the Tourist Information Centre next door. Here the helpful lady found contact details for John Murphy who runs walks to Piel Island and who gave me some information on Foulney. Barrow is an interesting town with its shipyard and giant sheds where submarines are still built. Particularly impressive is the Victorian red sandstone Town Hall opposite the modern Forum Theatre.

The town is protected by the eleven mile long, but narrow and slightly crescent shaped Walney Island. This is joined to the mainland by a bridge, and although there are proposals to build a second crossing, a few locals would like the current one removed and Walney to revert to true island status. Barrow Island and Ramsey Island are now part of the dock system and permanently joined to the mainland, but south of the town are six very different islands. Piel and Sheep Islands are tidal and I would be visiting them on my next trip. Headin Haw and Dova Haw are tiny islets, too small for me to include, but they can be walked to, although access is muddy and one should not attempt it without a local guide. Roa Island is linked by a permanent causeway that carries a road which rarely floods, and branching off this is the path to Foulney Island.

The bus runs along the Roa Island causeway, but I chose to get off in the village of Rampside and arrive on foot. On the shore is the impressive and unusual Rampside Lighthouse, a stunning remnant of the area's industrial history. Erected around 1870 by the Furness Railway, the narrow square brick-built tower is known locally as The Needle, and was one of a series of 13 lights built on the approaches to Barrow. It is still used by vessels negotiating Walney Channel.

It was only a few minutes walk to the half mile long Roa causeway, a dead straight and solid construction, just wide enough to carry the road. Before this was built in 1847 Roa was a true tidal island. Now it is cut off only for an hour or so a couple of times a year. Originally a railway ran along the causeway, taking goods and passengers to Piel Pier from where steamers ran to Fleetwood, but these ceased after the pier was badly damaged in a freak storm. In summer however a small ferry still runs from Roa to Piel Island.

It has been proposed to build Europe's longest bridge linking Heysham to Rampside, with the 12 mile structure also producing electricity from a tidal stream system. Opponents argue that the projected reductions in journey times are inaccurate and there is great concern about its environmental impact. What cannot be disputed is that the Furness Peninsula would lose some of its peace and tranquillity, and the part of its character that comes from the area's remoteness.

The Foulney causeway leaves to the left about a third of the way along Roa Island Road, where there's a small car park. It's a reasonably easy walk over a mixture of grass, mud and shingle. To the left is an area of salt marsh, formed due to construction of the causeway, and beyond this the extensive sands of Morecambe Bay. Depending on your point of view, either Rampside, Foulney or the southern tip of Walney Island mark the northern tip of this huge bay. To the right were views of Roa and Piel Islands, with Walney beyond. Roa, with its close knit buildings, no two of which appeared alike, and rooftops of varying heights, reminded me of the Italian Islands in Lake Garda. Protruding from the end of the island is the substantial lifeboat station which serves Morecambe Bay and the Irish Sea. Some might have described Piel, with the outline of its ruined castle in the mist, as spooky, others may have thought it romantic.

The embankment widens slightly with a wide shingle beach on the left and here I met a man sitting on the stones. He told me his name was Dave Kendall and that he often comes here, sometimes to fish from the end of the island where good sea bass can be caught. As we looked out across the mudflats he told me that it looks very different with the tide up on a sunny day, and that the area between Foulney and Roa is popular for wind and kite surfing. Dave thought that Foulney causeway was constructed with the intention to create docks on the easterly side, but as I was often finding, the first information I obtained about an island was not always the correct version. The causeway was actually built around 1860 by the Furness Railway for tidal protection, diverting most tides to the south of Foulney and preventing Walney Channel from silting up.

Now it's owned by Cumbria Wildlife Trust and is an important nature reserve. In summer a warden lives here in a caravan, monitoring bird colonies and protecting them from the few visitors that venture onto the island. Foulney is part of the South Walney and Piel Channel Flats SSSI and its make up of shingle, some of which is vegetated, provides ideal nesting habitat for large numbers of ringed plover, oyster catchers and terns. Skylark and meadow pipit nest on the coastal grassland, as do eiders, this being the southernmost limit of their breeding range on the west coast of Britain. The eiders mostly feed on mussels from the extensive beds around Foulney, swallowing them whole and crushing them in their stomachs. If well fed the female can sit on her eggs for 28 days without leaving the nest. Once hatched the young are tended by groups of females in 'crèches', but soon taken out to sea away from ground predators such as foxes.

Large numbers of gulls breed here, with the southern tip of Walney and Foulney Islands supporting 1% of the international population of herring gulls and lesser black-backed gulls. It is however for its tern populations that Foulney is probably best known. Although in the past all five species of British terns have bred here, in recent years only arctic and little terns have nested, laying their eggs in slight depressions in the shingle. The arctic tern is the ultimate long distant migrant, spending summer in the UK and winter in the Antarctic, its migration of up to 22,000 miles being the longest of any bird. It is said that the arctic tern sees more hours of sunlight than any other living creature. Foulney is the only place in north west England where they regularly breed.

Leaving Dave on the beach I continued along the embankment, passing a relatively modern white lighthouse which still shines a light guiding ships into Barrow. Close to this is Foulney's only other building, a small concrete workman's hut now somewhat worse for wear and containing just sacks of rubbish. To protect ground nesting birds dogs aren't allowed beyond this point.

The island soon widens out, with an area of rough grass at its tip. The path, which had changed from stony to easier walking short grass, ends at a small dry stone windbreak, which looked to have been fairly recently made. I was told that there had been a windbreak here for many years, made by local fishermen for protection in adverse weather, but that this was almost completely washed away and a local man rebuilt it about seven years ago. Planks of wood were positioned either side for the walker, angler or bird watcher to rest. On the sea side was a recess in the wall, and in this had been left some attractive shells and a number of children's toys – a plastic bear, ball and some lego. Stuffed between stones in the wall were several coloured tennis balls and a green plastic toy shovel. I wondered if this had any significance, but apparently it is simply flotsam and jetsam put there by fishermen during long hours waiting by the sea. I found a nice piece of ground green glass and a small plastic shell to add to the collection.

Beyond the island, shingle, rocks and little pools stretched for a mile into the gloom; a mysterious and inhospitable area at low tide, but under water for several hours a day. Unusually there was very little wind in what is often a wild and blowy spot, and the sound of bird calls drifted across the shingle. Bricks lying on the shingle are the remains of a lighthouse that once stood at the tip of the island. Of similar design to the one I'd seen at Rampside, this was no longer needed when the channels moved. As the first in the line the Rampside tower could be retained, the other lights sited to align with its position. I turned to the left, walking along Slitch Ridge which almost encloses an area of salt marsh. This is closed during the nesting season and access to the whole island restricted to designated paths. Ahead of me appeared to be two people sitting on the ridge, but as I got closer realised it was just a large piece of driftwood – a tree trunk that had been cleanly cut at the base. I wondered where it had come from and what stories it could tell.

Foulney's mixture of shingle, vegetation and salt marsh is not only important for birds, but also supports important plant populations, particularly on its relatively rare habitat of vegetated shingle. Sea campion, thrift, viper's bugloss and yellow horned poppy thrive here. The high organic input from drift seaweed enables dense strands of sea beet, sea-kale and curled dock to grow on the ridge. Common vetch, meadow saxifrage, ladies bedstraw and bird's foot trefoil inhabit the higher grassland, the last of these being the food plant for the caterpillars of the common blue butterfly, which can be seen here in huge numbers in early summer. Small copper butterflies and the brightly coloured burnet moth are also found on the island.

Foulney is different from all our other tidal islands in both make up and shape. It is formed entirely from pebbles that were brought to the coast from the Lake District by glaciers in the last ice age. More than a mile long, but only 40 acres in area, it has more the appearance of a spit that happens to get cut off, than a true island. Indeed with the tide low and the sea well back, it was hard to imagine that it can be cut off, but the causeway is regularly over-topped for up to four hours. The wall is gradually breaking down, meaning that it is likely to be covered more frequently and with the island no more than 10 feet above high tide level, it will be severely affected if climate change leads to significant sea level rises.

A month before my visit Barrow inshore lifeboat had rescued two ladies and a dog who were trapped on Foulney. They had gone for a walk, but on returning found that the tide had come in and the causeway was covered. After they attempted to walk through the water the lifeboat was called, which took the very wet, cold and a little shaken ladies back to Roa Island. Strong currents pass through the gaps in the causeway and the pair were fortunate not to have been swept away. Barrow RNLI Coxswain Alec Moore offered wise words of advice, 'These situations can be dangerous, we had a few incidents of this nature last year, but fortunately today was perfectly calm. If walkers do find themselves stranded by the tide, all they have to do is remain on Foulney Island where they are safe. The tide will go out and then they can continue their journey. Never try to cross the connecting wall when it is covered in water, it is dangerous'. The Cumbria Wildlife Trust sign at the end of the causeway warns of the danger, although amongst all the wildlife information it could easily be missed, and an RNLI spokesman said that they were liaising in an attempt to have a sign erected to warn of the dangers of the incoming tide.

Before visiting I'd contacted Susannah at Morecambe Bay Partnership and she passed my email to Dave Coward who lives at Biggar on Walney and knows the islands well, having once wardened on Walney. Dave gave me some useful information and promised to let me know when the Walney Liberation Front succeeded in tearing down the bridge so I could include the island in my book! He said that some Roman coins were found here in the early 20th century, which led some to believe that there was a signal station on Foulney, but with no evidence of this he thought it was just a nice story. However I have read of further Roman coins being found in 1959 and 1974, so maybe there was some truth in it. Perhaps there was indeed a signal station here, run by a careless Centurion with a hole in his pocket.

Although this low lying stony island appears to be a pretty inhospitable home, old charts show a building here in the 12th or 13th century. It is thought that is was once inhabited by monks from Furness Abbey, who used the island as a look out. We shall hear more of the monks and their activities in the next chapter.

The promised rain and snow hadn't materialised, so I was able to sit for a while on the dry, if rather cold stones, with a drink and cake, looking across to Piel Island, before setting off for Barrow. I stopped at the end of the causeway to investigate an old wooden trawler on the mud. A man with his dog appeared, asking if I wanted to do it up. He said that the boat had been brought here from Barrow docks about 15 years ago and was owned by someone in Rampside, but they hadn't got round to renovating it. The vessel was now in a sorry state, with the bridge fallen off and lying upturned on the mud.

It's a four mile walk back to Barrow – a walk of contrasts; first the Roa causeway than a pleasant footpath over Beacon Hill. Paved all the way, it's part of a nature trail and very easy walking, with excellent views across Piel Channel to Walney. At Westfield Point countryside changes to industry, with the path running alongside huge gas terminals, a power station, then sewage works. From here the tiny Headin Haw could be seen, just a pimple on the mud half a mile from the shore. The nature trail heads inland but the route to the town centre continues, now on a muddy potholed road between derelict Victorian factories. At any moment I expected to come across a burning car with a body in its boot. The last section was on a main road, passing Morrisons whose café drew me in for another cake, then through the town centre to the railway station and back to Manchester. Furness is certainly an area of contrasts and I looked forward to returning to visit its remaining two tidal islands.

# CHAPTER TEN

# PIEL AND SHEEP ISLANDS

*I was thy neighbour once, though rugged Pile!*
*Four summer weeks I dwelt in sight of thee:*
*I saw thee every day: and all the while*
*Thy Form was sleeping on a glassy sea:*
*So pure the sky, so quiet was the air!*
*So like, so very like, was day to day!*
*Whene'er I looked, thy Image still was there:*
*It trembled, but it never passed away*

*William Wordsworth 1805*

And so to my final trip to Cumbria and the last two Furness Islands. Once again I was to be walking over the sands with a guide from Morecambe Bay Partnership, this time the former Port of Barrow marine surveyor Matt Sanderson. Both Sheep and Piel Islands are between Walney Island and the mainland Furness peninsula, an area that few know better than Matt. With the starting point at Snab Point on Walney being some way from the nearest bus route and several miles from Barrow, he had kindly offered to pick me up from my guesthouse.

I'd left visiting these islands until the guided walk, however as I was to find, this was probably not necessary. Hence it was almost a year after I'd walked across the sands to Chapel Island that once again I was passing over the Leven viaduct and looking at the little speck of tree covered land now surrounded by water. I wondered how many of the thousands of passengers who pass by each week give the island a second glance and how few know its remarkable history. This was however not the only island that I was keen to see from the train this beautiful sunny morning. On my last trip to Barrow, near Grange-over-Sands I'd noticed a tree covered island linked to the mainland by a causeway. Could this be another tidal island?

Initial plans to stop at Grange to investigate however proved unnecessary when I found that Holme is a mere 'nearly tidal island', or more precisely an 'ex tidal island'. The substantial causeway does not flood, although before this was built in the mid 19th century the island was cut off at high tide, but walkable at low. The walled causeway is in keeping with the grandeur of the island, which is approached past a lodge and has hidden in its trees an impressive house and fake Roman temple. Less grand is the almost obligatory smuggling connection, a cave on the island according to legend being used to store whiskey and brandy illicitly traded from Ireland. Another local legend says that the island was given to the man who killed England's last wolf in the 14th century as reward for his bravery. Now privately owned, Holme Island is not open to the public.

It was an early start next day, Matt picking me up at 7.45 on a bright and sunny morning. At strategic points on the drive across Walney Island we stopped to put up signs, some of his walkers apparently being 'navigationally challenged' and not only requiring guiding over the sands. While he sorted out things at Snap Point, I made my way to the first island of the day, Sheep Island, ¼ mile off the shore of Walney and only a few minutes walk over safe but slippery mud.

Matt had warned that fencing may prevent me getting onto the 15 acre island and whilst I found a gap in the barbed wire, pretty much impenetrable scrub kept me close to the edge. Apparently the farmer put up the fence to keep people off, although with no livestock grazing, one wonders why. Matt thought it was to stop campers. The remains of a stone wall also surround the island, most of it fallen, but a few lengths intact. Presumably sheep were once kept here and since they left vegetation has grown up, but it's a shame that the island is not in a condition that would allow it to be enjoyed by visitors (or is that the intention?).

Although there are no buildings on the island there was once a small isolation hospital, erected by Barrow Borough Council in 1892 at a cost of £257. Not much more than a large wooden hut, returning ships carrying sailors with an infectious disease such as yellow fever, would drop off the patient at Sheep Island to save infecting the people of Barrow. Some sources say that local people were also admitted to the hospital, although it was probably seldom used and closed in 1922.

Back at the car park people were arriving and it was good to see Suzanne again, this time walking with her young daughter. Matt gave his short safety talk and Suzanne added hers. She'd been on a health & safety course all week and Matt totted up her seven warnings about slipping and sliding!

At 9.00 just over 40 of us set off across the sands, the group ranging from a toddler who was carried over, a lad of about 6 who was in tears, a group of students from Lancaster and assorted ladies and gentlemen of 'more mature age'. Most bizarre were a group of girls in pyjamas who were making the crossing as a sponsored walk. Suzanne's warning was well founded as the first section was very slippery. The pyjama clad girlies screamed at every slip and the crying lad pleaded to go home.

Once past Sheep Island it was more sandy and firmer underfoot, making for easy walking. With differing paces the group soon stretched out; a straggly line of brightly covered walkers across the mud. There's a 'firm track' that Land Rovers use to get to the island, although drivers must remember to switch off their engine if they stop for any reason, otherwise the vibration softens the sand and the vehicle sinks. Matt however took us further out in the bay, to extend the walk a bit. Twice we stopped to allow stragglers to catch up, but soon the line reformed.

Unlike Chapel Island, there were no rivers to cross and Matt assured me, no quicksand. I didn't sense that we were in such a dangerous place, but maybe that was partly due to having read Edwin Waugh's account just before I'd set off from Ulverston. Although guided walks are run regularly to Piel, mostly by John Murphy, Matt surprised me by saying that it's quite acceptable for people to go unaccompanied. In fact he wished more people would, taking appropriate care of course. The sands can be crossed for roughly 3 hours either side of low tide, although one should leave in plenty of time for the return journey. Anyone overstaying can catch the Roa Island ferry, but it's a very long walk back to Walney to collect a car. The guided walks provide a safe way for those less confident about venturing onto the sands and Barrow Tourist Information Centre can provide details of these, plus advice on tides for those who may wish to make their own way.

Matt had said that there'd be one small channel to cross just before the island, but by the time we arrived it was no more than a yard wide and just a few inches deep. Soon we were on Piel Island. The girlies were still giggling, and the little lad who'd been in tears now smiling happily, dwarfed in his father's jacket. We were met by one of the island's four permanent residents, Steve Chattaway, the King of Piel.

I was to meet many interesting people on and around our tidal islands, but only on Piel did I meet a real live king. The 'monarchy' is thought to go back to 1487 when Colonel Martin Swartz with 2,000 German mercenaries landed on the island as part of an attempt by Lambert Simnel to seize the crown. Simnel claimed that he was Earl of Warwick and therefore rightful King of England, but after setting off across Furness for London was defeated at the Battle of Stoke. When he finally arrived in the capital it was as a prisoner of Henry VII. It's thought that the tradition of the King of Piel began as a slightly mocking homage to Simnel's invasion.

Unlike most kings, the position is not hereditary, but is bestowed upon whoever becomes landlord of the island's pub, the Ship Inn. Steve Chattaway and his wife Sheila have been King and Queen since 2007, his predecessor Rod Scarr having held the post for the previous for 20 years. There is however one further qualification, the King being expected to be 'a free drinker and smoker and lover of the female sex', although perhaps that doesn't preclude too many of Barrow's male population. The new King is crowned in a ceremony of uncertain origin which involves him sitting in an ancient chair, wearing a helmet and holding a sword, while alcohol is poured over his head. Steve's coronation was filmed by ITV for Martin Clunes' *Islands of Britain* series.

One of the King's rights is to bestow upon worthy subjects the honour of being a Knight of Piel. Recipients are expected to be of good character, moderate smokers, ardent lovers of the opposite sex and generous in the buying of drinks. In return should a Knight be shipwrecked on the island he is entitled to lodgings, food, drink and the choice of any woman that he wishes. 'Sir' Jack Turnough, who was knighted by Rod Scarr, claimed he'd been trying to get shipwrecked for years!

Piel was my fourth Furness tidal island and all were very different. Chapel is small and wooded, Foulney mostly vegetated shingle, Sheep covered in scrub and Piel 50 acres of mostly green grass, dominated by its ruined castle. I set off to explore.

At one end of the island is a row of grey stone houses which were constructed for Trinity House pilots. These fell into disrepair after the pilots moved to the more convenient base of Roa Island where Trinity Terrace was built for them, but in the latter part of the last century were renovated as holiday cottages. When Thatcher's Poll Tax was introduced in 1990 the cottages became a matter of dispute between the tenants and Barrow Council. Those using the cottages as second homes said they shouldn't have to pay, as Piel belonged to the people of Barrow. It was given to the town in 1920 as a memorial to those who lost their lives in the Great War. A council official thought he had neatly resolved the problem by handing over the cottage deeds so the residents had to pay the tax, so now the island still belongs to the council, but the cottages are privately owned.

From the cottages I walked along the shingle beach towards the quiet north east corner of the island, but was soon aware of a great deal of noise above. A pair of oystercatchers were squawking alarmingly and just as I thought maybe they had a nest here, I looked down to see a pair of beige speckled eggs lying on the stones at my feet. The island is a popular breeding area, although sometimes the oystercatchers misjudge the tides and have to move their eggs up the beach. With other birds close by I quickly turned back to explore the other end of the island and the castle.

Much of Piel is surrounded by shingle beach and as well as the birds, this provides home to a good selection of wild flowers, many of which were in full bloom on a sunny June morning. The impressive English Heritage owned castle is now a semi-ruin, although the massive keep still stands. There is evidence of human occupation on the island as long as 3,000 years ago and it is likely that the Romans came here. Its first recorded name of Foudray or Fotheray comes from Norse for fire island, meaning a fire beacon to guide boats. In 1127 the island was given to Furness Abbey and a house built here for the Abbot. In 1327 Abbot John Cockerham gained permission to fortify the dwelling house and the stone castle was built.

The castle's primary use was not as you might expect, to repel invaders, but to protect the monk's smuggling operations. Piel was then the only local deep water harbour (Barrow wasn't built until much later) and the

Furness monks used the island for their lucrative, but illegal trade in wool and fine wines. The castle was probably used as a fortified warehouse to keep cargoes safe from pirates and other raiders, but also had the benefit of keeping the customs men at a distance. The French weren't too happy about the monk's illicit trading, a petition being issued in 1423 by merchants in Calais complaining that Furness Abbey had been smuggling wool from Piel without paying the necessary dues.

After the dissolution of the monasteries the island passed from Abbey to King, but whilst some effort was made to upgrade the castle when the Spanish Armada was threatening to invade, it was soon neglected again. The southern and eastern parts are being eroded and part of the curtain wall has fallen into the sea, but it remains an impressive building. Although it's no longer safe for visitors to climb the keep, there is plenty to see and as the pyjama girls were finding, a brilliant play area for children.

Completing my circuit of the island I wandered through the camping field where a dozen or so tents were dotted about in no particular order. At the back of the field are the island's freshwater pond and a couple of small animal enclosures. The first held pigs and the second hens.

Jack Nicholson, King of Piel from 1964 to 1970, once kept 20 bantams on the island. He writes in his *Tales of Piel Island* of the problems they had getting them to lay. First they were told to feed the birds, but no eggs arrived. Then the order was, Starve them! Again no eggs arrived. Keep them in; Let them out – still no eggs. Next advice was to feed them laying pellets, which they duly did until the birds couldn't face another pellet. Still they refused to lay. Then the problem was found – all 20 were bantam cocks! After that they were given the run of the island – free range, but without the eggs. Soon numbers began to dwindle, with suspicions that they may have been ending up in various cooking pots. Eventually there was just one, who became quite cheeky and was christened Bertie Bantam. He took to visiting the Ship Inn at around dusk, announcing his arrival by rapping on the kitchen window with his beak, and soon learned that he'd get fed scraps there.

Bertie developed a pre-dinner routine and a spectacular method of arrival. When he thought it was time for his evening meal he'd amble over to the castle and climb the spiral staircase to the top of the tower. Standing no nonsense from the colony of rooks who lived here, he'd put them to flight and appear on the battlements. Here he'd spread his wings, give them a good shake, compose himself, then launch in the direction of the walled garden by the kitchen window. With a good following wind he'd make it in one go, otherwise it was an early landing and a comical rolling gait as he hurried to dinner.

Initial island exploration completed I stopped where most visitors end up, the Ship Inn. This had been closed for renovation for some time and only recently re-opened. Inside is the ancient wooden throne used for coronations and knightings. A notice on the chair advised:

BE IT KNOWN THAT WHO SO EVER NOT BEING OF THE ORDER SITS IN THIS ANCIENT CHAIR OF PIEL SHALL BY TRADITION FURNISH REFRESHMENTS FOR ALL THOSE PRESENT

I moved the sign for a quick photo, but with perhaps 200 people on the island thought better of a brief sit down.

It's thought that the Ship Inn is over 300 years old and was developed from a former chandlery established in the 17th century. A description in 1813 paints a vivid picture of the innkeeper's life, an 'old Scotchman', who whilst kept busy in summer admitted that when there were no ships around 'found his situation rather too lonesome and apt to drive him to his beer barrel for company'. Sometimes however it was the inn's customers who imbibed a little too much, with boating accidents resulting. In one case the coroner stated that 'the landlord of the Ship Inn should not supply drink as to make incapable men who may have to take charge of a boat'.

Outside I found the King again and he told me a tale that suggested that it was not just in the 19th century that the landlord may have drunk a little too much. Steve said that he was looking for a new tractor, but it needed to be an old fashioned type with no electrics as modern ones couldn't cope with the sea. The previous king had encountered a water related problem with his tractor. Well more to the point he'd turned it over on the sands and by the time it could be retrieved several tides had covered it. Mind you, according to Steve he was 'drunk as a skunk'!

Normally one would expect an audience with a king to be in stately surroundings, perhaps with a dainty cup of tea and maybe a few cucumber sandwiches. My conversation with the King of Piel was outside a burger van (The King's Kitchen), while he cooked bacon and sausages for the visitors. He told me that whilst the island is busy in summer with campers and day visitors, in winter months the ferry doesn't run and few visit. Often the only people on the island are Steve and his wife, plus now a couple who had recently moved permanently into one of the cottages. The island has running water, but with just a one inch pipe from the mainland supply is limited. There's a toilet block and even showers, although with cold water only.

As you may note, I often enjoy bacon sandwiches on my travels, so it was a great pleasure to be able to buy one on a tidal island. In such circumstances it seemed inadequate to just have bacon, so I while Steve cooked me the full breakfast bap I popped back into the Ship Inn to collect a drink. Enjoying these sitting on the grass watching the two little ferry boats sail back and forth was one of my more pleasurable island experiences.

Soon it was my turn to catch the boat. The walkers were setting off back to Walney at 1.30, but I'd decided to take the ferry and experience both methods of Piel Island travel. The arriving ferry was full with campers, laden with rucksacks and tents, but just I and two others were leaving the lovely island of Piel. In the tiny motorboat I was close to the still water, across which Piel looked perhaps more romantic than from the approach over sand. Although even with Walney's shelter the sea can be rough here, today it was the proverbial mill pond. There would be no call for a 'Farne Island bucket'.

The crossing takes just a few minutes, landing next to Roa Island's impressive lifeboat station. Earlier we'd seen the lifeboat set out for sea, on what I later learned was a special voyage to scatter the ashes of a former crew member who'd recently died. I took a look in the RNLI shop, leaving with two pens and a comb that I didn't really need, but as the only customer felt I should support both the charity and the two ladies who were giving up their time to serve there.

Matt had arranged for me to visit Anton Allen, a former Barrow pilot, who lives on Roa Island. He told me the story of a collier boat whose captain was having an affair with one of the nurses on Sheep Island. One evening he moored the ship in the channel between Piel and Sheep Islands and leaving the crew in charge, went ashore to see his lady friend. However, with a pub close by on Piel Island, the crew neglected their duty, choosing instead to spend the evening in the Ship Inn. All would have been well had not the tide fallen and the ship run aground. Even that might not have been a major problem, were it not for the ship coming to rest on its anchor, which punctured the wooden hold. The vessel never floated again and for decades afterwards residents of Piel used to collect free buckets of coal from the sands. Whether the captain or crew took the blame doesn't seem to have been recorded, but until well into the 1960s two masts in the sands remained as a reminder of their folly.

From Roa I repeated the enjoyable walk along the coast to Barrow that I'd done on a somewhat colder day returning from Foulney in February. As I looked back the very different islands of Foulney, Roa and Piel were behind me. Sheep Island could just be seen off Walney and a few miles round the coast Chapel Island was waiting to allow me one last glimpse as I returned on the train. My travels to Furness and Morecambe Bay were almost over, but just one more mystery remained.

Had I been writing this book four hundred years ago there would have been one more island to visit. Somewhere in the bay was an island about which almost nothing seems to be known. It was called Hurst Island, but its location is a mystery. However what is known is that one night a fearsome storm or perhaps even a tsunami struck the area and in the morning Hurst Island had gone. As illustrated by the castle wall lying on the beach of Piel, the sea is still nibbling away at our islands, a process that mankind must be accelerating as he causes our climate to change. I wonder how many more islands will have gone the way of Hurst Island in another 400 years?

# CHAPTER ELEVEN

# ROUGH ISLAND and HESTAN ISLAND

The Solway Firth is a part of Britain I'd never visited before. Just north of the Lake District, and protruding further west than the Isle of Man, Dumfries & Galloway is the most southerly part of Scotland, a little known area, but one which promised much. Described by Visit Scotland as 'the perfect location for an amazing break that will leave you relaxed and refreshed', the coast is an Area of Outstanding Natural Beauty, notable for its scenery and wildlife. The Solway has fewer islands than most of Scotland's west coast, but with its huge expanse of sand and mud, there are four which are tidal. This trip was to take me to the Urr Estuary, to the little known Rough and Hestan Islands, my first Scottish isles. The Islands of Fleet, further west along the coast would be my next trip. Tides, distance and shortening daylight hours meant that the islands would have to be visited on separate days, so I booked two nights accommodation in the small village of Kippford, near Dalbeattie.

I arrived from the north, having travelled up the previous night on the sleeper for a morning meeting at Kilbarchin west of Glasgow. I wish I could say that the day was straightforward, but all did not proceed smoothly. Waking at 6.50 the train was just stopping at Motherwell, 13 miles short of Glasgow. An hour later we were still at Motherwell. There were problems with the overhead wires and no trains moving. Eventually we were all put on a diesel train, which headed off in the opposite direction, giving us a tour of Strathclyde and eventually arriving at Glasgow Central. There, on Platform One, was the sleeper, with its staff chatting on the concourse. As I queued to buy my ticket to Dumfries the man ahead of me was berating the poor clerk, although I somehow doubt it was her fault that the wires had been repaired faster than expected and he'd missed his meeting. All credit to ScotRail though, who in response to my letter sent a full explanation and vouchers for the cost of the single journey.

On completing our glue discussions, I mentioned that I was heading off to tidal islands, which raised considerable envy from our customer Graham. Firstly he was working and I wasn't, and secondly he has an interest in islands, although hadn't been to either Rough or Hestan. I left the meeting with two litre pots of glue, not ideal to have to carry (my rucksack was already chocker), but I was keen to get them back to our lab for testing, a decision that proved to be profitable as by matching one we gained some useful new business. Should you be interested, the adhesive is put onto the black supermarket labels which are positioned over the original label when there's a price change.

The scenery on the ride to Dumfries was excellent, with lakes, rivers, forests and hills – the Southern Uplands. Even away from the more famous mountains, almost every train journey in Scotland has scenery that deserves looking out the window, but I was the only one to be doing so today. What the locals take for granted would merit National Park status in England.

At Dumfries things started to go wrong again. With a disappointing lack of transport integration trains arrive at one side of the town and buses leave from the other. Hence I missed the 14.00 to Dalbeattie. With unexpected warmth I was carrying two jackets, two pots of glue, one folder and a very heavy rucksack, so although Dumfries looked to have much of interest, a walk round the town wasn't welcome. Instead I found a cafe serving toasted tea cakes, always a good way to spend half an hour. I was able to marginally lighten my load, taking a now completed book to the Oxfam shop, the effusive thanks from the elderly lady serving being somewhat disproportionate to the value of the gift. Back at the bus stands by the river I suddenly realised I was missing something – the pots of glue. Hoping they were in the café, back up the hill I went. Fortunately the waitress had found them, putting the pots behind the counter with no question as to why I was carrying glue.

Dumfries's bus system isn't designed with the visitor in mind. There are half a dozen stands, each with a list of numbers and destinations, but no proper timetables. If you know the number you want or its final destination, all you have to do is go round each of the six stands until you find it on the list. If like me all you know is the departure time and one calling point, not only do you have to tour the stands, but you have to guess where your bus might be eventually heading. Fortunately there were only two departures scheduled for 15.00 and I knew it wasn't going to Glasgow, so the Castle Douglas bus was mine.

Again the scenery was excellent and absorbed in watching the passing hills we arrived at Dalbeattie sooner than I expected. Leaving the bus in a hurry and concentrating on asking the driver where I should catch the Kippford service, I made another error. As the bus drove off I realised my folder was still on board. In it were the notes from my meeting, information on the islands, but most importantly a sheet of bus, train and tide times. To compound the annoyance, as the Kippford bus drove off, with me the only passenger, the one I'd been on from Dumfries sailed by. It must have done a tour of the town after I'd got off, but now it was heading for Castle Douglas with my red folder containing all those crucial times on the second seat. Bother! I had to call my wife in the evening and ask her to look up the most important times again.

The bus dropped me on the waterfront at Kippford, and what a contrast to the world of glue and industry. Stretched out along the riverside, Kippford is a most picturesque village on the Urr estuary, popular with visitors and yachtsmen. After gratefully dumping my bag and glue pots at the very friendly Mariner Hotel, I set out to explore in the remaining two hours of daylight. I hadn't planned to walk to an island but on reaching the causeway to Rough Island saw it was clear. High tide had been 3½ hours ago, but it seemed that a quick impromptu visit may be possible. Walking onto the cockle banks that run part way to the island, I approached a couple who were returning. They said that the tide had only just turned and I had time to walk over. I knew the tide was well on its way in, but judged that provided I kept a close eye on the sea, there was time for a quick visit.

## Rough Island

The couple had warned me not to continue to the island directly from the end of the cockles, as here the mud was soft, but to cut across to the slightly raised hard causeway. The advice was good and I arrived with feet still dry. The causeway is fairly straight, but whether it is man-made or natural is unknown. Missing the path to the top of the island, I headed to the right around the shoreline, finding a remarkable rock formation resembling a camel. After my visit I read that this is quite well known locally, but was pleased that I'd found it and correctly identified the animal likeness.

Knowing the tide was rising this had to be a fleeting visit, a bonus trip with the main island exploration to follow. As I crunched my way back across the cockles the tide was coming in rapidly around me. There were no waves, but the water moved across the mud and shells at a great rate. It was quite eerie watching it spread so quickly, yet silently, and hard to believe that this was being caused by the pull of the moon 240,000 miles away. Timing the water to cover a few paces I reckoned it was coming in at about 5 metres a minute. It's easy to see why there are so many stories of people being stranded on tidal islands, or worse still, washed away by inrushing sea. The Kippford lifeboat is apparently regularly called out to Rough Island.

As I stood on the cockles, a close eye on the water either side, a collie dog bounded up to me. Seemingly pleased to find company he repeatedly ran into the sea, picking up a shell and dropping it at my feet. One thing that I could never be short of here was shells, but he obviously enjoyed the game. Concerned that he seemed to have no owner with him, when we got back to the shore I was pleased to see him run into a house by the water. Maybe he waits there every evening, ready to run out and play his shell game with anyone spotted on cockles.

It isn't possible to walk along the shore to the next little village of Rockcliffe, but a path runs through the woods, and with just enough light left I followed it up the hill, stopping every so often to spy the island through gaps in trees. Rockcliffe has a lovely little shell covered beach, and is the closest landfall to Rough Island. It is walkable, but possibly muddy and the causeway is probably easier. Beyond Rough Island I could see the headland of Almorness Point and peeping out behind, Hestan Island, clearly distinguished by its lighthouse. I watched the sun set over the estuary, although not as spectacular as I and a lady with her camera on Rockcliffe beach had hoped. As dusk fell it was time to return to the hotel for a welcome dinner and to plan island walking to come. The next day I was to visit Hestan Island, then return to Rough Island the day after, as being less remote it would give more time to travel back to Glasgow. For simplicity however I will complete writing about Rough Island, before moving on to Hestan.

The island is owned by the National Trust for Scotland (NTS) and they put me in touch with the Property Manager, Karl Monday. We had made tentative arrangements to meet and for Karl to show me the island, but he called in the morning saying he had matters to deal with and very apologetically had to decline. As Property Manager, Senior Ranger and Naturalist he is a busy man, however he gave me some background to the island and we arranged to speak after I'd visited. We eventually met when I travelled back to Dumfries and Galloway to visit the Islands of Fleet.

Rough Island was an important breeding site for birds, although Karl told me that numbers have declined sharply in recent years. He thinks that this is due to a combination of factors such as an increase in the number of corvids, stock being moved off the island, loss of habitat due to vegetation encroachment, land management, but mainly due to disturbance from the public. Hence visitors are asked to keep away from March to May, however due to the Land Reform Scotland Act (2003) the NTS are no longer permitted to put up notices forbidding access. For the rest of the year the island may be visited at any time, subject of course to tides.

A walk before breakfast confirmed that the tide was high and I'd have to wait for the causeway to clear. I sat in the hotel bar for a while, writing on my new net book computer, a useful tool for both work and book writing, but additional weight in my rucksack. Two children were fishing from the Solway Yacht Club jetty and I watched one catch a little silver fish. It must have been all of four inches long but father rushed along with camera to record the event. A few minutes later father was summoned again, this time when the bending of the girl's rod suggested she had caught at least a whale. Dad taking over to land the monster found that it was just a very large clump of seaweed.

Returning two hours after my pre-breakfast walk, the scene had completely changed. The causeway was clear and the whole area between the island and Rockcliffe now mudflats. The water certainly moves fast round this island. With Karl's directions this time I found the path to the top of the island, passing between high bracken, through recently cut meadows and coming out at the cairn on the summit. From here I could see Hestan, with clear water between it and the mainland. The 60 turbine Robin Rigg wind farm and the Lake District mountains that I'd seen clearly on the first evening were however hidden in the mist.

A narrow and steeper path runs down to the far end and wilder part of the island. Here spectacular rock formations outlined against the sea, interspersed with autumn colours of fading heather and berries. I'd bought a postcard in Kippford's little shop, The Ark, which showed a riot of colour on the island, but had arrived too late for the best of the wild flowers. Rough Island was nevertheless a lovely place and like all my tidal islands, didn't need the best of weather to display its beauty and atmosphere. As so often I was the only person on the island, but with a bus to catch I couldn't linger. Before leaving however I walked around the east side of the island, to investigate poles in the water that looked like the fish traps I'd seen near Chapel Island. Karl told me that these are pole nets which catch flounders, mullet and sea bass, but that he has occasionally had to remove guillemots from the nets. These are just one type of traditional fish traps still used in the Solway, stake nets and paidle nets also being employed along the coast, plus salmon nets which are licensed for use around Hestan Island.

Karl sent me two most interesting documents covering the NTS Rockcliffe Estate, which includes Rough Island. The first was an assessment of the areas notable plant species and the second headed Property Statements 2007 – 2012.

On the western side of Rough Island there are three colonies of the Nationally Scarce seaside centaury, a small biennial herb with pretty pink flowers. Small numbers of lax-flowered sea-lavender were found at the north end of the island, which although Nationally Scarce is relatively common along the north Solway coast, its UK northern limit. Sea spurge, which is vary rare in the area can be found on the shingle bank to the west side of the island, and two scarce species Centaurium littorale and Limonium humile grow on the areas of salt marsh. Two Nationally Scarce varieties of eelgrass (Zostera nolti and Zostera marina) can be found in the intertidal area between Rockcliffe and the island, especially around the causeway. Eelgrasses are the only marine flowering plant in the UK, forming underwater meadows that provide shelter for crabs, anemones and young fish.

Rough Island was donated to the NTS in 1937 by John McLellan and Major James McLellan in memory of their brother the late Colonel William McLellan CBE. It was given with the condition that the Trust would not allow any structural developments, camping or disturbance of nesting birds. The island was designated as a bird sanctuary and on my second visit, close to the start of the path onto the island I'd found a fine old brass sign with 'The National Trust for Scotland' written around the rampant lion and 'Rough Island Bird Sanctuary' beneath.

In managing Rough Island and the areas of mainland which it owns around Rockcliffe the Trust works to a set of Guiding Principles. With regard to Rough Island most notably it states:

*The Trust will conserve and enhance the landscape character through appropriate management of landscape features and views.*

*The Trust will aim to maintain the mosaic of habitats and, where possible, enhance species diversity through management that allows natural processes to thrive.*

*Responsible access and public appreciation of the property will continue to be enriched by the Trust through offering recreational experiences and enhancing interpretation.*

*The Trust will continue discussions with local communities to generate awareness of the cultural and natural heritage to ensure effective consultation and positive collaboration.*

As with so many areas, a balance has to be found between the often differing requirements of local people, visitors and nature, but for Rough Island the problem of access is particularly difficult. There is concern that the most significant factor causing the visible decline in bird populations may be human activity, but despite this and the island having been donated on the condition that birds will not be disturbed, the Scottish Outdoor Access Code allows the NTS only to discourage but not prevent people going onto the island during the nesting season. The Trust prefers not to erect signs and in any case people walk to the island from several directions or may arrive by boat, but the message doesn't always get to prospective visitors. The NTS website has no page for Rough Island and I only found the information on the Undiscovered Scotland website. Visitors may arrive here not knowing that they shouldn't be going to the island, then locals who perhaps feel that with greater knowledge they are less likely to disturb the birds, say it is unfair they cannot visit. Efforts are however being made to determine why bird colonies are now more established in other areas of the Solway coast, if there is potential for them to return and what levels of human disturbance are acceptable for the remaining populations.

Rough Island was grazed until the early 1960s, but locals say this was stopped as dogs were scaring sheep off the island. With it totally surrounded by mudflats for several hours each tide it was easy for stock to wander off, just as wild animals like roe deer often come onto the island. Without grazing to keep vegetation down the nature of the island and its habitats gradually changed, however since the late 1980s the Trust have been managing the meadows, encouraging conditions for biodiversity. Grass is cut and paths maintained to encourage visitors to walk to the summit cairn rather than wander.

Little appears to be known about the history of Rough Island, although there is evidence suggesting that it was cultivated with visible remnants of field boundaries of pre-enclosure land divisions showing management prior to the early 18th century. It is not thought to have been inhabited and there's no indication of there having been any buildings on the island. Indeed there seem to be few stories about Rough Island, nor the religious or smuggling connections so common in the histories of our tidal islands. Its past may be mysterious, but its present is being carefully managed. Hopefully the island's future will see a balance found where people can enjoy its beauty but birds return to breed in numbers once more.

## Hestan Island

I had two dreams of death last night. The first involved a speeding train with failed brakes and the second some sort of fairground ride that threw people into the Thames. Of course they both ended before finding out whether I'd survived, but a third dream finished when I woke having been talking to the ranger while he was in the process of warning of the dangers of Hestan Island. If the book ends here then I should have heeded the warnings. After a bacon sandwich for breakfast I put the TV on – to see that they were showing a programme about helicopter rescues. Was this a sign too? Was this the day I'd come home in a Chopper?

Dumfries Tourist Information Centre had told me that walking to Hestan Island is discouraged due to the fast tides, however the few accounts I'd read of those who had visited all seem to have returned safely, not one reporting that they'd drowned. Hence I decided to go ahead, but with due care. The safest route appeared to be from Almorness Point, as although some said they'd walked across Auchencairn Bay from Balcary, other sources advised that this was highly dangerous without a local guide. I was told later that a Belgian couple drowned walking across the sands this way in the 1980s. Today however was to be a day that showed the importance of being well informed before visiting a tidal island. It was unfortunate that the copy I'd ordered of *On a Galloway Island* by Beryl Scott, who lived on Hestan in the late 1950s, had arrived the very day I was in Scotland and heading for the island.

With time to spare I went for a short walk after breakfast. The Urr estuary was beautiful. Dead still with tiny wisps of cloud on the highest hills. A heron stood sentry like on the mud, hoping his breakfast would swim by. A quick chat with the lady who served my breakfast confirmed our mutual appreciation for the area's beauty. Like me she enjoys the train journey to Glasgow, but wasn't at all surprised that I was the only passenger watching the views as most people just take it for granted. She had been to Hestan Island and said it's lovely. She'd been to Rough Island too, and got covered in mud.

Two short bus rides took me to the village of Palnackie. With no glue pots or folder to leave behind today, this time I left my notebook on the bus. The one with all the bus, train and tide times that my wife had kindly looked up again for me, and the only paper I had to make notes. At least I'd be able to make quicker walking progress, with stops just for photos, not scribbles.

From Palnackie it was a most enjoyable 3 mile walk to Almorness Point opposite the island. The route starts on a narrow lane, passing the 15th century Orchardton Castle, the only fortified round tower house in Scotland. Unpaved after The Holm, at Almorness House it turns into a track. Here I met a farmer on his quad bike and as I held the gate for him, took the opportunity to mention Hestan Island. He assumed that I'd be staying over the tide as on his visits had found that by the time they'd walked to the end of the island the causeway was covered. He confirmed that the tide was falling and I assured him I'd be careful and was planning just a quick visit. From here it was a beautiful walk through Gibb's Hole Wood, the trees looking their best in early autumn colours but with few leaves fallen. The path divided, although only the left fork is shown on the O.S. map and after some deliberation I took this. It may have been less direct but I was concerned the other may come out at the top of a cliff, with no way down to the sea.

At Horse Isles Bay the track ended, changing to a narrow path across a marsh, which was quite wet in places and only just possible to negotiate with dry feet. The path brought me to the sea at the delightful little spot of White Port Bay. This little bay with shell beach, rocks and rugged but colourful low cliffs, is one of hundreds in Scotland, which like the hills are largely taken for granted by most who live here. Studying the map I'd been unable to find a path beyond here and quick investigation confirmed this. I'd thought that it would be possible to walk round the headland on sand, but the sea came right up to the rocks. The only way forward was to scramble over them. This wasn't easy and great care was needed, especially when climbing down two steep gullies. The rocks were less rugged closer to the sea, but I was concerned about slipping on the wet seaweed. This was a very remote spot and not a good place to break a leg, especially below the tide line where water may arrive before rescue.

As I clambered to a pinnacle of rocks on the headland a view of the whole of Hestan Island opened up. I could see the island's single cottage and below it the beach, the closest part to the mainland. The Rack, a raised shingle bed covered with thousands of mussels, which were harvested for many centuries by local fishermen, was partly visible, but there was still a channel of water between this and the shore. Finding a sheltered spot I settled down with my lunch, waiting for the water to recede. The mussel promontory was gradually growing, but closer to the mainland was still sea. Low tide was due at 14.17 but with half an hour to go not only was the island still cut off, but the wide area of Auchencairn Bay shown on the map as sandbanks, was still mostly sea. According to the map Mean Low Water exposes sand all the way to the island and for some distance both sides of Almorness Point.

It was becoming clear that either I had the tide time wrong, or there wasn't going to be time for a safe visit. I would like to have checked the tide, but the table I'd printed from Easytide was in my red folder on the 501 bus and the notebook in which I'd written down the times after my wife's search the previous night, was on the 505. By quarter past two there was a small patch of mud below the rocks, on which a grateful oystercatcher poked about looking for lunch. He too must have been anxious for the tide to fall. I waited another half hour until I could see the mud starting to cover once more. The sea wasn't going to allow a visit to Hestan today. I'd assumed that the causeway was clear every day and none of the people who'd told me about their visits had said otherwise. I had seen Hestan Island but like St Catherine's, a visit hadn't been possible. Had I have obtained Beryl Scott's book a few days earlier I would have read that on days with small (neap) tides, the island remains cut off. If I was to visit Hestan I would need to come another day and this time look at the tide heights as well as times.

With the tide a little lower the walk back was easier, as away from the point of the headland a narrow strip of exposed mud allowed flat, if sometimes squelchy walking back to White Port Bay. I lingered at this lovely spot for a while, before negotiating the marsh once more and stopping at Horse Isles Bay to eat a cake I'd chosen in Dalbeattie. Opposite the bay Rough Island was totally surrounded by mud, a much easier tidal island to reach than Hestan. Despite its name Horses Isles is not an island. Although surrounded by sea on one side and low marshes on the other, a small area of higher ground links it to White Port Bay, so it would need a large sea level rise for it to be cut off. Not so however Glen Isle, which is opposite Kippford and which only a marshy area prevents being an island. It may be very occasionally cut off by exceptionally high tides, but only with a few inches of water if at all, however if sea levels rise as predicted this will become a tidal island, whilst Hestan will eventually be permanently cut off. Further west, St Mary's Isle near Kirkcudbright is also not actually an island, being attached at all tides.

Without my notebook I relied on memory for the bus times, but thought there was one at 17.04. Arriving at Palnackie with time to spare, a look at the timetable showed it wasn't due until 17.42. Fortunately the Glen Isle pub opened at five, with welcome liquid sustenance for the thirsty walker.

The 505 is a true rural bus; an ancient minibus, with friendly driver and passengers who all seemed to know each other. On this bus no screens separate driver from passengers and the fare money is kept in a tuppaware sandwich box. As I showed the driver my return ticket, he showed me my notebook. 'Had I left this?' With grateful thanks I put it safely in my bag, texting my wife to cancel the request to look up train times for a third time.

Despite its remoteness and comparative obscurity, Hestan Island has its own website, www.hestan.co.uk, and I'd like to thank Dave who runs it for his permission to use information from the site. I've also taken some stories from Beryl Scott's book, although was warned not to rely completely on its accuracy. Beryl writes 'Heston', but although I'd seen that elsewhere, the most common and Ordnance Survey spelling is 'Hestan', so it is that which I shall use.

Measuring 460 by 270 metres, Hestan is small by Scottish island terms, but with a maximum height of 54 metres (175 feet) is one of our higher tidal islands. Its shape is said by some to resemble that of a horse with its head down drinking, which was indeed the origin of its name, Hestan being Scandinavian for horse. Others say it looks like a beached whale, which to me seemed the greater likeness.

There is evidence that Hestan was inhabited by Mesolithic folk, with Hugh Paton's *History of Auchencairn* describing an oyster shell midden at the top of the raised beach, immediately below the cottage. Living between 5000 and 4000 BC the Mesolithic people had no axes, so unable to clear forests lived around the coast, collecting shellfish, harpooning fish and hunting seals, deer, otter, badger and wild cat.

Like so many islands, Hestan has religious connections, being owned by Dundrennan Abbey in the 12th and 13th centuries. The monks called the island Estholme and used it for grazing and fishing. The remains of a walled enclosed, 'Monk's Pool' in which they used to trap fish as the tide receded, are still just visible.

The island was once home to a former King of Scotland, Edward Balliol who built a fortified manor house here in the 14th century. Balliol was crowned King in September 1332 after victory at the Battle of Dupplin Moor, but his position was far from secure, so he had the house built on Hestan as a safe retreat. The remains of his house can still be seen here above the cottage.

In the 1840s copper mines were built on the island, the ore being shipped to Swansea with its huge smelting industry. Hestan's cottage was built in the 1840s on the sheltered north end of the island. The island's website says it was constructed to house the first lighthouse keeper and was later used by miners, however as the lighthouse wasn't erected until 1893, it appears to have been the other way round.

Through the website I made contact with Wendy Haynes from Wolverhampton whose ancestors lived on Hestan in the mid 19th century. She told me that the 1861 census showed James McVinnie, a sheep farmer, his wife Margaret and three of their children living on the island. Their elder daughter Agnes, who was Wendy's great great grandmother, had by then married and moved to Birmingham. The 1871 census shows Hestan as uninhabited. Wendy however suspects that the enumerator couldn't be bothered to go across there, as she has been unable to find the McVinnies recorded anywhere else and has found an entry in the Dumfries and Galloway Saturday Standard of 15th November 1873 noting the death on Hestan Island of Margaret, wife of James McVinnie. By the 1881 census the McVinnies had moved away.

Samuel Murdoch Crosbie in *The Gallovidian Annual* writes that in August 1882 the proprietor repaired and reconditioned the cottage with a view to occupying it occasionally in summer. He tells how two cart-loads of furniture were sent to Auchencairn, but that the two men charged with bringing them to Hestan set out late and were caught by the tide. With the sea threatening to engulf the whole party the traces were cut to release the horses, so that they and the men could swim for their lives. One horse reached the shore, but seeing its companion in difficulties, swam back as if to render aid – 'a wonderful act of animal comradeship'. Fortunately both horses were rescued and some fishing boats picked up the furniture, the owner having to pay salvage before he could reclaim his property.

It is many years since Hestan was permanently inhabited, but within the last 100 years a number of tenants have lived on the island. Bob and Nancy

McWilliam came here in 1929, their daughter May being brought up on the island in the 1930s. Fifty years after the family left Hestan the then May Fraser wrote a most interesting article describing her childhood here for the *Auchencairn News*.

She was to come into the world in November 1930, so with the weather forecast poor and small tides approaching, two or three weeks before the due date Bob took Nancy by boat to his mother's house in Auchencairn where she was to have the baby. Nancy had expected to be able to rest for a while, but May appeared to have other ideas and was born at 9.00 the next morning. It had been arranged that her grandfather would light a fire so Bob would know that all was well, but the tide was such that it was several days before he could cross to the mainland to find out whether he had a son or daughter. A few weeks later May was brought to Hestan in a clothes basket and grew up here as her parents worked hard to maintain an independent life on the island.

They kept cows for milk, making some of the cream into butter and grew vegetables, digging in manure from the cows and sometimes seaweed as fertiliser. A pig was kept for a while, but May thinks this was stopped as they found it too personal rearing one pig then eating it. They had bought a large horse called Geordie from the previous tenant, a Mr Tweedie, and found him to be a willing and hard worker. He pulled the plough, reaper and hay cart on the island, and carried produce to the mainland, bringing back groceries and animal feed. May tells of an occasion when as a toddler she was sat on a blanket while her parents worked with the hay, but when her mother looked had disappeared. She was soon found, having crawled under Geordie, sitting playing with the long hair on his fetlocks.

One of their cows by the name of Mayflower was a particular character and on one occasion was being taken across the sands to be serviced by a bull belonging to a Mr Cuthbertson of Seaside. Mayflower knew where she was going and for a while trotted along the sands on a halter, but gradually speeded up until she was going at a full gallop and Bob had to let her go. Mr Cuthbertson saw her coming and by the time Bob reached the farm Mayflower was standing ready for him to take her back home, the deed done. Mayflower was probably a little spoiled and came to associate people with food. One day a group of visitors arrived by boat at high tide and spread out a picnic on a large white table cloth near the copper mine, before going for a swim. Attracted by the noise in the water, the cow made her way down the cliff path and finding the feast laid out, pretty much demolished it. The visitors came knocking at the cottage door complaining that a cow had eaten their picnic and Nancy had to do her best to replace as much food as she could.

The time came when May had to start at Auchencairn School, staying with her grandparents and getting home at weekends if the tides were suitable. Sometimes she was allowed to leave an hour early on a Friday or arrive an hour late on a Monday to enable her to cross the sands, something of which the other children were envious, although May recalls that maybe she envied their simple journeys home. Sometimes she brought friends back to Hestan, but remembers one girl's mother saying no, as they wanted the family to be together if Hitler came. The McWilliams eventually left the island, which May calls a magical place, recalling that her parents always said that their years on Hestan were the happiest of their lives.

Hestan is owned by the Houston family and in the early 1950s James Houston gave up a career in law to come here, living alone with only the birds and occasional seal for company. He moved out in 1957, being replaced by the last permanent residents, Beryl Scott and her husband John, who took over the cottage and lighthouse duties. Her book gives an insight into life on a tidal island.

A recently married young couple from near Birmingham, Beryl and John had a dream of living on an island, and found Hestan while holidaying in Galloway. Returning the following year and hearing that Mr Houston was thinking about leaving, they arranged to travel to the island with mussel fishermen from Kippford. A few months later they moved to Hestan, although initially in a tent as the cottage was in such a state that it had to be fumigated before they could stay in it. Mr Houston sounds quite a character and as Beryl writes 'obviously not used to housework'. The cottage was packed with piles of dusty old books, including hundreds of western novels, but he made a bit of effort to impress when the couple first visited, hastily brushing the dead flies off the bit of the table from which they were to eat. He apparently had just one meal a day, which consisted of a whole loaf of bread, a large pan of bacon cooked until blackened, plus some jam. When helping him pack his belongings the couple were surprised to find that he insisted on taking a sack of old bread crusts growing a mould, but he assured them he never wasted food.

The two specified duties of Hestan's tenants were to tend the island's lighthouse and its sheep. Both had their temperamental moments. With rich deep soil over most of the island Hestan grows succulent grass and the Scotts were paid to take care of forty to fifty sheep over winter when the mainland pastures had been grazed bare. The flock from a farm in Nether Linkins, a few miles from Auchencairn, was brought over the sands with the aid of three sheepdogs. Sheep are still kept on Hestan and I was told that they are taken across by riders on horseback, the 'old fashioned way'. Beryl and John had to count them regularly and often rescued missing animals who'd got themselves entangled in the thick brambles on the cliffs.

The Urr estuary was once an important route for shipping, exporting granite from Dalbeattie quarry, but with its shallow tidal waters the Solway Firth claimed many vessels. Often they got into difficulties around Hestan Island and after much campaigning a lighthouse was built here in 1893. The island's tenants were required to look after the light, keeping it clean and ensuring that it didn't go out. In the McWilliam's and Mr Houston's time the light was powered by acetylene which was produced by dripping water onto carbide, but before the Scott's took over engineers changed the mechanism to run from acetylene gas cylinders, which were brought to the island by Kippford mussel fisherman. Later in their tenancy engineers came to change the system to propane fuel and in 1996 it was converted to solar power. Beryl and John sometimes spent weekends on the mainland, often staying with the minister of Rockcliffe church where John played the organ every Sunday, and later at a house they bought in Dalbeattie. They sought out various viewpoints from where they could check the lighthouse and on occasions had to return urgently to Hestan when the light had blown out, sometimes braving heavy seas to get back.

May Fraser recalls the Northern Lighthouse Commissioners instructing that the light must be put out and the building painted grey at the outbreak of war in 1939. Her parents were horrified at the thought of camouflage on the lantern which they kept sparkling, so her father fashioned a cover from a piece of canvas and painted this grey. There was much pleasure at removing the canvas and re-lighting the lamp when hostilities ceased.

Hestan has a number of natural features of interest, including the intriguingly named Daft Ann's Steps. The story says that these rocky outcrops at the southern end of the island were named after a girl from the village of Auchencairn, who not being blessed with the greatest of brains, set out to walk the dangerous route from Hestan to Balcary, laying stepping stones ahead of her. The poor girl drowned and the rocks were named after her.

Like Rough Island, Hestan has its own peculiar rock formation, the Elephant Rock on the foreshore to the west of the island. Somewhere on Hestan's rocks is a Water Benchmark, a marker used to link heights between land and oceanic maps. Unfortunately a few years ago when men came from the Ordnance Survey they couldn't find it and ended up making another on the mainland.

Hestan Island is probably best known as Rathan Isle in Samuel Rutherford Crockett's novel *The Raiders*, a romantic and loosely historical adventure. Published in 1894, the story is told by Patrick Heron who inherits the island while still a teenager, and is caught up with gangs of outlaws, gypsies and smugglers. Rathan Isle is central to the smuggling, with contraband being stored in a large cave beneath the cliffs. Whilst *The Raiders* is fiction, its tales of smuggling are probably based on a certain amount of truth, as in the 18th century Hestan was indeed a centre of illegal trade, with goods being stored in its caves, one of which is reputed to have shelves cut into the rock. The big cave which Crockett described was however based on one he had seen in Ireland, not on Hestan.

It was only on returning home and speaking to Keith Kirk, Countryside Ranger for Dumfries & Galloway Council, that I got the information on access that I really should have found out before setting out. With a normal tide one can have one to two hours on Hestan and it is possible to cross on most days, but not neap tides. The tidal range on the day I visited was just 3.8 metres and low water height 2.6 metres. A week later it was as low as 0.6 metres with an 8 metre range, explaining why the amount of sand uncovered varies so much.

Keith also gave me information on walking to the island, although it wasn't really what I wanted to hear. He used to run guided walks there, but recently stopped due to 'Health and Safety', although he still visits Hestan himself a few times a year. He always walks from Balcary, as although you have to wade through a river channel, this is much easier to get to than Almorness Point. However he confirmed that the crossing is dangerous unless you know the route and that I should not attempt it. He told me that when the lighthouse had to be repaired workmen ignored advice not to take a short cut and their digger got stuck in the sands, being covered by 3 or 4 tides before it could be freed. Although the sands between Almorness Point and the Rack are usually safe, he couldn't be sure as they shift each year.

Keith confirmed that the path I had declined that headed over Moyle Hill does lead towards the island, but said that in summer one has to fight through high bracken. A winter visit would therefore be a better option.

I considered trying to get to Hestan when I came back to Galloway for the Islands of Fleet, but with concerns for safety reluctantly decided against. The marsh by Horses Isles may well be impassable in winter, so I'd have to follow the track over the hill, with nothing shown on the map to guide me, then cross to the rack over sands which shift and may not be safe. Walking alone in a remote place, with freezing weather and possibly quicksands that could have appeared since the last person crossed to Hestan was just too risky. I didn't want to be featured on the front page of *Auchencairn News,* pictured with a bearded Mountain Rescue man in a woolly jumper under the headline 'Bloody Idiot!'.

Just over a year from my first attempt I tried once more to get to Hestan. Again I caught the train south after a meeting near Glasgow, but this time stayed the night in Dumfries, making an excellent selection with Glenlossie Guest House. After a walk by the River Nith and looking for shelter in an afternoon of continuous rain, I remembered the toasted tea cake café. It was the same waitress as last year, but if she recalled me as the man who forgot his pots of glue she didn't let on. Returning from the town, damp clothes became sodden as a car swished through a deep puddle, covering me with spray. As I stopped in disgust, wondering if he'd done it on purpose, the car following went straight through the same puddle, depositing a second layer of muddy water on my soaking trousers.

Not wishing to soak my spare clothes by walking back into the town centre, I dined conveniently but more expensively than planned, at the hotel next door. The meal was enlivened by the couple on the next table arguing as to whether the wine could correctly be described as Chilean when it had been bottled in the UK. The wife said she wasn't nit picking and the husband that they shouldn't fall out over it, but they didn't seem far from doing so.

The rain had gone by morning, although the grey sky suggested more may arrive at any moment. I planned to walk from Almorness Point, as although Keith Kirk had again warned of possible quicksands, I felt even less happy with the long walk across mud from Balcary. Keith had helped me with tide times but I still wasn't sure if there'd be time to cross by either route. In Dalbeattie where I bought lunch, locals added to the conflict of opinions about walking to Hestan Island. Three ladies in 'Snax' (purveyors of fine ham rolls) warned of soft mud and suggested I should take a flare. One had walked from Balcary many years ago, as had the man in Dalbeattie Visitor Information Centre. He said however that the sands from Almorness were firm, although added that as volunteers they don't have to worry about being sued.

This time I walked straight over the hill rather than continuing on the track to Horses Isles Bay. It was shorter and I thought might be easier with no marsh to negotiate and rocks to climb. It was a lovely walk in autumn colours (I even saw a red squirrel), but the path ranged from good to non-existent. I could understand Keith's warning that in summer vegetation makes it hard going, although soon found that after the heavy rain some sections were very wet underfoot.

As I reached the top of the hill Hestan Island came into view, looking just as I'd left it a year ago with its little cottage and lighthouse, and surrounded by sea. Just a short section of The Rack was clear and like last time I sat eating lunch watching the tide fall. This time though The Rack was clear an hour before low tide and the sea starting to pull back from the sands. It looked as if the crossing was to be on.

It was quite a scramble down to a little inlet in the rocks – a tiny shingle beach from where I watched the tide fall. With half an hour to go there was just a narrow channel of water close to The Rack, and when a gull landed I could see that it was no more than a couple of inches deep. Very gingerly, warnings of soft mud and quicksands very much to the fore, I stepped out onto the sands. I counted the paces – forty five to the channel, eight across and twelve more to The Rack. From here it was easy over the bed of cockle shells. Ten minutes and I was on Hestan Island. Hoorah!

I stayed for only a few minutes, mindful that the tide would soon be turning and that daylight would be running out for the long walk back over the hill. The cottage was in better condition than I'd expected. It used to be let for holidays, but last year I'd been told that its condition had deteriorated so that only someone used to living rough would wish to stay there. An application for funding to renovate had apparently failed, but it seems that some work has been done and I was later told that despite having no electricity or running water, it is still occasionally let out.

Having read so much of the island's tenants it was quite strange to at last be outside their house. Little seemed to have changed since the Scotts left over fifty years ago. The animal sheds were a bit worse for wear but the house in remarkably good condition. The garden where they and the McWilliams had grown vegetables still showed the furrows of cultivation. By the beach was the rusting remains of a boat trailer that had probably lain there since the Scotts departed.

It was with much reluctance that I left this little known island, but an island with so many stories. I stood on the beach and imagined Beryl and John Scott struggling with their little boat in rough weather, little May McWilliam with Geordie the horse, Mayflower the cow bounding over the sands to her romantic encounter with the local bull and James Houston's solitary life here. Most of the islands have an interesting history, but having read so much about the lives of its tenants, Hestan's seemed more real. This Galloway island had become a special place to me too.

# CHAPTER TWELVE

# THE ISLANDS OF FLEET :
# ARDWALL ISLE & BARLOCCO ISLE

*'Britain Under Siege. Arctic Freeze and Snow Wreak Havoc. 7000 Schools Closed. Panic Buying as Heavy Snow Hits. Motorists Urged to Avoid Motorways. More Chaos as Snow Turns to Ice.'*

Maybe everyone else was right and I was mad to be walking to a Scottish island in the first week of January, with the country in the grip of the harshest winter for 27 years. Roads were closed, airports shutdown and trains disrupted, but despite snow falling in London the Glasgow sleeper slipped out of Euston bang on time. Vaguely conscious that the train was stationary, I woke at 6.30, pulling the blind to see that we were in a world of white. Shiny metal rails poked out of snow that must have been eight inches deep. Distant town lights reflected orange, but everything else was white. Half an hour later the train was still stationary. Soon my breakfast arrived, the attendant saying that we were outside Carstairs, but should be on the move soon. True to his word, within minutes the train was moving again and before long crossing the frozen Clyde as it drew into Glasgow Central. Stage one of the journey successfully completed – I was back in Scotland.

Before heading south I had another meeting at Kilbarchin, where this time Graham, although interested in my island visits, didn't appear quite so envious. Maybe he too thought I was mildly insane to be walking to islands in the snow. With parting warnings not to trouble the Mountain Rescue Services, I was on my way. Changing at Killwinning, I joined the Stranraer train and what a lovely ride it was. First running close to the sea with views across the Firth of Clyde to Arran and its snow covered mountains, then as we approached Girvan, the famous rock of Ailsa Craig, often picked out by TV cameras from golf at Troon or Turnberry. Leaving the sea we headed inland, climbing to the remote station of Barhill, then across wild and snowy moorland with views to the hills of the Southern Uplands. Like the Dumfries line, the route passes through scenery that in England would have National Park status, but this single track line was wilder and more remote – it could easily have been in the far north of Scotland, not this little known corner of the south west.

At Stranraer more than half the passengers headed for the ferry terminal and the boat to Belfast. I too went to the Stenaline terminal, not for a boat, but the Hertz car hire office, for this was to be the second trip where a combination of public transport and Shank's pony wouldn't get me to the islands. I could have caught a bus to the village of Gatehouse of Fleet, where I was staying the night, but from here it's a seven mile walk to the islands of Ardwall and Barlocco. In summer I would have walked it, but with January weather and short daylight hours, car was regrettably the only realistic option.

The hotel had called while I was on the train, warning of icy roads and wondering if I was still coming. Of course I was. Despite others' doubts, I'd got as far as Stranraer and wasn't going to turn round now. They gave me an orange car, perhaps so I could be seen in the snow, like the orange balls once used for winter football matches before the days of under-soil heating and over zealous Health & Safety officials. Maybe they thought it would help guide in the rescue helicopter should I be stuck in island snow or estuary mud.

The A75 was reasonably clear, although with much care still needed especially as I headed east and the snow became deeper. A driver flashed his lights as he passed me, increasing my alertness, but rather than ice or snow drifts, round the corner was a policeman with a speed camera. With the conditions ensuring that everyone was staying well under the 50 limit I resisted the temptation to stop and suggest he may be better employed elsewhere, perhaps with a shovel. Passing Gatehouse of Fleet I continued to Castle Douglas, where I was to meet wildlife rangers Keith Kirk and Karl Monday. It had been hard to coincide diaries with these two busy men, our glue customer in Glasgow, the tides of Fleet Bay and of course the West Ham fixture list, so it wasn't only my natural stubbornness to defy the weather that encouraged me to go ahead with the trip.

We met in Keith's office, a cottage opposite the frozen Carlingwark Loch, Karl soon joining us from his base just down the road at Threave Estate. First Keith proudly showed us a wonderful photo of a red squirrel that he'd taken in the snow that morning, then presented me with a pile of papers about the islands. As we chatted the knowledge and affection that both men held for the area and its wildlife shone through. I had seen its beauty in my stay at Kippford and again today from the train then drive from Stranraer. Dumfries and Galloway Council are trying to promote the area for tourism, but as with the Borders, people tend to drive past, heading for the more famous Highlands. I can thoroughly recommend it as an unspoilt area, with hills, valleys, beautiful coast and of course islands.

My home for the night was the Murray Arms Hotel, a listed building built in 1760 and originally a coaching inn on the Dumfries to Stranraer stage. Robert Burns is said to have written his poem *Scot's Wha Hae* here, having composed it while walking over the hill from New Galloway. There were only two other guests and the restaurant was closing early to allow the chef to leave early in the snow, but I was in time to enjoy a fine dinner.

With temperatures forecast down to twelve below I was reluctant to leave my warm bed next morning. It was minus 10 degrees in the car. The bottle of coke I'd left there overnight had frozen solid. Without a scraper I removed as much ice from the windows as was possible with a credit card and set of in search of islands. Heading to the mouth of Fleet Bay each road was slightly narrower and a bit more snowy than the last, but all were passable with care. My biggest worry, that I'd travel all this way then find the lanes blocked had proved unfounded. Taking the little lane signposted for Carrick, I parked just before a steep downward slope, concerned that Orange Car may not get back up again. From here I had my first view of the Islands of Fleet.

I'm sure that even without the snow Ardwall would have been beautiful in today's bright sunshine with blue sea and sky, but with all around covered in pristine snow the whole area was exceptionally picturesque. The sort of view you see on calendars but are rarely lucky enough to experience first hand. Today was one of those days. How glad I was to have persisted despite the weather and ignored the advice of those telling me to stay at home.

So leaving the car (it felt strange not to have arrived on foot), and wearing as many layers as I could physically fit on, I set out for Ardwall Isle. Heading up the lane I met a gentleman walking with his two black labradors. This was too nice a place and too remote just to say Good Morning, so we stopped and chatted for a while. Obviously the weather was the first subject of conversation, followed by the view, but he was most interested that I was writing a book on tidal islands. He told me that Ardwall was beautiful and that I'd find the cottage over the hill. He said there's a smugglers cave nearby and warned me not to fall into it. Then he related a sad tale about the cottage. Last year some people had parked a caravan near to where I'd left my car, but unfortunately they weren't the type of people one would want in a beautiful place like this. The farmer had problems with them and eventually had to get the police to remove them. Soon after this Ardwall's cottage was found to have been attacked with axes. The wooden shutters were broken down and crockery and furniture smashed inside. The assumption was that the caravan residents had attacked the cottage in retribution for being made to leave.

There's no causeway to Ardwall, just mud, although Keith had assured me that it was firm. Setting out from the pretty little Isle Mouth bay I realised just how cold it was. There was snow on the beach and even a crust of ice on the rock pools. It's only about a third of a mile to Ardwall and I headed in a straight line, deviating only to skirt patches of shallow standing water. I soon found that the mud wasn't all what I'd call firm. Whilst most was hard, areas were squelchy and on one footstep my boot completely disappeared. Without Keith's reassurance that this was a safe walk I'd have been quite concerned. Yesterday I'd told him about Ray Porter's safety talk for the walk to Chapel Island, but Keith's advice was the opposite – 'if you feel yourself sinking, stop!' I was certainly happier to turn round rather than keep going as we'd been told at Ulverston, and soon found my way round the softest patches.

The obvious route onto Ardwall is across a lovely little beach, again covered in snow and ice, then up the path through a gulley. The only footprints were of animals; rabbits and foxes I guessed, so I must have been the first human visitor since the snow fell two days ago. The track passes the remains of an old chapel then opens out into small fields. With the snow covering it was hard to choose the best way and I was wary of falling down an unseen rabbit hole, or worse, the smugglers cave. With no sign of the cottage I scrambled up a bank to the cairn at the highest point of the island, from where the views around the bay were superb.

I'd been told that the cottage had its own orchard, so headed down the hill towards trees and found the track which took me to the boarded up building. Keith had said that in spring an avenue of daffodils leads up to the house, but today all around was white. Functional rather than pretty, the cottage however lacked the life that it must have had in years gone by when Ardwall was inhabited. People still stay here in summer months, but in winter it is left to the birds, animals and the occasional human visitor.

Little is known of the island's first occupants, but Brian Blake in *The Solway Firth* (published in 1955 – I found a copy in a second hand book shop in Hay on Wye), tells us that an inscribed cross was found that could be dated back to the 12th century. Much of the island's forty or so acres were divided into three or four holdings, Blake reporting that traces of the dykes can still be seen. Excavations of the chapel area in 1964-5 however provided more information on the island's history.

A sequence of occupation was found, starting with a local lay cemetery possibly dating from the 5th or 6th century, to which a slab-shrine of Irish character was added around AD 600. A timber oratory was built in the mid 7th century and further burials aligned on this structure rather than the slab-shrine. This was in turn replaced by a larger stone chapel around AD 700 and burials aligned with this until the 11th century, although the building had collapsed well before this time. The site was enclosed by a bank, possibly built as far back as the timber structure phase, and may have contained small cells which it is thought were probably an eremitic (recluse or hermit) monastery serving the Gatehouse and Borgue district. Next on the site was a hall-house which was built in 1250 – 1350 and followed by a tower around 1780 – 1800.

In the 18th and 19th centuries there was a tavern on Ardwall and this could have been the building that the archaeologists found to overlay the hall-house. Blake suggests that it may have been built to cover the comings and goings of smugglers who were very active here, and writes of underground chambers on the island which could be entered until 'some years ago'.

He tells an identical story about Ardwall as J.H. Ingram does for Hilbre

Island. Around 1850 there was an inhabitant on the island by the name of Laurie (or Larry) Higgins, an Irishman who lived in poverty until coming into money by dubious means concerned with a wrecked ship. He eventually took over the pub, perhaps unwisely, as he drowned one night crossing the sands. It is to him that Ardwall once owed its other name of Larry's Isle. As covered in chapter seven, it is unsure whether Mr Higgins actually ran his pub here or on Hilbre, but from the limited evidence available my feeling is that Ardwall is the more likely.

Ardwall is a fair sized island, rising to around 100 feet and I had found it to be one of the most beautiful of our tidal islands. Maybe I saw it at its best in snow and sunshine, but with little bays, trees, a small hill and superb situation in a lovely bay with distant hills, Ardwall was possibly my favourite island so far.

Before leaving I stopped to take some photos looking towards the nearby Murray's Isles. These two small islands are tidal in that they can be reached at the very lowest of tides, but not often enough for inclusion in my list. Estimates vary but it seems that on only around four tides a year can you walk across the sands to them. Like Rough Island, the Murray's are owned by the National Trust for Scotland and under the care of Karl Munday, but he always visits by boat. They were gifted to the Trust in 1991 as a bird reserve, and hold regionally important colonies of gulls and cormorants. The larger and more northerly of the islands has a small derelict stone house with no roof.

It's only a mile or so around Knockbrex Bay to Barlocco Isle, but with the tide coming in rapidly I took the car rather than walking along the shoreline. Parking behind Bar Hill, I walked through a field to the track that runs close to the island. Barlocco is closer to the shore than Ardwall, although the shortest access is over rocks rather than mud. On the rocks I met two men with buckets and sacks collecting shellfish. One told me his name was Ray and they were collecting them to eat not sell. They'd pick mussels, whelks, cockles, or 'anything else worth having', whatever that may be. Not being a lover of shellfish I declined the offer of a whelk, despite his attempts to persuade me it was a great delicacy.

Barlocco is accessible for only 3 to 4 hours each tide and by now the gap between the incoming sea either side was only a few yards wide. My visit to the island would have to be brief. I climbed over the rocks and looked across to the grassy centre of the island, but with sub zero temperatures and no shelter this was not an island to risk getting trapped on. There is however little of note to see on Barlocco, which is not thought to have ever been inhabited and has no buildings or obvious remains. It rises to only 30 feet and much of the island's 25 acres is rocky, although there is sufficient vegetation for cattle to be grazed here in summer.

Barlocco Isle experienced brief notoriety in March 2006 when a 60 foot fin whale beached on the rocks here. It was discovered by two whelk pickers who were drawn to the spot by its high pitched cries. They told the *Galloway Gazette* of hearing 'an indescribable noise, almost like crying' and that the whale's eyes followed them as they walked around the sad creature, its tail flapping on the barnacle encrusted rocks. The men called the SSPCA, but when Senior Inspector Iona Brooke arrived from Dumfries an hour later the animal was beyond help, its body lacerated by efforts to get free. Ms Brook told the *Gazette* that although still breathing, the whale was no longer moving and experts had advised it was best to leave it as pressure on internal organs would quickly lead to death.

The sad tale however did not end here, there being the small matter of what to do with a 60 tonne carcass. The cartoon under the caption 'Save the Whales' with a stereotypically bearded man standing next to a decomposing corpse and saying 'I've been saving mine for years – It's gone a bit smelly though', comes to mind. The fin whale is the second largest creature on the planet and doesn't normally come close to our shore, so it is thought that this one may have been unwell before it beached. The head alone was estimated to weigh 15 tonnes and its tongue said to be bigger than an estate car, so Steve Brown Barlocco's owner had a bit of a problem. Meanwhile the creature had become quite a tourist attraction with Mr Brown's son taking people out to see it at a charge of one pound for charity.

First Mr Brown contacted the local environmental health agency who told him that because the whale was over 15 metres long it was the property of the Scottish Executive. Then they said that as it was above the high water mark the carcass was the responsibility of the landowner. This Mr Brown pointed out wasn't true as it still floated at high tide. One wonders quite how they thought a whale could strand above the high water mark. As the local council and the Executive wrangled over who was responsible for the whale's removal the poor creature still lay rotting on the rocks, its skin starting to peel, seagulls pecking away at the corpse and the smell worsening. Eventually it was confirmed that the Scottish Executive would foot the bill for removal and options discussed with Dumfries and Galloway Council; cover the whale where it lay, roll it down to the sea and cover it, or cut it up and have it taken away. The first two options may have required a licence from the Fisheries Research Services which could have taken weeks, so the decision was made to cut up the body. Rather than move it from Barlocco, it was eventually decided to bury the whale here and diggers managed to excavate to a depth of 8 feet on the rocky island.

A month after it died on the rocks the last of the rotting remains were finally interred, although the story still didn't quite end here. The cost of disposal had been considerable (I hope the poor workers who had to cut up the less than aromatic remains were handsomely paid) and the matter was raised at the Scottish Executive. Alasdair Morgan SNP member for South of Scotland asked whether the Executive would attempt to recover costs incurred from the Crown Estate. The written answer was that the Crown Estate has no responsibility for dealing with 'Royal Fish' (stranded whales measuring more than 25 feet from snout to the middle of the tail).

Leaving the island I went to look at what appears to be a small fort nearby, but is in fact a folly belonging to Knockbrex House, then climbed Bar Hill for the view across Fleet Bay. Barlocco was now cut off, but I could see Ray and his companion still picking shellfish off the rocks. With bare hands they must have been frozen. Ardwall was surrounded by water which had quickly covered the mud I'd crossed only an hour before. On the far side of the bay I could just pick out Garvellan Rocks which Karl told me he fishes from, catching good sea bass, and had suggested I may want to include in the book. Just off Ringdoo Point, these are linked to the mainland by a sand bar (tombolo) that floods on higher tides, but are too small for my definition, as is Cat Craig a tiny tidal islet further up the bay. A magnificent backdrop to the bay was the snow covered 1,500 foot peak of Cairnharrow. Further away, but remarkably clear was the Isle of Man. Snaefell Mountain was easily identified towards the centre and the small island Calf of Man at the southern tip. I think I could even pick out Chicken Rock beyond this.

Although still below zero, with the sun shining and energetic walking I didn't feel cold. In such clear weather, with snow enhancing the beauty of what I'm sure is always a lovely spot, this was another of those days when I didn't want to leave the islands. Back on the mainland it wasn't tides that were telling me to leave, but the infrequent trains from Stranraer, plus the prospect of being charged for another day's hire if I didn't get the car back by 2.00. Perhaps I should have dragged myself out of the bed covers a bit earlier this morning.

I stopped once on the drive back; at Cardoness on the A75 from where I could look down the bay for a last glimpse of the little known but beautiful Islands of Fleet. Arriving at the ferry terminal a whole three minutes before the car was due back, there was just time for a bacon roll before catching the 14.43 back to Glasgow. I was one of only seven passengers boarding at Stranraer, as we set out on another snowy journey through the wilds of south west Scotland. With the sun still shining it was again a beautiful ride, although with the train's heaters struggling in the icy weather, a little chilly. The sun was setting as we passed Ailsa Craig, beyond which I could just make out the tip of the Kintyre Peninsula which I'd be visiting for my next Scottish island.

Alighting from the train at Glasgow the cold hit me as soon as I stepped onto the platform. Trudging through the snow on Ardwall I'd felt quite warm, but with darkness now fallen it was going to be a cold five hours until the sleeper could be boarded. Usually I find that however cold the weather, with suitable attire and brisk walking I soon warm up, but tonight was different. The longer I walked around the city the colder I got. Finding a warm restaurant and spinning out a meal for as long as seemed reasonable without being charged rental for the table, then doing the same with a drink in the pub on Central Station, I made it to ten o'clock without getting frostbite. The sleeper left on time and the hour late arrival in Euston allowed me a welcome lie in.

I emailed ScotRail to thank them for keeping the trains running while others gave up in the snow. Jane Gill, Customer Relations Adviser, replied promptly, expressing delight at receiving such a nice letter, thanking me for my encouraging comments and assuring me that I would continue to receive this standard of service in future. The response may have been standard wording, but at least they'd read the email, unlike Virgin Trains who once sent me an apology and £10 compensation voucher in reply to my letter of praise!

So despite all the warnings I'd made the journey without difficulty. I had greatly enjoyed my second visit to this lovely part of Scotland and been fortunate to see two of our least known tidal islands with their beauty enhanced by the wintry weather. I had discovered a beautiful area of Britain, somewhere to which I hoped to return before too long.

# CHAPTER THIRTEEN

# DAVAAR ISLAND & EILEAN MHIC CHRION

That closest railway station used to be Ballycastle in Northern Island illustrates the remoteness of Davaar Island, which lies off Campbeltown on the Kintyre peninsula. When this closed the nearest station became Girvan, 32 miles away over the sea, and from where I'd looked across to the peninsula back in snowy January. With spring arrived it was time to find a way to my next Scottish Island.

Despite extending well south of Glasgow, Kintyre is one of the least accessible parts of Britain, and Campbeltown the furthest town from any other on the British mainland. Options for travel were varied, but not easy: A four and a half hour bus ride from Glasgow – no thanks. The Kintyre Express executive charter power boat from Troon – memories of Farne Islands 35 years ago still too vivid – I think not. Plane from Glasgow – unnecessary flying – no way. Drive from Glasgow – 139 miles – not keen. Cunning plan to take ferry to Isle of Arran, hire car, drive across island, ferry to Claonaig and drive down peninsula – thwarted by only car hire outlet on Arran not allowing vehicle to be taken off island.

There was actually once a railway to Campbeltown, but it ran for just three miles across the peninsula to Machrihanish, wasn't connected to the main system and closed in 1934. Steamers used to run from Glasgow and more recently there was a ferry from Ireland, a service which locals are campaigning to have reinstated. It's still possible to get here by train, boat and bus, but conscious of comments that I was neglecting work for islands, time had to be a factor. I opted for the shortest drive from a railway station – 89 miles south from Oban, with the bonus that I could visit Eilean Mhic Chrion on the way.

After a long day of meetings in Glasgow I boarded the 18.21 to Oban, leaving thoughts of glue, sticky labels and equally sticky price negotiations behind. Soon the city was gone and the train running along the banks of the Clyde, as it headed north west on one of Britain's most scenic railway journeys. Climbing steeply above Gare Loch we looked down on the Faslane nuclear submarine base, then as the scenery started to get wilder, followed the slender Loch Long. Like the Stranraer and Conwy Valley lines, this is an essential service, a lifeline for the isolated towns and villages, and not simply a tourist route. There were a few walkers on board and no doubt in summer the trains fill with tourists, but today most of the passengers were locals, returning to Oban or some of the small stations along the way.

Tonight however the beauty was not restricted to lochs and mountains, for on board we had the pleasure of Natalie, a particularly attractive young lady working the refreshment trolley. My gaze was of course firmly out of the window, but to the two ex soldiers sitting opposite she provided welcome diversion. At Arrochar and Tarbert where we waited to pass a freight train, half a dozen 'enthusiasts' adorned with cameras provided amusement for some of the passengers. As the tanker train pulled by a large diesel engine approached, they took their photos, then legged it along the platform with tripods trailing to snap it once more as it waited at a signal. Our two ex soldiers took the opportunity of the stop for a quick smoke outside, soon being joined much to their delight by the lovely Natalie.

After running through the trees above Loch Lomond, we stopped at Crianlarich where the train divided, two coaches for Oban and two for Mallaig. From here the line heads west, through mountains, past little streams and tiny lochs. The rides to Dumfries and Stranraer had been beautiful, but this was wilder and more remote – real Highland scenery. Passing through Glen Lochy we reached Loch Awe, the ruined Kilchurn Castle atmospheric in the mist as dusk fell. There was just enough light to see across this narrow but surprisingly large loch (the third largest freshwater loch in Scotland), however with darkness falling views of Loch Etive would have to wait for my return in two days time.

The Mull ferry was arriving as I left the station at Oban, 'Gateway to the Isles', from where boats run to ten Hebridean islands. Glenroy Guest

House provided a friendly welcome with all the comforts I could need, and at half the price I was to pay for an inferior room in a disappointingly impersonal Campbeltown hotel the next night.

Picking up a hire car (a little blue one this time) I set off on the long drive to Kintyre. Heading south along the B816, then turning right onto the single track B8002 where a huge wooden finger points the way, I was aiming for Ardfern, a village of 400 people (but once 4,000) and the largest settlement on Loch Craignish. First however I had to investigate Eilean Traighte, a tiny island near the head of the loch that is linked to the mainland by a short causeway. Whilst too small to make my list, I don't pass a potentially tidal island without stopping, so made the short walk over the grassy causeway. Seaweed on the grass suggested that it is sometimes covered, although dipping my finger into one of the little pools showed that the water was not salty. The island is mainly covered with low trees and scrub and there appeared to be no evidence of buildings having been here.

Ardfern is sheltered by the narrow but mile long Eilean Mhic Chrion, which rises 200 feet above the loch. It was once known as MacNiven's Island or Eilean Mhic Naomheim, having been part of the MacNiven estate (MacNiven is from the Gaelic MacNaomhain, meaning 'the son of the saint'). This was an island about which I had been unable to find much information, least of all regarding access. Various references said that the island was tidal and the map shows mud and sand between it and the mainland, but also a channel running most of its length. The map suggested that access would be easiest at the eastern end by Ardfern Marina and Falcon Scott from Eilean Buidhe (more of which tomorrow) confirmed this. My first contact with the marina however advised that I would need wellies or waders to reach the island, but asked me to make myself known on arrival. The staff in the marina office couldn't have been more helpful, showing me where to cross, saying that there's normally access for a couple of hours but today a spring tide would be coming in quickly, and telling me to call if I got stuck as they'd send a dinghy over.

It's only 30 yards or so to the island and a stone wall runs part way. From the end of the wall it was seaweed covered rocks and cockle shells, slippery, but quite easy to cross. Certainly there was no need for wellies or waders, so Eilean Mhic Chrion definitely qualifies as a tidal island which can safely be walked to. There's a low lying area of marshy grass at the eastern end, but then the island rises steeply, with a long ridge running most of its length. A tiny path ran up to the cairn at the highest point, from where there were good views down the loch and of Eilean Righ, a similar shaped but slightly larger island on the opposite side of the water. The only sounds were from birds singing and the island's sheep, and apart from the cairn there was little sign of human activity. Conscious of the spring tide and the need to get to Davaar Island this afternoon, I returned down the steep hillside rather than walk further along the island.

Two folds by the crossing point are presumably used to hold sheep before they are taken to the mainland, grazing being the main use for the island. There is a holiday house on the far side, but the owners always travel here by boat and it seems that visitors to Eilean Mhic Chrion are few. Although only 35 minutes after low tide, the water was rising and I had to step over it between the rocks as I walked back to the marina. Much longer on the island and I'd have had to summon the dinghy.

There are four buses a day from Oban to Ardfern, so the journey can be done by public transport, but for me time dictated that a car had to be used. Hence I set off south again along the highly scenic road through hills and mountains. At Cairnbarn I reached the Crinan Canal, which runs the nine miles across the peninsula from Ardrishaig on Loch Fyne to Crinan on the Sound of Jura. Opened in 1801, two years late, significantly over budget, and not properly finished, the canal was designed to provide a quick link between the Clyde Estuary and west coast, avoiding the long voyage around the Kintyre peninsula. Until the coming of the railways the fastest way to travel from Glasgow to Inverness was by steamer using the Crinan and Caledonian Canals, usually calling at Oban en route.

The canal could be said to make the Kintyre peninsula and Knapdale above it a bridged island. Whilst I suppose this is strictly true, the same criteria would make the whole of Scotland north of the Caledonian Canal from Inverness to Fort William an island, so common sense classes Kintyre as mainland Scotland. However according to Norse sagas, it is indeed an island. King Magnus Barelegs (more correctly King Magnus 2nd, but he was normally referred to by his nickname which came from his penchant for wearing kilts) was told by King Malcolm of Scotland that he could take ownership of all the islands off the west coast of Scotland around which he could sail his boat. Determined to have the Kintyre peninsula, Magnus had his warriors drag a Viking longboat across the narrow isthmus, while he sat inside taking hold of the helm. Hence he gained possession of Kintyre and the peninsula became an 'island'.

I had considered turning west at Cairnbairn, then driving down the narrow Tayvallich peninsula, which separates Loch Sween from the Sound of Jura. At the southern end of the peninsula is the remote Danna Island, which whilst described as tidal, failed however to meet my definition, being cut off only around four times a year. It took much research before I was able to find information on the island, but eventually I made contact with James Johnston, one of Danna's two residents, who told me that the height of the man-made causeway means that it rarely floods. Without the causeway the island would be cut off on every tide. James said that the 1881 census showed a population of 49 souls, but by 2001 this was 5, and making a living from sheep and cattle farming, he is now 50% of the population. It used to export potatoes (or tatties as James called them) to Ireland and harvest kelp for potash production. To visit Danna Island would have added another day to the trip, so as just a 'nearly tidal island' I had to give it a miss.

I stopped to buy lunch at Lochpielhead, a nice little town with an attractive outlook onto Loch Fynne. A cake in the bakers took my fancy, but not recognising the seemingly unpronounceable name, I indicated my choice by pointing. I shouldn't have worried, marsbarkrispie cake being a combination of a popular chocolate bar and well known breakfast cereal, and not a traditional Gaelic delicacy.

The next section of the drive southwards was along the bank of Loch Fynne to the little town of Tarbert then onto the Kintyre peninsula. Crossing back to the west coast, the A83 runs alongside the beautiful West Loch Tarbert, then by open sea with the islands of Jura and Islay just visible. Closer to the mainland was the community-owned 7 mile long Gigha Island, linked by ferry from Tayinloan and the island I decided I'd most like to visit of all those seen today. South of the islands the road was now by the Atlantic Ocean, where waves ended their long journeys, splashing up on little rocky bays and sandy beaches. Seals lay on one beach and apart from the odd car driving by there was hardly a person to be seen. Oh what a wonderful place is Scotland!

Set at the head of a deep loch, sheltered by Davaar Island and surrounding hills, Campbeltown is one of the largest towns in Argyll. I checked into my hotel, repacked the rucksack with clothes for the four seasons that Scotland can have in an afternoon, and set off for the island. It's a couple of miles to the causeway, but roads all the way, so preferring to maximise time on the island I took the car.

The Doirlinn, the natural shingle causeway to Davaar Island, is uncovered for roughly 3 hours either side of low tide, allowing a good time to be spent on the island, which at 140 acres is slightly larger than Eilean Mhic Chrion. Rising to 378 feet, it was the largest so far on my clockwise tour round the UK, and I was glad to have plenty of time to explore. Its name probably derives from the two summits, Dr Hugh Gillies in his *Place Names of Argyll* agreeing with the popular derivation of the Gaelic Eilean Da-Bharr (meaning double-pointed island), and the more commonly used English version Davaar Island.

The Doirlinn is easy walking, heading first north to a marker light, then turning almost 90 degrees and arriving at the westerly dip of Davaar. Roughly a mile long, the walk took me 20 minutes, although it's advised to allow more. This corner of the island is quite flat with short sheep cropped grass, but beyond it the hill rose steeply.

A track runs along the north of the island to the lighthouse and cottages, but I headed right, over lush green grass towards the cliffs on the south. Beneath these are seven caves, one of which holds Davaar's greatest claim to fame, a life size painting of Christ's crucifixion. The painting was discovered by fishermen in 1887, who thought it must be the work of a miracle, but in fact it had been painted in secret by the local art teacher Archibald MacKinnon after he saw a vision in a dream telling him to paint it there. It couldn't have been easy and apparently he had to lash a paintbrush to his walking stick to reach the top. There was much interest in the cave from local people who considered the painting to be a sign from God. However, once the townsfolk discovered that it was MacKinnon and not The Almighty who had made the painting there was uproar and he was exiled from Campbeltown indefinitely. In fact he returned in 1934 at the age of 84 to restore the painting, by which time the town had forgiven him and he was given a civic welcome.

Restoration was carried out again in the 1950s and 1970s, fittingly by art teachers from Campbeltown, with a lead strip fixed above the painting to afford some protection from dripping water. It has become a place of pilgrimage for some, with visitors having walked over the Doirlinn for over a century to see MacKinnon's work. Every year on Easter Saturday the churches of Campbeltown gather here, holding a service outside the cave.

In July 2006 the painting was found to have been vandalised, a red and black image of the Argentine born Cuban revolutionary Che Guevara being sprayed over Christ's face. Nobody claimed responsibility for what was thought to be a political rather than random attack. A young man was apparently reported having been seen leaving the island with a bag at around the time of the attack, but with nothing else to go on the police investigation failed to find the culprit. The image was soon removed and the picture restored as closely as was possible to its 1887 original.

The springy grass ends abruptly near a ruined stone building, once a primitive shelter known as the Sheep'oose, where the hills meet the sea. From here access to the caves is over the stony shore under high cliffs. I had read that the route was over rocks, with stout shoes required, but walking was reasonably easy, although the footwear advice good. The first six caves are of varying size and apparently some link together beneath the cliff, but it was only the seventh that I was to explore. A sign outside helpfully indicates 'Cave Painting' and on the wall ten yards or so into the cave was MacKinnon's work.

The much restored image is clear and the shaft of light from the entrance enough to see it well. I did wonder how much of what I was looking at actually remained from the 19th century, or if this was like the proverbial hundred year old axe, that had only needed three new shafts and five heads.

To the right of the main painting of Jesus on the cross is a smaller image, with the face of a younger man, perhaps the younger Christ, and the words 'I did all this for thee, what will thou do for me'. Alone in this isolated cave on an island I found the paintings strangely moving, but then thought why strangely? Whatever your religious beliefs, it cannot be disputed that there is no other man whose face would have been painted in such a way nearly 2,000 years after his death.

Back at the grassy shore I stopped for a snack, observing oyster catchers and cormorants by the water. I'd bought a small pair of binoculars in the hope of spotting the minke whales and basking sharks that occasionally pass by, or the seals, otters and mink that can be seen on the shore, but today their use was to be restricted to viewing the island's many sea birds and later some of its more unusual land animals. Amongst the varied birdlife are auks, black guillemots, shags, peregrine falcons and even the occasional golden or white-tailed sea eagle.

The track on the northern side of Davaar runs along the shore, passing the island's jetty and a small white stone hut, ending at the walled lighthouse compound. A sign warns that this is private with CCTV in operation. The white lightkeeper's house, which was built as recently as 1952, is still occupied by the island's caretaker and the low stone buildings to its left, which were once the keeper's home, are now holiday cottages. Also now a holiday home is The Lookout, a square building standing on a small knoll, which was built during World War Two to house naval crews, whose task it was to stretch anti-submarine nets across the water, protecting Campbeltown.

The lighthouse was built in 1854 by David and Thomas Stevenson, sons of the famous Scottish engineer Robert Stevenson who built many Scottish lighthouses. (Thomas was the father of Robert Louis Stevenson, the writer of *Treasure Island*.) It was first constructed as a mock up on the mainland with numbered bricks, which were then brought over to the island and the lighthouse rebuilt. In 1983 the light was fully automated and with no need for its keepers to live on the island the cottages lay empty until 1992, when they were converted to self catering holiday homes. Although the cottages are still let, today all the buildings appeared empty and yet again it seemed I was the only person on an island.

Many tidal islands have tales of tragedy, but Davaar experienced a recent loss which was particularly sad and poignant. Len Bennett had lived in Mold in North Wales, commuting to his job in Liverpool for 30 years. In his spare time he worked as a volunteer in the RNLI shop and the local visitor centre. Whilst helping to organise a summer camp for Merseyside children he met his wife Rose and when Len reached his early sixties the couple decided to move to Kintyre, taking over as caretakers for the lighthouse cottages on Davaar. They loved the island and Len used to drive across the Doirlinn several times a week to buy provisions from

Campbeltown or pick up visitors. He was a popular man, who touched many lives and was said to have a smile for everyone.

On the afternoon of 4th January 2008 Len set out for the mainland, a journey he'd done a thousand times before, but this time he failed to return. Rose raised the alarm and a full scale search was launched with lifeboats, coastguards and a Royal Navy helicopter. In the early hours his Land Rover was found on the shingle, but it was empty. Despite continuing searches there was no sign of 70 year old Mr Bennett. More than a week later a walker discovered his body washed up on the shore of the Isle of Arran over 10 miles away. The exact circumstances were never discovered, but it was thought that he had simply misjudged the tide in gusting winds. Mrs Bennett decided that his ashes should be buried on the island with those of their golden retriever Mabel, who had recently had to be put to sleep. She moved to Campbeltown but how hard for her it must have been to look out across the loch where her husband had perished. Most commonly it is the reckless or ill-informed visitor who gets into difficulties, but so sadly on Davaar it was a man who knew the island and its tidal causeway, yet still lost his life to the unforgiving sea.

A very narrow path ran in front of the compound wall, but with a sheer drop to the rocks below meaning a slip would result in almost certain death, I sought another route to continue my exploration. Finding a path behind the houses I climbed the hill into Davaar's interior. This was wilder than any island I'd been on so far, with rough moorland, bogs and large areas of dormant bracken and heather ready to sprout once summer came. One could easily spend half a day exploring here.

Returning to the track I spotted on the beach what I'd hoped to find on the higher part of the island, four of Davaar's wild goats. Long haired, bearded, horned, and foraging for food amongst the rocks, they were clearly wild. Goats have been on the island since the mid 19th century, with the cliffs, rocky bays, shingle beaches and heather moorland particularly suited to them. James P. Hynes booklet 'Davaar Island', which was designed, illustrated and produced by Len Bennett, and to which I am indebted to some of information in this chapter, says that they were originally introduced to prevent sheep from being tempted onto dangerous ledges. Presumably the sheep are supposed to look up at the cliffs and say, 'Look at that silly goat up there, I think I'll stay down here on this nice green grass'.

I watched the goats snuffling around on the rocks for a while, then continued my way along the track, over the Doirlinn and to Little Blue Car, who'd waited patiently all alone in the lay-by.

Declining the over-priced hotel dinners I set off in search of food. There's little in the way of places to eat in Campbeltown, but down a side street I found a small chip shop. Not fancying mushy pea fritters I decided on a nice piece of fish, but options were limited; 'Fish' or 'Special Fish'. The former I was informed was cooked in batter and the latter in breadcrumbs. The type of fish was not advertised and nor was the fact that it had absolutely no flavour. I ate it on a seat by the harbour, watching a seal who I suspect would have enjoyed it more than me. How disappointing in a town with its own small fishing fleet.

Campbeltown is indeed a strange town. I was told that the people here are very different to the rest of Argyle, but my informant declined to say more on grounds of political correctness. It is poorer than Arran or Islay, but the tall stone buildings bear witness to the town's prosperity in the 19th century when fishing and ship building industries were booming and 34 distilleries manufactured Scotland's famous amber liquid. Now just three remain. Shops and businesses seemed to come into three categories; spruced up and making an effort, little changed in 30 years, boarded up and closed. It has great potential, a lovely setting, but the long and slow journey means that few visit. Perhaps the one bright spot for the local economy is golf, a championship standard links course at nearby Machrihanish, which if it were not so isolated would host tournaments, but still attracts players from across the UK. Flybe offer golfing packages with flights from Glasgow and the participants bring some wealth into Campbeltown, perhaps helping to keep its hotels and craft shops in business.

After some excellent porridge for breakfast I set off not back north, but first south to the end of the peninsula, the Mull of Kintyre. Although it would add to the day's driving time, I wondered if I'd ever get the opportunity again, and anyway I wanted to sing the song. It was a detour well worthwhile. The hills rise at the end of Kintyre and a single track road provided spectacular views of high cliffs, little bays and rocky shores. Ireland was clearly seen less than 15 miles across the sea.

I stopped four times on the drive back, once to wait for an obstinate hare to get out of the road, once to eat lunch at a lovely spot overlooking West Loch Tarbert and twice at almost tidal islands. The first was Ceann na Creig, a small island in West Loch Tarbert from where ferries run to Islay and Colonsay. It is linked to the mainland by a sturdy causeway which doesn't tend to flood and was built to facilitate access to a new terminal when larger ferries were brought in. I watched the Islay boat arrive and cars, lorries and foot passengers queue to board for their journey to the island. Most appeared to be locals, with just a few early season walkers and cyclists travelling to an island famous for its sandy beaches, moors and single malts. Earlier I'd seen the tiny ferry to Gihga and both gave a desire to one day visit islands further afield. Mind you today the sea was dead calm. I'm sure my feelings would have been different had the boats been going up and down Farne Island style. Indeed the voyages aren't always straightforward. In 1960 the MV Lochiel struck a reef in the loch and slowly sank. Apparently the Argyll & Sutherland Highlander Territorials were on board, and pushed the sheep overboard knowing they'd swim to safety, then retired to drink the bar dry, aided by the barman who stuck valiantly to his post handing out bottles to all comers despite water almost up to his armpits.

The final island of my trip was one which whilst not tidal, is particularly interesting. Until the early 1980s, Eilean Buidhe in Loch Shuna on the north side of the Craignish peninsula, was an uninhabited islet used for sheep grazing and separated from the sparsely populated mainland by 200 yards of sea. Now it is home to a family of four, plus three luxury holiday cabins and is permanently linked to the thriving little village of Craobh Haven (pronounced 'Croove Haven'). Falcon Scott, owner of the island's house, invited me to visit and we chatted around his dining room table.

Causeways were built to Eilean Buidhe (pronounced 'booie') and its sister islands of Eilean an Duin and Froach Eilean (which are now linked), in order to provide a sheltered area in which to build Craobh Haven Marina. Where there was once a small hill the 30 houses, shops and pub now stand, the spoil having been used to make the substantial causeways, which don't flood even on the highest tides. Falcon told me that construction was almost halted when the marina owners went bust, but the foreman pretended not to have received the message to stop work and continued building. His masters weren't happy but the causeways were completed. The Bond film *From Russia with Love* was filmed close by in Lunga bay and Sean Connery apparently showed interest in building a golf course here. It was decided that the terrain wasn't right for golf, but that the location an ideal base for sailing, hence the marina plan. Falcon and his wife Jane moved to the island in 1999 and have raised their two boys in this beautiful setting. He built the house himself and they offer B&B, plus the self catering Loch Shuna Lodges.

I took a walk around the little island with its tiny shingle beach and rocky foreshore. Fifty yards out into the loch I counted 15 seals lying stretched out on a rock, 4 light coloured pups and the rest adults. One plopped into the water and soon appeared closer to the island. He looked at me for a while and on deciding that the Englishman on the beach was bringing neither threat nor food, returned to the little colony. Falcon told me that the seals come onto the island sometimes, but prefer the rock. They see otters too, but not often as they are both shy and few in number.

I'd seen some beautiful scenery from train and car, but it's only when you get to walk in it, feel the breeze, breathe the air, hear the wildlife and see everything up close, that you can really experience the true qualities of Scotland. It's like the difference between watching a football match from close to the pitch where you can see the player's faces and hear their shouts, to viewing from high in the stands or on television. Eilean Buidhe isn't the most famous or even the most spectacular place in Scotland, but on the shore here, the rocks of Davaar, and the hill at Eilean Mhic Chrion, I had experienced the real beauty and atmosphere of Scotland, something that you just can't get from the inside of a car or train. What a lovely place this little island must be to live or stay. Sadly for me now it was time to drive the 20 miles back to Oban and the long train journey home.

# CHAPTER FOURTEEN

# WEST HIGHLAND ISLANDS

The sleeper to Fort William is a special travel experience and one of the world's great railway journeys. On a warm May evening the train was full, but in winter just a handful use it, hence this unique train was almost withdrawn a few years ago. That it is used by some influential Highlanders, giving it the unofficial name 'Deerstalker Express', may not have been entirely coincidental in its reprieve. I didn't sleep as well as usual, perhaps because we stopped more often than the Glasgow train and perhaps because I was at the end of the coach with my bed over the wheels making for a rougher ride. I dreamed that our house was shaking and woke just as it fell down, to realise that it was just the train lurching around another bend. At 7.00 I pulled up the blind to look out on mountains reflected in the dead still water of Loch Long. Half an hour later I was sitting in the lounge car eating a bacon panini as we trundled above Loch Lomond. It's easy to see why the West Highland Line was twice voted the world's top railway journey in the Wanderlust Travel Awards.

Stopping at Upper Tyndrum and looking across the valley to the Oban line that I'd travelled three weeks before (the village is the smallest place in the UK to have two stations), we picked up two passengers. The guard returned to the lounge car quite triumphant that she'd sold some tickets! Soon the line traverses a horseshoe curve, built because there wasn't enough money for a viaduct, then after Bridge of Orchy we were on Rannoch Moor. A desolate place only skirted by roads; to construct the route here 19th century engineers floated the line on a mattress of tree root, brushwood, earth and ash. A herd of deer stood close to the track, watching the train approach, something they must see every day. As far as I know it hasn't yet jumped off the rails and chased them, but the herd still ran off across the moors as we passed.

The moors were higher after Rannoch Station, which is surrounded by a horseshoe of mountains, with the pointed peak of Schiehallion in the distance just like a child would draw a mountain. Snow shelters and avalanche fences protect the line. 1347 feet above sea level we stopped at Corrour, made famous in the film Trainspotting (which incidentally is not about trains) and my favourite station in the whole of Britain. I came here once after a morning meeting in Glasgow, and found a perfect place – a railway station but no cars, a rough track but no road, a loch surrounded by mountains, wild moors and next to the station a single house offering B&B and meals. That afternoon I'd walked round the loch, enjoyed scampi & chips, then travelled home. Today I was continuing north with islands beckoning. Soon running downhill, we passed high above Loch Treig, over the rocky waters of Monessie Gorge, under snow capped Ben Nevis and into Fort William. I said that everyone should ride the Cambrian Coast line once in their lives. Well you should do the Fort William sleeper twice!

After a couple of hours wandering round the town I was back on a train, this time heading towards Mallaig and the first of the plethora of potentially tidal islands in this area of the West Highlands. The final section of the West Highland Line is often considered to be the most spectacular. There's more water as it runs beside lochs and sea, but it's not quite as remote as Rannoch Moor. At Glenfinnan the guard announced that we would be crossing the famous viaduct and the driver slowed to allow the many camera wielding passengers to take their snaps of the monument commemorating the point where Bonny Prince Charlie raised his standard at the start of the 1745 Jacobite Uprising. This is the viaduct that features in Harry Potter films with Harry travelling over it both by steam train and flying Ford Anglia. At Loch Nan Uamh we had our first view of the Hebrides, the 'Small Isles' of Rum and Eigg across the Sound of Arisaig. According to local hearsay, when the line was built in 1898 a horse and cart fell into one of the piers of the viaduct over the end of the loch. State-of-the-art scanning in 2001 proved the story to be true. The remains of a horse standing vertically against the wall above the wreck of a cart suggesting that the cart had fallen into the cavity, dragging the poor animal with it.

I left the train at Arisaig, the most westerly station in Britain, and set off for my first island, Eilean Ighe. Like several islands on this trip I wasn't sure if it could be visited on foot, so my journey was one of investigation.

Ann from the Land, Sea & Islands Centre, an information centre by the harbour, had told me that the she thought it could only be walked to on very low tides in spring and autumn when high tides reach 5 metres. Today's was due to rise to 4½ metres. The lady in the centre this afternoon didn't seem to know anything about the island, but recommended that I walked there on the road and not the two mile path round the headland. This she said is overgrown and warned me that there's a fierce dog at the house on the way. With memories of my walk to Sully Island, I hesitated but decided to go for it. I was however not a little relieved at finding no sign of a dog, fierce or otherwise, at the lone house. The path, whilst somewhat diffuse, took me over the hill to the shore where two men collected shellfish. From here the path through a wood was shall I say, sporadic, but with some pushing through undergrowth and bog hopping the other side, I eventually came out by the white sands of Gortenachullish.

It was 25 minutes before low tide, but bar a foot wide channel the sands to the island were hard and dry. I was on my first West Highland Island. Eilean Ighe was larger than I'd expected (about 85 acres), rising to 20 metres. The island is in two parts, joined by a narrow isthmus. I'd arrived on the northern section, which is almost bowl shaped; rocks around the edge, with flat, boggy, rough grass and heather in the middle. The southern section is partly wooded. Climbing a rocky outcrop on the far side of the island there were superb views to Rum, the distinctive flat top of Eigg, and back across the island to the mountains around Loch Morar.

The remains of three buildings on the island were surveyed by The Royal Commission on the Ancient and Historical Monuments of Scotland in 1974. The first two are defensive structures on separate rocky knolls, which it is thought were medieval forts. The stretch of water between the island and mainland is called Coalas Eilean Ighe, meaning 'channel of the forts'. Local tradition is that they were defences against cattle raiders, but it's thought more likely that they were the stronghold of a small clan chieftain. The third building is the remains of a corn-drying kiln with well preserved draught passage. Not knowing the exact location and with at most an hour to explore, I didn't find the remains. On the southern part of the island is a cave, which was found to contain midden deposits of animal bones and a shard from what was possibly a medieval vessel. It seems therefore that although no one has lived on the island for many centuries, people were here at least temporarily in medieval times.

I returned to Arisaig along the road, and was the sole passenger boarding the train back to Fort William. After dinner at the very comfortable and convenient Alexandra Hotel right by the station, I set off on further island investigation, this time on foot. Just north of the town is an inlet where the River Lochy drains into Loch Linnhe. The map showed an island here which looked as if it may be tidal. Following the Great Glen Way, passing Inverlochy Castle and with superb views across to Ben Nevis, I reached the river. Crossing the footbridge, I turned left along a road and scrambled down a bank. A man waiting at a bus stop looked at me as if I was mad – surely not? Fifteen yards or so of what looked like stony riverbed, but was at high tide a hidden part of the sea loch, separated me from the land opposite.

The tide was coming in and I had time just to cross and watch the water creep rapidly over the stones. Standing at the edge I timed the sea as it moved in from either side – 40 seconds for about 10 metres. Hopping across the still narrow but rapidly filling channel I returned to the mainland, content that I'd found another tidal island, even if my visit had been measured in seconds. It was only on returning to the hotel and looking closely at the map that I realised I had crossed only to a short peninsula and not the island. The island tally for the trip was still at one.

My travels were now to take me to the beautiful but remote area east of Fort William. With little in the way of public transport the only way to get to several islands in a reasonably short time was once again to hire a car. I'd considered using a combination of the sparse local buses and cycling, but was very glad to have thought again. A couple of weeks before the trip my youngest son and I hired bikes at a local country park, the first time for more than 30 years that I'd been on a bicycle for more than a few minutes. Whilst my legs are quite content with walking, they were definitely not so keen cycling and little used muscles quickly raised their objections. Worse complaints came from slightly higher, where a bottom that is used to soft chairs found a hard bicycle saddle far from comfortable. This was on the flat paths of Essex, so it's a jolly good thing I'd decided against riding for miles across Scottish hills. My days of cycling 25 miles each way to Southend must be over (OK I only did it once – 34 years ago!).

Next morning a little car (silver this time) was delivered to my hotel precisely as arranged and I set off for a long day in search of islands. First the short distance back to the little peninsula I'd visited last night, but this time crossing a second dried stony bed and onto the island proper. Marked on the OS map as Eilean a Bhealaidh (meaning 'The Broom Island'), but also as Eilean Mor ('Big Island'), it is of reasonable size at roughly 400 x 500 metres. Much of it is covered with mature trees and shrubs, the flowering gorse, daffodils and bluebells making it an attractive island. It would not have been so peaceful in 1431 and 1645 when the Battles of Inverlochy were fought close by.

Little seems to be known about the islands around Fort William but Ian Abernethy, a local journalist and owner of Ben Nevis Book Corner, was able to give me some help. It's not even easy to work out how many islands there are around the mouth of the River Lochy. There seemed to be six islands but only four names.

The Ordnance Survey Explorer map and a town map I'd picked up in Fort William both clearly show Eilean a Bhealaidh and Eilean Mor as one, but Ian said they are different islands. He told me of two other islands, Eilean Uaine ('Green Island'), which is joined to another at low tide, and Eilean na Craoibhe ('The Tree Island'). These could be the unnamed cigar shaped island shown on the O.S. just south of Eilean Mor and the unnamed island shown close to the shore to the west. Two further small islands in the south east corner of the basis are also not named on the maps. The flow patterns and channels however change rapidly and tidal status of the islands could alter over a relatively short period of time. Hence maps may not always be up to date. I consulted Google Earth and found this pretty much matched the O.S. Returning to Ian for help, I sent him copies of the maps, but his reply was that whilst Fort William is his specialist subject, his expertise is mainly people and buildings, and he could assist no more with the islands.

I shall therefore conclude that the relatively large island I walked to is either a joined or co-named Eilean a Bhealaidh and Eilean Mor. It has been suggested that this may have originally been man-made, having been constructed by the early Celts when they lived in crannogs, artificial islands in the middle of lakes or bogs. Ian Abernethy however is convinced that this is not the case and the island is natural. There are no buildings on the island and it seems to have been left to nature. Its size, proximity to Fort William and the battle sites, its flowering bulbs and possibility that it was man-made however justify sufficient human activity for inclusion in my list. Eilean Uanie and Eilean na Craoibhe however I shall consign to my list of nearly tidal islands on account of their size and apparent lack of human activity.

Before moving on I went to investigate An Caol, a small island on the bend where Loch Linnhe becomes Loch Eil. The map suggested that it might be possible to walk to it at low tide from the beach at Caol, an outlying village of Fort William, which with a population of 6,500 is the largest village in Scotland. With the tide now approaching its high point this however appeared unlikely. It was though a magnificent view down the loch with mountains reflected in still water. Fort William may be the wettest town in the UK, but for the second day running the weather was perfect, with bright sunshine and just enough cloud to make the sky interesting.

Leaving the town I drove south on the A82 along the banks of Loch Linnhe to the tiny Eilean Stalker, dominated by its castle and immortalised as Castle Aaaarrrrrggghhh in the final scenes of the 1975 film *Monty Python and the Holy Grail*. I had read much conflicting information as to whether the island was tidal and it was only after calling into Oban Tourist Information Centre on my previous trip that I'd been able to find the answer. I was given the phone number for Ross Allward whose father bought the island in 1965 and whose family still own it.

Ross gave me the information that I had been seeking, although his initial answer 'yes and no' suggested further uncertainty. The answer is that yes one can walk across soft mud close to the castle on spring tides (perhaps once a month), but no it isn't possible to walk all the way to the castle with dry feet as there's always water around it. Almost like a moat and a couple of feet deep, it would require wading rather than paddling, so there is no doubt that despite what many sources say, Castle Stalker is not on a tidal island. Ross said that the water helps keep people way from what is still a family home, although now used more as a holiday home than a continuous residence. The castle is open to the public for 5 weeks each year, dates which are chosen when the tides are high, as visitors are brought here by boat.

The stone castle was built in the mid 15th century by Sir John Stewart, Lord of Lorn, probably in place of an earlier fortified building. For hundreds of years there were many bloody battles and murderous uprisings, particularly between the clans Stewart, MacLaren, McDonald and Campbell. In 1520 Sir Alexander Stewart was fishing off the small island next to Castle Stalker when he was surprised and murdered by a party of Campbells. According to tradition the nurse of his baby son hid the child in the castle and when the Campbells had left found him still alive in his hiding place.

Despite all the bloodshed, it was as a result of a drunken wager in 1620 that the castle first passed into the hands of the Campbells, in exchange for an eight-oared wherry. The Stewarts regained the castle in 1689, but then forfeited it to the Campbells after defeat at the Battle of Dunkeld. The Campbells continued to reside here until around 1800, when they built a new house on the mainland, the castle remaining merely as a storehouse. In about 1840 the roof fell in, or was perhaps removed to avoid roof tax, and the castle abandoned. In 1908 it was purchased by Charles Stewart who carried out basic preservation work to stem the decay. Continuing the bloodshed his successor Duncan Stewart who was Governor of Sarawak, was murdered in the Far East. In 1965 Lt. Col. D.R. Stewart Allward negotiated terms for purchasing the castle and with the help of friends and family spent ten years rebuilding and restoring it to the fully habitable state it is today. He sadly died suddenly while out walking in 1991, his wife and four children taking over responsibility for the castle.

The tide was well up when I arrived, but from the viewpoint above, the castle stunning in its watery setting. Most of the castle scenes in *Monty Python and the Holy Grail* were filmed at Doune Castle near Stirling, but Castle Stalker appears in the final scene. It was on the far grassy bank that King Arthur's army prepared to attack the castle and claim the holy grail, before with typical Python ludicrousy a couple of 20th century policeman intervened. The King (Graham Chapman) was arrested and a constable's hand over the camera lens brought an immediate end to the film.

Next I took my little silver car onto the Corran Ferry for the short crossing over Loch Linnhe which provides access to the remote Morvern, Moidart and Ardnamurchan, where I was to be spending the next two days. The ferry is the only direct link to the southern half of the area. The school bus uses it and as I drove off a hearse was waiting to board. I stopped briefly at the little village of Strontian, then continued along a single track road on the banks of the beautiful Loch Sunart. Most of the roads in the area are narrow with passing places, but provided drivers read the road ahead progress isn't as slow as one might think and reversing to allow passing generally avoided. It is law that slow drivers must pull into a bay to allow faster ones to pass – what a good idea!

Ardnamurchan is a peninsula along the northern bank of Loch Sunart, its tip marking the most westerly point on the UK mainland. It is a remote and beautiful area, with no towns, and most of the few settlements barely justifying village status. Had time permitted I'd have made the long drive to the lighthouse at the most westerly point, or nearby Sanna Bay, where there is a potentially tidal island. The OS Explorer map names as Sanna Island a rocky area off the beach just north of the tiny hamlet of Sanna, although most maps show it unnamed and probably barren. Like many of these remote Scottish islands it was hard to find information, but eventually I made contact with Louis Costella, a local photographer and owner of a website about the bay. He told me that although it can be walked to at low tide, the 'island' is a rocky outcrop and not named locally. Hence I shall just add it to my list of 'nearly tidal islands'.

Turning right at Salen, then left after Archaracle down a tiny lane following the River Shiel, I soon found one of the tidal islands that I'd been most looking forward to seeing. Castle Tioram (pronounced Cheerum) on the 6 acre rocky Eilean Tioram in Loch Moidart, is a comparatively well known tourist spot. Indeed there were several other visitors here already, a change from most of my islands, but a fraction of the number who would visit if this were in a less remote location. Hence there are no tea rooms, craft shops or ice cream vans. The island can be walked to at all but high tide, either along a sand and shingle bar that's covered for only a short time, or across firm sand either side. Unlike Stalker the castle only covers part of the island, although its grey stone walls dominate not only the island, but views of the whole area. I ate my lunch sitting by the loch with the castle behind me. A beautiful and peaceful scene, although like Stalker, Tioram has a long and often bloody history.

This is a rare Scottish tidal island about which much has been written and I have taken information from a booklet *Castle Tioram in Moidart* by Christian Aikman that I spotted in Strontian Tourist Information Centre, and an article by Sandra Evans published on the Moidart Local History Group website.

It is likely that the dry island, flanked by beaches ideal for pulling up boats and with a deep anchorage on the north east side, would have been used even before the castle was built. The discovery of a 7th century bronze bowl in a castle midden suggests that the site was of importance before it was chosen as a medieval base, and small pieces of worked soapstone found on the beach point to the probable presence of Vikings. According to local tradition the castle was built by Amy MacRuari (or Amie NicRuari) in the 14th century, but it is likely that she improved an existing 13th century building. It appears in records from 1373, being part of the lands given to Ranald Clanranald by Lord of the Isles John of Islay and became the principle seat of the chief of the clan, Captain of Clanranald.

The castle remained in the family's possession until the early 20th century, although in a violent age it was not without its struggles. Clan leader Alan Clanranald successfully fought with Highland forces against the Scottish Crown at the battle of Harlaw in 1411 and imprisoned the defeated Macintosh chief in the castle dungeon. It is thought that Alan was eventually executed by James 1 in 1509, and that his son Raonuil Ban met a similar fate at the hands of the Crown. The next chief, Dugall, was unpopular with the clansmen who eventually murdered him and excluded his sons from succession. Hence his uncle, Alexander, took over, who seems to have been less warlike and more popular (could these perhaps be connected?), dying peacefully around 1529.

The next 150 years were no less turbulent, with clan chief John of Moidart's involvement in the 1544 'Battle of Shirts' when the Highlanders threw off their surplus clothing and fought in shirts, his grandson Donald receiving a knighthood for maintaining 'King's Peace', but the next chieftain, another John, turning to piracy. In 1685 Allan the 14th chief chose to live elsewhere and from then Tioram was no longer the family home. In 1692, when despite having sworn allegiance to the British Crown he joined the Jacobite Court in France, the castle was seized by Government forces and fell into disrepair. Allan recaptured it in 1715, but then torched the castle apparently to keep it out of Hanoverian hands, before leaving for the battle of Sherriffmuir where he was mortally wounded. It may have been partially inhabited for a short time, but in 1748 was described as an abandoned ruin, which it has remained to this day.

The castle has been used as a location in a number of films. It briefly appears as the Duke of Argyll's castle in a night scene in *Rob Roy* and can be seen in the 1984 *Supergirl* movie. Workers on the film made themselves unpopular by leaving litter by the loch and abandoning a support that had been used to stop the crane employed for flying scenes from sinking into the sand. Prior to filming, the portable toilet trailer that was to be used by the cast and crew came off the road and ended up in the River Shiel.

Sadly the castle is now in an unsafe state and several signs warned visitors not to walk beneath the north side as masonry may fall at any time. The door is blocked as it would be dangerous to enter. There has been much dispute between the owner, millionaire businessman Lex Brown who purchased it in 1997, and Historic Scotland, an executive agency of the Scottish Government, who are charged with safeguarding the nation's historic environment. In 2002 Mr Brown's plans to turn the castle into a 15$^{th}$ century style home and clan museum were approved by Highland Council, but refused by Historic Scotland, who argued that the proposals would 'produce a building which does not reflect any known historic form'. The decision was later upheld at a public inquiry, but the wrangle continues.

Mr Brown told the Sunday Herald that 'Hell will freeze over' before he'd sell to Historic Scotland, but as a scheduled monument they have to agree to any alterations. Local opinion is divided, some would welcome the increased visitors that Mr Brown's proposals would bring, but others agree with Historic Scotland that the building should be preserved as the ruin it has been for many years. It is a common debate as to whether our heritage should be 'preserved in aspic', or allowed to change as it often has over the centuries. Each case probably needs to be considered on its merits, but I'm inclined to the view that a preserved but ruined castle is more appropriate on the remote Loch Moidart than would be a renovated home and museum. Unfortunately if no decision is made the elements will make it for us. Part of the north west curtain wall has already collapsed and the whole building is in a dangerous condition. It is a truly beautiful spot and a historic building. What a shame it would be if the castle falls down before the dispute can be resolved.

Close to Tioram is the small tree covered Riska Island and behind this the joined islands of Eilean Shona and Shona Beag, my next destination. It had taken a lot of research to discover the layout of the islands and whether they were tidal. Eilean Shona is often described as a tidal island and the smaller Shona Beag (meaning 'Island of the Ford' or 'Small Island') is joined to it on the easterly side. Shona is the larger at roughly 2½ by 1½ miles, with several peaks, the highest being Bein a Bhaillidh at 265 metres. The eastern end of the island is wooded, but most of the remainder is rough hilly moorland. Both islands are inhabited. The magnificent eight bedroom Eilean Shona House, with its own billiard room and tennis court is surrounded by large informal gardens and let out as luxury holiday accommodation. In the 1920s the house was rented by J.M. Barrie as a summer home for his family and friends, and he wrote the screen play for the 1924 film adaptation of Peter Pan here. There are five other cottages on the island, plus a schoolhouse, which was apparently built two miles from the other houses because the wife of the 19th century island's owner didn't want to be disturbed by children.

Estate Manager Rose Martin told me that Eilean Shona can only be accessed by boat, however Google Maps shows a road running between the linked islands. Rose said the map was wrong and the OS Explorer map confirmed that there's no road or even path between them. I'd read a couple of accounts from people who had managed to walk from Beag to Shona, but who did not advise others to do the same. Reading that 'Crossing Shona Beag is very rough, cleg and tick ridden, with a steep and awkward descent to the isthmus' and 'the crossing of the bracken and bog infested hill will not easily be forgotten' didn't enthuse me about trying to reach Eilean Shona. In any case there's no way it could be done over one low tide hence I would only be visiting Shona Beag, but as the islands are linked, they would count as one.

Although less than a mile across the water from Castle Tioram, the drive around the end of Loch Moidart took half an hour. I parked at the top of a track just as the road turns inland and walked a pleasant half mile through woods to the loch side. Here a short causeway runs to Shona Beag and can be crossed for roughly 2 hours either side of low tide.

The track continues through woods on the island and here I met Steven Lindsay, one of its population of four. He and his wife live in the island's house and another couple in its cottage. His grandfather owned Eilean Shona and he's lived here for 40 years, bringing up four children, although he was in the army so away quite a lot. Modestly he didn't mention that he reached the rank of Lieutenant Colonel and was Regimental Secretary to Black Watch for 10 years. What a wonderful and peaceful retreat he must have found the island each time he returned here from army postings. He retired in 2005 after 45 years service, but said there's still plenty to do on the Shona Beag, which I found to be a delightful place and one of my favourite tidal islands.

About half is covered with ancient oak woods, for which the island is an SSSI, whilst the higher areas are rough and boggy moorland. Mr Lindsay told me that the path to Eilean Shona is long gone, but I walked a little way across the boggy upland, although not as far as the highest point which is just over 100 metres. He said they see deer, otters, seals, mink (which are not welcome) and pine martins (who are troublesome). Wildcats used to live here but he hadn't seen one for a long time. People on holiday on Eilean Shona put out jam to attract pine martins, hence they are now accustomed to people. They've nested in the Lindsay's attic and broken china in their larder, but as a protected species cannot be harmed.

Mr Lindsay said that few visitors come to the island (although more venture as far as the causeway), and told me of one man whose stay was longer than anticipated. A gentleman from Lancashire contacted him and asked to visit Shona Beag as he wanted to set a sequel to Treasure Island here. Unfortunately he missed the tide and as the Lindsays were away had to find a place to spend the night. He sat in the stone barn for 7 hours and being used to town life, said he'd never realised how dark it could be. Mr Lindsay never saw the book, but I assured him that mine would come to fruition.

Continuing across the island I passed the fine house (built in 1860) and its well tended gardens with neatly cut lawns, flowering shrubs and blossoming fruit trees, then followed a path through the woods to the little white crofters cottage on the banks of the loch. This narrow path is the only land access for the couple who live here and the man travels by boat to his work on Eilean Shona. A postman used to visit the island by boat, but now mail has to be picked up in Archaracle. Several tree covered tidal islets lie off Shona Beag's south shore and sitting on a jetty opposite the cottage I became aware of a presence on the islet. A lone deer was watching me, but soon decided I presented no threat and continued with the serious business of nibbling the grass. Shona Beag is a most beautiful island, from which its lucky residents have stunning views across the lovely Loch Moidart.

I checked into Salen Hotel on Loch Sunart, but with the long Scottish summer evenings my day of island exploration continued after dinner. At high tide Kentra Bay, four miles north west of Salen, is a large body of water almost enclosed by hills and marshland. At low tide the water drains through a narrow channel leaving an expanse of mud. In the bay are a number of islands, mostly small, but all potentially counting as tidal. John Rye, an expert on the area and leader of many walks, had told me that those in the north of the bay were just rocky outcrops, but that those at the south end have some cultivation marks on them and possibly the remains of old habitations.

I parked at the south east corner of the bay, where the road ends and a track continues along the bottom of the bay. With the tide well on its way in I wasn't optimistic of getting to an island and investigation was the main aim. However Eileanan nan Gad, the largest island in the bay, was looking promising. From a distance there appeared to be sand between island and shore and on approaching there was indeed 20 yards or so of firm sand, with grassy salt marshes either side. The only footprints were of birds and deer. Soon mine were added and I was on my fourth island of the day. Eileanan nan Gad rises to around 10 metres, with rocky outcrops, rough grass, heather and a few small trees. The island is grazed and a sheep with its single lamb wandered around on the grass.

Just beyond Eileanan nan Gad is a most attractive island, which the O.S. map doesn't name. Of similar height, it is smaller and almost totally tree covered. Wedge shaped it slopes down from the shore end. There are just a couple of yards of mud between the salt marsh and island, so it must be accessible at all but high tide.

I walked another mile until the track heads uphill into the trees, stopping at a little bay where the only sounds were from the woods – an unseen waterfall and a cuckoo. By the time I got back to the islands the mud was covered and the incoming tide filling the little channels on the marsh. As I stopped to look at Eileanan nan Gad a lone deer appeared. It walked over the marsh, stood for a while at the waters edge, then waded through, the water coming almost to her flank. Once on the island she bounded off, then moments later appeared on top of the rocks, silhouetted against the evening sky. Such magical moments are experienced only when you get out of the car.

Next morning the sun had gone and low cloud gave more familiar Scottish weather. At Glenmore, eight miles along Loch Sunart, I stopped at the Ardnamurchan Natural History Centre, an excellent exhibition of local wildlife, shop and cafe. Owner John Polak told me about Eilean Mor, a tidal island opposite the centre. The island is owned by Michael Macgregor, a professional photographer based in Glenmore, who keeps highland cattle on it. Whilst cut off only on higher tides it recently had regularly been an island. An area of grassy salt marsh separates the island from the mainland, with little channels that fill as the tide rises. To the right a tiny path runs through rocks, making the easiest access when tides allow.

Once on the island the path disappears and walking is hard going. Rough grass, heather and bracken cover the centre, with woodland on lower slopes around all but the northern edge. If the owner permitted John hoped to start running guided walks here later in the summer, and to cut some vegetation to make a path. The island is deceptively large, roughly 2/3 mile long and 1/3 mile wide, with rocky outcrops rising to more than 40 metres.

An old wall suggests that it was once divided and farmed, but there's no evidence of habitation. I climbed to the highest point at the far end of the island, looking out across the loch and scanning the water for dolphins. None were to be seen but John told me he'd spotted one 2 days earlier when the water had been dead calm. Neither did I see a golden eagle, although these are regularly seen in Ardnamurchan skies, however with food less plentiful their density is less than on nearby Mull. Nor did I see the cattle, for which if I'm honest I have to admit to not being too sorry – those horns aren't just for show you know. There was however plenty of evidence of them having been here – and not just the footprints! There were few human footprints on the island and yet again I was the sole visitor.

After lunch in the Centre I headed north for further island investigation. I'd read that Samalaman Island near Glenuig in the Sound of Arisaig is tidal, but John Dye had told me it can only be walked to on very low tides. Today's was 4½ metres, so quite large but not exceptional. Arriving at the picturesque little bay 2½ hours before low tide, the island with its tiny white sand beach was the other side of a wide stretch of water. It was going to be a long wait, but there could be worse places to spend it. Working on the watched kettle never boils policy, I went for little wanders, noting how far the sea had retreated each time I returned. For a while I watched a lone tern flying over the water then suddenly dropping like a stone as it dived for fish. A heron stood in still water by the rocks, his more sedate tactic waiting for the fish to come to him. Twenty minutes before low tide there was still 40 yards of water. The sand was firm and it probably could have been waded, but this time local knowledge was right, and the beautiful little Samalaman Island would just make my 'nearly tidal' list.

The drive back along Loch Ailort, then the A83 'Road to the Isles' by Loch Eilt, past Glenfinnan and finally Loch Eil, was no less spectacular than those in Moidart and Ardnamurchan. Just before Fort William I made a short detour. With the tide now low I went again to investigate An Caol, and how different it looked. The water had gone and there was firm sand all the way from shore to island.

In ten minutes I was on the narrow strip of partly vegetated shingle that makes up this little island. A few shrubs and gorse bushes grew, but otherwise it was just rough grass and stones. The loud calls of gulls and oystercatchers suggested I wasn't welcome, so not wishing to disturb the birds I ventured only onto the end of the island, leaving after just a minute or so. A couple of small wrecked boats lay on the eastern bank, but other than them there appeared little sign of human influence. The island is so low and narrow (An Coal means 'narrow isle') that it's hard to spot from the shore and few probably know it is here. Sixty years ago however it was larger and grassy. The island was part of the Kennedy croft (Charles Kennedy MP and his father still live just across the loch) and the young Charles used to be taken out to the island on horseback. Now An Caol seems just to belong to the birds.

This was my fourth trip to see islands in Scotland and as I moved up the west coast the scenery had become increasing spectacular. I chatted to a couple in the sleeper lounge car as we trundled back over Rannoch Moor. This was their first visit to Scotland and they'd been quite taken aback by the place. Certainly it's a special country, viewed by many as the most beautiful in Europe. It's hard to make comparisons with say Switzerland, with its higher mountains, glaciers and lakes, but what makes Scotland different is its wildness. The Alps tend to be farmed up to the snow line, with well marked paths, and above this only mountaineers can venture at will, but much of Scotland is wild – rough ground, with few paths, but in the main accessible to the determined and well prepared walker. Perhaps only in Scandinavia can such terrain be found elsewhere in Europe. As darkness fell I returned to my little cabin with thoughts of the next trip that was to take me even further north in this wonderful country.

# CHAPTER FIFTEEN

# THE SANDAIG ISLANDS

*The islands formed a chain of perhaps half a mile in length, and ended in one as big as the rest put together, on whose seaward shore showed the turret of a lighthouse. Splashed among the islands were small beaches of sand so white as to dazzle the eye. Beyond the islands was the shining enamelled sea, and beyond it the rearing bulk of Skye, plum-coloured distances embroidered with threads of snow.'*

*Gavin Maxwell – Ring of Bright Water*

I'm not generally someone who likes to jump out of bed immediately on waking (the snooze button on our alarm clock is well used!), but on a sleeper train the anticipation of discovering an unknown view outside is usually enough to tempt me from under the covers. Pulling up the blind this morning revealed a scene of Highland beauty. Early morning sun was lighting up the mountain tops, but had not yet gained the strength to burn off layers of mist that lay over nearby fields and more distant lower mountain slopes. Breakfast was enjoyed with a backdrop of the Cairngorm Mountains.

Although on the west coast, ten miles south of Kyle of Lochalsh, the easiest route to the Sandaig Islands is via the east coast of Scotland. Hence for the second time I'd boarded the Highland Sleeper at Euston, this time heading for Inverness. It's actually three trains in one, the 16 coaches dividing in Edinburgh, with sections running to Fort William, Aberdeen and Inverness.

At Inverness we were met by three policemen and a dog which sniffed at every passenger, young or old. There was not a word of greeting and my attempt at light hearted conversation, 'Is this customs?' met with a gruff reply. My email to Visit Scotland suggesting that this was hardly the friendly Highland welcome they advertise was forwarded to the local police. Acting Detective Inspector Derek McGillivray phoned me to explain that there had been a major drugs operation that day, and that as well as raiding houses, officers had targeted the bus and railway stations. He explained that although the Northern Constabulary Force area is one of the safest places to live in the United Kingdom, many people don't realise that Inverness and even the remoter towns on the west coast have drug problems. A follow up letter advised that at future similar operations 'the benefits of good interaction between police and public will be emphasised to the officers deployed'. Hopefully next time the drugs dog sniffs a little old lady he'll do it with a smile on his face.

From Inverness I headed west on a little train to Kyle of Lochalsh, another famously scenic ride, which featured in Michael Palin's series of 'Great Railway Journeys'. The 80 mile route runs from coast to coast, starting by the Beauly Firth and ending opposite the Isle of Skye. Heading inland from Dingwall we started to climb over the Highlands, reaching the still waters of Loch Garve which mirrored surrounding hills and trees. At Garve a coach party boarded, a sea of grey hair clustering around a single door as if the train were a coach. Their driver waved them off then set out to follow the train to Kyle.

The line follows the River Bran, which runs through lochs and meanders across a glacier-cut U shaped valley – a geographer's paradise. A buzzard flew alongside, only yards from the train window and a lone deer stood by the river's edge. More mountains reflected in the glasslike waters of Loch Achanalt. Ruined crofts reminded of the Highland Clearances when landowners cruelly evicted their tenants because more money could be made from grazing sheep. I made a note of Achnasheen as a place that I shall one day return to and walk along this beautiful valley.

The two coach train was surprisingly busy, with hardly a spare seat. Tourists heavily outnumbered locals, American and German accents mingling with those from England and Scotland. To the lady sitting opposite me however this was a vital transport link. She was returning from art college in Inverness to her home on the island of Benbacula, a journey that would take 8 hours, involving train to Kyle, bus to Uig on

Skye, ferry to North Uist and finally a bus north and over the causeway to Benbacula.

Approaching the west coast the line runs along Loch Carron, twisting and turning around inlets of this sea loch that extends 13 miles inland. Although we had reached the sea at Strathcarron it was another 45 minutes before the train pulled into Kyle of Lochalsh, from where ferries once ran to Skye. It is now bypassed by most visitors who drive straight over the bridge.

These were the only islands that I didn't visit alone. My parents happened to be staying in Kyle of Lochalsh as part of their Scottish holiday and were waiting on the platform to greet me. How strange to see them so far from both our homes. Perhaps now is a good time to thank Mum and Dad for their help in proof reading this book and particularly my father's incisive questions which caused me to repeatedly check various facts.

Also waiting at Kyle station was Sarah from Kyle Taxi Company, with a silver Peugeot 307, a larger car than I'd wanted but all that was available for hire. With two passengers however the extra room was appreciated. A family business which Sarah is learning to take over, this was the friendliest hire firm I used on my travels. The car had only been returned 20 minutes beforehand and both she and it were still wet from a high speed washing.

Such is the geography of Scotland's west coast with its inlets and sea lochs, that the quickest route to Sandaig was via the Isle of Skye. We crossed the bridge, then soon turned left along a single track road through the spectacular glens of Arrock and Kylerhea. The road ends at a slipway from where a unique little ferry crosses the Kylerhea Narrows back to the mainland.

The Glenachulish, the single boat that operates the community owned Glenelg Ferry, is the last manually operated turntable ferry in the world. Cars are driven onto the deck which is then rotated 180 degrees by the crew, allowing vehicles to drive straight off the other end. This ingenious design ensures that the ferry can be loaded at any state of the tide and that drivers never have to reverse. Operating only in the summer months, it provides a vital link for the area's tourist economy.

Just one other car accompanied us on the Glenachulish as we crossed the beautiful stretch of water, the ferry taking an exaggerated arc as it battled the tidal race, one of the fiercest in Britain. It can take only six cars (and that must be a squeeze) and a maximum of twelve people. When we returned a minibus was making the crossing, but with two cars already on board, half its passengers had to wait for the next trip. Also making both trips was Nak, the skipper's border collie, who spent the entire journey running perilously around the edge of the boat, almost as if the passengers had to be continually rounded up lest we should stray into the water.

Ferries such as this were once an essential part of Highland life, but new roads and bridges have seen them off. The Glenelg Ferry is the last, a Scottish national treasure and a unique travel experience.

It had started to rain while we were on the ferry and the boatman told us that with the wind from the south west this had set in for the day. Local knowledge however proved to be wrong. Within twenty minutes we were sitting on Bernera Beach in bright sunshine eating a picnic and looking across to the hills of Skye. There was to be no more rain until tomorrow, but plenty then to make up. A tug boat sailed slowly by, towing a platform on which was a section of bridge. A little later we saw it heading back north, still with the bridge in tow. My parents had seen it pass Kyle of Lochalsh in the early morning and we reckoned it must be sailing around Scotland looking for two bits of land exactly the right distance apart where it could leave its bridge.

The coast road took us through the little village of Glenelg and past Bernera Barracks, an impressive and surprisingly complete 18th century building that acted as a base for Government troops stationed here to keep order after the Jacobite uprisings. With the tide soon to turn there was no time to explore, particularly with some uncertainty of the route to the islands and how easily parents would cope with the steep paths. Continuing south we stopped by a shallow lake at Upper Sandaig (a settlement of just one house) and leaving the car set off along a forestry track towards the sea.

Knowing I was taking my parents I'd put more than the usual research into the walking route, but a combination of the OS map and Google Earth didn't show an obvious way. Then on the website of Eilean Ban Trust I came across an excellent set of directions, although involving a path that's not on the map.

Eilean Ban is a small island under the Skye Bridge. It was for a short time home to the author Gavin Maxwell, best known for the book *Ring of Bright Water*, which describes his life with otters and sold over a million copies worldwide. Maxwell bought the Eilean Ban cottages in 1963 and moved here after his cottage at Sandaig burned down. He had lived by the Sandaig Islands with his otters and wrote the book here. The 1969 film starring Bill Travers and Virginia McKenna was set at this remote spot. This literary connection brings a few visitors to the Sandaig Islands, the Trust's directions and several signposts, making the walk easier than I'd initially expected.

After half a mile or so on forest tracks, a small white sign indicates a narrow path that runs above a steep ravine. Far below the waters of Allt Mor Shantaig could be heard gurgling over rocks as they ended their journey from mountain to sea. It was a lovely walk through a mixture of deciduous and coniferous trees, which in most places allowed through enough light to support plants and flowers on the forest bed. The path was sometimes steep and might be difficult when wet, but to my parents who although in their mid seventies are used to walking, it presented little problem. I too was glad that the route wasn't too hard, as with my walking boots having virtually fallen apart, I was wearing a relatively new pair of trainers. These were not ideal for walking, having not yet reached that very short time window of maximum comfort gained from prolonged wear, before disintegration and nasty odours creep in.

As we rounded a bend, through a gap in the trees we got our first glimpse of the islands, bathed in sunshine. Beyond was the Sound of Sleet then the hills of Skye. This was yet another superb Scottish view. The path took us down to the burn where the directions indicated we'd find stepping stones. These were no more than a few rocks, mostly below the water level. The alternative, a very basic rope bridge tied to trees either side elicited a predictable immediate reaction from Mother – 'There's no way I'm crossing that'! The path continued on our bank, but appeared to run to the north of a headland and may or may not have allowed us to reach the islands. Returning to the crossing and having seen me scamper over, she decided that even grandmothers can get their feet wet, so rather more cautiously than me, both Mother and Father negotiated the rocks. (For the return journey we found a path through bracken to the north of the burn so crossing the stepping stones, and wetting of feet could have been avoided.)

Under a tree on the south bank of the burn is a stone memorial to Edal, Maxwell's otter who died in the fire at his cottage. The inscription reads:

*Edal, The Otter of Ring of Bright Water*

*1958 – 1968*

*Whatever joy she gave to you give back to Nature*

Close by is a boulder with a plaque in memory of Maxwell, whose ashes were buried here. Apart from the loss of the cottage, of which no signs now remain, little seems to have changed here since he left Sandaig in 1968.

From the memorial it was a few hundred yards to the islands, over rough meadow then shingle. The burn had to be crossed again, so once more toes were wetted. The first island is Eilean Carach, where we sat on the grass and just as she used to when we were children, Mum produced shortbread from her bag. As parents rested I set off to explore.

There are six named islands; Eilean Carach, Sgeir Mholach, An Gurraban, Fraoch Eilean, Sgeir nan Eun and Eilean Mor. At high tide these are distinct islands, but now with the tide low several were linked by rocks and sand. Sgeir nan Eun is just a rocky outcrop, however the others are small but true tidal islands, with grass, bracken, trees, rocks and tiny sandy beaches. Looking back to the mainland a small white cottage lies at the foot of the tree covered hill, with the bare Beinn a Chapuill mountain rising majestically behind. These are beautiful islands in a magnificent setting.

I clambered over rocks, investigated pools small and large, left my footprints on pristine beaches and crossed a little sandy strip to the narrow channel in front of Eilean Mor. An hour after low tide the water here was too deep to paddle and as far as I can ascertain it is never dry. Hamish Haswell-Smith's *The Scottish Islands*, a superb guide to all Scotland's islands, but which other than a quick mention doesn't include tidal or bridged islands, states that this is the only one of the Sandaig Islands that is not tidal. There is a small lighthouse on the island, but more of this later.

Although the other islands are small and other than the occasional footprint show no sign of human activity, I considered the Sandaig Islands as worthy of inclusion in my list on the basis that they are a group, the outer (but not tidal) island has a lighthouse and because of the Gavin Maxwell connection. They are remote, but accessible with a car by those able to negotiate the steep path, or in summer by an infrequent bus and a five mile walk from Glenelg. On a day when the sun was shining, but with enough fluffy white clouds to enhance the scene, and with mountains all around, these were wonderful islands to take my parents to.

When Gavin Maxwell came here in 1956 he brought with him Mijbil, an otter he'd acquired from Marsh Arabs while living with the explorer Wilfred Thesiger in Southern Iraq. Mij became a constant companion, living in the house, sharing Maxwell's food and bed, and accompanying him everywhere. The author was however ahead of his time in his love for otters – to many people they were vermin who depleted fish stocks and should be exterminated. Thus, little more than a year after coming to Sandaig, when for once out of sight of his owner's, Mij met his end under a road workman's pickaxe. Maxwell was naturally devastated, but resolved to replace the otter who had become a major part of his life.

Edal had been brought to Scotland from West Africa by a Dr MacDonald, but with him due to return to Africa, was destined for a zoo. A chance meeting with Maxwell however resulted in the otter coming to Sandaig and taking over Mij's place by the fireside. After two years she nearly died, a septic tooth leading to infection of the brain and a personality change that meant she attempted to savage anyone who went near her. Partly paralysed and unwilling to eat, the advice from Maxwell's London contacts was to put her down. The local vet however would have none of it and despite her aggression managed to inject her with antibiotics daily until she began to respond. After seeming to be a hopeless cause Edal never looked back, thriving in this beautiful spot by the sea, burn and islands.

The third otter to come to Sandaig, or Camusfearna as Maxwell called it to try to protect its location, was Teko. Like Edal, Teko was an African clawless otter whose owner was going abroad. From the outset it was clear that Edal was possessive of her home territory and a friendship out of the question. New quarters were built and separate exercise regimes devised to keep the otters apart and happy.

To Gavin Maxwell Sandaig was not just a place but a way of life, living with and caring for nature. Not much more than a year after the cottage burnt down and Edal was tragically killed, he died of cancer. Two weeks later Teko died of a heart attack.

Mum and Dad now understood why so often I want to stay longer on islands, which perhaps I claim as mine for an hour or two. To Gavin Maxwell this idyllic spot was home for twelve years. Who could not envy him sat writing at his desk, otter by his side, looking out on the mountains, sea, islands and the little burn curving across the shingle – his Ring of Bright Water.

Back at the car we continued south along the dead end road that leads to Loch Hourn. As we turned a bend by a gap in the trees there was another magic Scottish moment. A huge red deer stag, resplendent with antlers, bounded into the road, stopped, looked at us for a moment, then leapt back up the hill. Mother still hasn't stopped talking about it! This majestic creature is the largest UK land animal, but from 1st July to 20th October may find itself in the sights of a hunter's rifle. With no natural predators numbers probably need to be controlled and it cannot be disputed that the 'sport' of deer stalking contributes to the Scottish economy, however what I question is why anyone should gain pleasure from killing wild animals. The website www.deerstalkingscotland states that 'The most popular type of deer stalking in Scotland is for Red Deer. These magnificent animals are a symbol of Scotland and a red deer stag with a full set of antlers is a sight to behold'. Then it tells you where you can shoot them!

We stopped on Loch Hourn to look at another tidal island, Eilean Tioram, by the little village of Arnisdale. Meaning 'dry island' there are a number of islands of this name, but only the one I'd visited on Loch Moidart met my definition. This Tioram rises to a reasonable height, with humps at both ends and a small area of trees on the westerly shore. It is walkable for longer than it's cut off, but shows no sign of human activity. If I were to include islands such as this there'd be at least another dozen to add on the west coast of Scotland.

The road ended at Corran at the foot of Glen Arnisdale. Surrounded by mountains this is a beautiful loch. On the far side is Knoydart, a remote mountainous peninsula that's often described as Britain's last wilderness.

Accessible only by boat (a ferry runs to Mallaig) or a 20 mile hike, its 7 miles of road aren't linked to the Scottish road system. The hundred or so people who live here are the most remote on the UK mainland. We'd like to have stayed longer at Corran, especially as there were signs to a tearoom (outings with my father generally necessitate a stop for tea or coffee every couple of hours), however there was now less than an hour until the last ferry back to Skye. If we missed this it would be a long drive across the hills and around Loch Duich.

At the ferry Dad found his cup of tea. By the slipway is a little octagonal lighthouse which once stood on Eilean Mor. Inside is a small exhibition and shop, with tea, coffee and snacks for people to serve themselves – all done on trust with profits helping to keep the ferry running. As we looked around a man turned up to collect the tea and coffee jugs – his daily job. He knew the Sandaig Islands well but didn't think you could ever walk to the outer isle. His only visit there had been in swimming trunks. He told me that when Gavin Maxwell moved to Sandaig the moors ran down to the shore, but the whole area was then planted with conifers. Now they are starting to be felled, although only when timber prices make this worthwhile. The plan is to clear the whole forest within five years, but he couldn't see it happening.

The lighthouse was built in 1909 on the Sandaig Islands and stood guard on Eilean Mor until 2004, when it was replaced by a modern solar powered light. Designed by David Stephenson, the lighthouse was a local landmark and the community decided it should be saved. Thanks to their efforts and funding from various sources, it was dismantled and rebuilt here by the ferry. Such was the workmanship and the quality of the design, that only the mild steel lamp gallery and railings had to be replaced, the cast-iron structure still being as good as new.

Back in Kyle I joined my parents for a night at the Lochalsh Hotel. Seeing the hotel on honeymoon in Scotland in 1958 they'd said that one day they would come back and stay here. More than fifty years later it was questionable as to whether they or the hotel had aged the better! The hotel's website and customer's internet reviews make for interesting contrasts. The website enthuses:

*Imagine an oasis of comfort and quality situated in the Scottish Highlands* amongst some of Britain's most wild and spectacular scenery. Imagine an impressive building resting astride a rocky promontory, commanding magnificent panoramas towards the mountains of the Isle of Skye, attractively framed through the arch of the nearby Skye Bridge. Add to this vision the warm Highland hospitality that is the hallmark of Gael, who will treat you as an old friend rather than a guest then you have conjured up The Lochalsh Hotel.

Internet reviews were shall I say 'mixed'. Typical were:

'Such Potential – I have always wanted to visit this hotel since watching Michael Palin in the 1980s. I am sure the bridge must have taken people away as the place looks in a sorry state. With a bit of effort, some money and some decent marketing this could be a really good mid-range hotel.'

'Needs Rescue – The manager / owner must have either given up or been negligent. The receptionist was not helping, the wall paper yellowed with age, the ironing board was torn and some old tea was remaining in the tea pot in the room. The view was beautiful. I could not believe it when my husband told me that this hotel used to be posh. He visited it 20 years ago and kept such a fond memory that he wanted to take me. It was heart-breaking. What happened? Is it because the bridge took the tourists away? But you have such a beautiful location and a building with atmosphere'

'Stay Here If – You appreciate a stunning location and view but are prepared to overlook tatty décor. You see the funny side of staying somewhere with all the old clichés of British hotels. Don't stay if you'd rather spend your fifty quid on spotless accommodation than on an astonishing location with a load of history'.

Perhaps of most concern to the owners, of the 41 reviewers only 39% said they would recommend the hotel to their friends.

Built by the Highland Railway Company in the late 19th century, the Lochalsh Hotel had clearly seen better days. The room rate reflected that it is no longer 'top of the range' but was quite reasonable for the standard of facilities. However the view from my bedroom could hardly be bettered – the deep blue waters of Kyle Akin with evening sunshine on the dark hills of Skye behind. This was worth any amount of mediocre service, threadbare carpet and peeling paint. Hence we chose to eat here – there may be better food elsewhere, but not many dining rooms have such magnificent views.

The hotel was up for sale. It has so much potential. With investment and marketing it could be restored to former glory, hopefully without losing its character or affordable rates. There are plenty of identikit, soulless modern hotels around and some very expensive private hotels in prime locations. With a bit of effort the Lochalsh Hotel could be something special once again.

Next morning the Isle of Skye had gone. All I could see from the window was mist. As I enjoyed a particularly large bowl of porridge the occasional outline of a mountain could be glimpsed, but we were in for a wet day.

It was to be a day of 'nearly tidal islands'. First the short drive nine miles along Loch Alsh to the village of Dornie, and Eilean Donan on which stands Castle Donan, said to be Scotland's most photographed castle. I find it hard to believe that more pictures aren't taken of Edinburgh, Stirling and perhaps Urquhart, but with a steady stream of coaches disgorging tourists from a host of nations, the castle is right on the tourist trail.

The once ruined 13th century castle that had been built for defence, was rebuilt as a home in the early 20th century, a bridge linking it to the mainland being constructed in 1931. From then it became an ex-tidal island. A guide in the castle told me that it can still be walked to at low tide over rocks and seaweed, but that during its five centuries of life as a fortress access was always by water. There were few roads and the sea was the main highway in this 'Sea Kingdom' of the Lord of the Isles.

It is indeed highly photogenic; an arched bridge leading to an archetypical Scottish castle on the still waters of Loch Alsh, surrounded on all sides by mountains. The best pictures are in sunshine, but today's cloud added atmosphere more suited to the castle's bloody past. Perhaps its most horrific episode dates from 1331 when Randolf, Earl of Moray had 50 men executed and their heads spiked on the castle walls, simply to demonstrate his power and impress a guest known for his strict discipline. The castle's end as a fortress came in 1719 when it was garrisoned by 46 Spanish soldiers who were supporting the Jacobites. Three heavily armed frigates sent by the English bombarded the castle, although with walls up to 14 feet thick, achieved limited success. After three days men were sent ashore and overwhelmed the Spanish. Following their surrender the Government troops found 343 barrels of gunpowder and used this to blow up what remained of the castle.

Castle Donan's position on the main road to Skye, its photogenicness (is that a word?), restored interior and facilities (a large shop and café) means that it attracts huge visitor numbers. 152,000 paid to go round the castle in 2009 and as many again visited the site but without paying to cross the bridge. It makes for an interesting contrast with Eilean Tioram in Loch Moidart, which is equally attractive, but a remote semi-ruin, with no facilities. When discussing the future of the Loch Moidart castle some locals made comparisons with Eilean Donan, expressing fear that should Eilean Tioram become similarly commercialised, the castle and area would be ruined. Whilst its location means that visitor numbers would never match Castle Donan, today's visit here confirmed my view that Loch Moidart's castle should not be developed. Decay should be stabilised but the peace and beauty of the quiet location not spoiled by the onslaught of tourists. Eilean Donan is a beautiful and historic island in a superb setting at the head of three lochs, but the more tranquil Castle Tioram is maybe even more special.

Close to Eilean Donan are two further tidal islands, both unbridged and walkable at low tide. The first, another Eilean Tioram, is a low lying grassy piece of land, best viewed from the castle's upper windows. Just two small trees stood at one end of the island, but size and lack of obvious human activity keep it from my main list. Leaving the hordes at Castle Donan we drove a mile along Loch Long (which is actually quite short) – a narrow loch linked to Loch Alsh, running north into the mountains. Opposite the settlement of Cardu is the tiny Sheep Island – tidal but too small for my list, although with one sign of human activity – a satellite TV aerial.

Back at Kyle, after a quick lunch and last look across the water to Skye, it was time for me to catch the train home. As we waited on the platform Mum disappeared for a minute, returning with a large bag of tablet, that most yummy Scottish fudge. Unlike my wife who once bought me a special cake from France, but then ate it on the boat back, I resisted temptation and delivered it home to grateful boys. A few minutes before departure was due a lady arrived with a trolley full of shopping from the Co-op. Putting the bags on the train, she hurried back to the shop with the empty trolley, returning at a trot just before we left. Today there was another coach party on board, but the line's most important passengers are the locals who use it all year.

Between Kyle and Strome Ferry we passed a number of little tidal islands, some named but none meriting promotion from the 'nearly tidal' list. The day before I'd arrived my parents had visited Plockton and walked to the tidal islet of Eilean nan Gamhainn, the only one visible from the train to show an obvious sign of human activity – a picnic bench. I could have spent several more days visiting small or nearly tidal islands on this part of the coast. Had there been time I'd liked to have driven the 68 miles from Kyle to Badachro on Gairloch where there's yet another Eilean Tioram, although this one seems to be more commonly known as Dry Island. There are two holiday cottages on the island, which would have made my main list were it not for the floating bridge that connects it to the mainland at high tide.

With three hours to wait for the sleeper in Inverness I enjoyed one of my favourite city walks – along the river to the Ness Islands, over the suspension bridges and back on the south bank. With mountains in the distance and fly fishermen by the river, Inverness is a fitting place to be Capital of the Highlands.

## Post Script:

Just before the book went to press I found someone who had walked to Eilean Mor, the outermost of the Sandaig Islands. Eric Peacock, a volunteer at The Lighthouse Christian café in the Essex village of Tollesbury, used to live in Scotland. He told me how he and some friends walked across the sand and shingle to the outer island. After just 15 minutes on the island they turned to come back, but found the sea rushing in. Wading through the currents of Khyl Rhea, an experience that Eric describes as 'hairy', is not to be recommended.

# CHAPTER SIXTEEN

# ISLE RISTOL & INNIS MHOR

A trip to our most northerly tidal islands, saying farewell to the west coast and to visit one of Scotland's few east coast islands.

Innis Mhor in the Dornoch Firth 40 miles north of Inverness, is a little known island and one that's not easy to visit. It's part of an active Air-to-Ground bombing range, for many years known as RAF Tain, but which just before my visit changed its name to Defence Training Estate Scotland – Tain Training Centre. I suspect it will be a long time before people stop calling it RAF Tain. Considerable research was required to find a contact for the range, but I eventually found Margaret Wilson who was most helpful.

First I was told that the range is in use by aircraft from RAF Lossiemouth every weekday from 9am to 10pm, but then that I could visit after 2pm on a Friday. After checking tides and making provisional plans, I then found that on Friday afternoons a team from Lossiemouth come to clear the range of ordnance. It might be possible to visit at a weekend, but Margaret would have to talk to the Squadron Leader. Three days later an email arrived. Squadron Leader John McKeown, Officer Commanding RAF Tain, would authorise my visit as long as I received 'Health & Safety and Range face to face briefings', could liaise with the ordnance clearing team who work at weekends and 'de-conflict' with them as to the best time to walk to the island.

Hence on a warm London evening I once again boarded the Highland Sleeper, arriving at Inverness on Friday morning. Whilst Tain has a railway station, nowhere in the town could I hire the car needed to get to the west coast, so had to pick one up in Inverness. My plan was to start at Tain with the safety briefing, then drive to the west and return to Innis Mhor on Sunday. With different tides on each coast careful planning was required.

I'd left London in shorts but arrived in Scotland to wind, rain and cold. I was to be glad of the extra clothes thrown into my bag at the last minute. A wet morning was spent in Tain, which I soon found was like many small Scottish towns – pleasant enough but not much to detain the visitor for long. Maybe because the scenery is so spectacular I was expecting every town and village to be a tourist trap, but most are primarily living communities and where there is beauty it's more often from the setting than buildings. I spent an hour or so looking round the main attraction and seeking information on Innis Mhor. Marketed as 'Tain Through Time' this is a reasonably interesting diversion, including a pilgrimage, St Duthis Collegiate Church and the town's museum. There were just two other visitors, a couple from Norway. The moustachioed husband could not have looked more Scandinavian if he'd had a ski under one arm and a whale under the other.

The pilgrimage is a nicely laid out exhibition telling the story of St Duthac, who lived in the 7th or 8th century and drew medieval pilgrims to his shrine in Tain, the supposed town of his birth. The shrine held a number of important relics including his skull, breastbone, shirt, staff, cup and bell. The bones, like those of many other saints, were believed to have healing powers and pilgrims would have been keen to touch them. The shirt was thought to protect its wearer from injury so according to legend, in 1333 Hugh, Earl of Ross, decided to borrow it to wear in battle against Edward III. Unfortunately for the Earl, Duthac's shirt let him down rather badly, the wearer dying in battle. Given that the shirt must have been at least 500 years old, I don't suppose however that it would have provided much in the way of protection from the cold, let alone the sword.

It was hardly weather for sitting out so I lunched at the Royal Hotel then drove the few miles to Inver, the nearest settlement to Innis Mhor and where the museum curator had told me I might find information on the island.

Inver has an interesting history, most notably as one of a number of places around Britain that were evacuated during the Second World War. On the 11th November 1943 villagers were summoned to Inver Hall and told that they must leave their homes as the area was to be used for battle training purposes. In four weeks, not only around 850 people and their belongings, but 1,600 cattle and 9,600 sheep had to be moved from the land. It wasn't until the following year that the people found out why they had been evacuated in such secrecy. The whole area was to be used to practice the Normandy beach landings, however perhaps they should have sought local advice first. The army hadn't realised how the tide moved the sand and water channels, and found it almost impossible to bring in their tanks by barge. Instead they transported them by land and used the area as a shooting range.

The village looks out across Inver Bay and the expanse of Morrich More, a huge area of sand dunes, salt marsh and heathland that protrudes into Dornoch Firth. From here I could see Patterson Island, a strip of sand dune almost joined to Innis Mhor that was once an island but is now permanently connected to the mainland. As the sands move it's likely that Innis Mhor will also one day lose its island status. The landlord of the Inver Inn told me that years ago 250 salmon could be trapped in a day in Inver Channel, but now you'd be lucky to catch one. Ships used to come up the channel but now even little boats have to pick their way through. This is very much a moving coast. Being largely unaffected by human activities, Morrich More demonstrates an almost perfect record of changes in the coastline that this part of Scotland has experienced in the last 7,000 years and is providing vital information for assessing the likely impacts of future rises in sea level.

The landlord gave me directions to RAF Tain, which I'd driven right past. I'd expected a grand entrance but was later told that the lack of signage is for security reasons. Not perhaps the greatest hindrance to the determined spy, who if he didn't notice the control tower and targets might just spot the jets which were noisily swooping overhead.

I was greeted by Site Manager Billy Livingstone. He works for Qinetiq who had recently taken over running the site from the MoD. With him was one of the ordnance crew to carry out the briefing. This was short and to the point. They used to bring someone in from the range to show a set of photos of shells and bombs. All of these the person being briefed was told they must not touch. Then one day someone asked whether this meant it was OK to touch anything else metal. 'No' was the firm answer. Then they realised that the photos were superfluous, so the briefing now consists of just one short sentence – 'Don't touch anything metal.'

Next, arrangements had to be made for me to access the site on Sunday. Since Qinetiq took it over 24 hour security had been stopped (maybe they thought it was unnecessary, the lack of a roadside sign being adequate to deter intruders) and there'd be no one here to let me in. Billy called Squadron Leader McKeown to see if he'd let me have the code for the gate lock. No, that wouldn't be possible. I'd have to leave the car outside and climb over the gate.

Arrangements made, I left, heading west to the little settlement of Drumbeg in the north of Assynt, a remote and mountainous corner of North West Scotland. It was a lovely drive along the banks of Dornoch Firth, then a single track road to Ledmore and north on the A837 & A894 National Tourist Routes. As I travelled west gentle hills and slow moving rivers gradually gave way to high mountains and fast flowing streams. Many views merited a stop, but with a tidal deadline there was no time to dally. The rain had stopped before I'd left Tain, but the further west I got the lower the cloud and the wetter it became. By the time I left the main road just before Kylesku bridge it was pouring.

A sign said that Drumbeg was 8 miles, but gave no indication that this is the start of one of the country's most spectacular roads. David St John Thomas in *Journey Through Britain*, probably my second favourite travel book, and one that like most of Bill Bryson's merits reading once a year, describes the 60 mile winding loop to Drumnerie north of Ullapool as 'Britain's most scenic minor road'. For good reason the route is nicknamed the 'Breakdown Zone' and the most testing part is the northern section to Drumbeg.

As usual I'd hired the smallest and most basic available car, minimising both cost and carbon emissions, but my little Kia Picanto (silver again) didn't let me down. Up steep inclines, round switchbacks and over blind summits we went. Its only complaint was to repeatedly flash a little number telling me to change gear, a strange choice of extra in a car that didn't even possess a clock. Even in heavy rain the views were spectacular, although I daren't take my eyes of the road for more than a couple of seconds. I stopped briefly at Loch Nedd, getting out for a better look at this tree lined slither of sea that cuts into the mountains. Like so much of Scotland, even in rain there is beauty and atmosphere.

I didn't plan to check in at Drumbeg Hotel until investigating Oldany Island, but as the road went past the door, made a snap and perhaps fortunate decision to go in. They were surprised to see me, my booking having been entered for the next day. Fortunately there was one room spare. After confirming availability of a table for dinner, I drove a couple of miles further west, to where a track heads north towards Oldany Island. This was an island about which I'd been able to find out very little.

Situated at the entrance to Eddrachillis Bay, at 500 acres and rising to 341 feet, it is of significant size. Although once inhabited the island has been abandoned for many years. A burial ground dating from the late 18th century has been surveyed and symbols for a cairn, chapel and cemetery are shown on an 1855 map. The cairn can still be seen, as can the remains of sheilings – small huts or houses where farmers and their families lived in summer while livestock were grazed on common ground.

What I hadn't been able to find out was whether one can walk to the island. Hamesh Haswell-Smith and a couple of internet sources described it as tidal, so like a number of other Highland islands, my journey was one of investigation. The track ended at a little bay opposite the south east corner of the island. The map suggested that any dry access would be just to the left of the bay, but a few minutes after low tide there was clear water between mainland and island. Without a dangerous climb around the cliff I couldn't reach this part of the shore to judge the depth, but there was no doubt that even if possible, on a now rising tide it would be far from safe to attempt to cross. It was a lovely spot and an island that invited exploration, but Oldany was to be one island I couldn't get to.

Back at Drumbeg, Dawn who runs the hotel with her husband Robin, told me that only twice a year on exceptionally low tides can one walk to Oldany. It was an island for my nearly tidal list and I didn't have to feel I'd failed in not getting there.

Even in rain, the view from the dining room looking out over Loch Drumbeg rivalled that from The Worm's Head and Lochalsh hotels for the best on my travels. Both the food and welcome were however better in this unpretentious but charming Scottish hotel. I would have liked to have stayed longer and explored this remote area with its excellent walks, but Isle Ristol beckoned.

Oldany was as far north as my travels were to take me. However, in the very north of Scotland, guarding the entrance to the Kyle of Tongue near Talmine are some more almost tidal islands – The Rabbit Islands. These are accessible on foot only a few times each year when a sandbank is exposed and they can be walked to from Ard Skinid.

An article by Ben MacGregor in *John O'Groat Journal* illustrates just how treacherous tidal islands can be. On a cold March day Ben set out towards the Rabbit Islands. The wind was howling, with snowflakes and hailstones mingling with blowing sand. He walked across the big sweep of sand as the tide fell, but with big rollers coming in from the north feared the wind could be piling up the water. He stopped for a moment, considering a choice of continuing towards the island and perhaps not getting back, or returning to the shore. As he looked, deciding whether to go forward or back, the water suddenly started rushing up the channel and his mind was made up. Maybe it was the tide or maybe the wind, but had he been further out tidal islands would have claimed another victim. After several further attempts to walk, later in the year Ben did get to the islands and to spend a night there, his mode of transport however not feet but kayak. A quick dash across a narrow spit of sand took him to the outer isle, where the only footprints in the pristine sand were those of an otter.

The weather next morning was even worse, so neither of my ideas to walk to Old Man of Stoer or take the long drive along the coast road appealed. Instead I decided on an early start, and a drive to Ullapool on the A837, still a beautiful route, but an easier road. I stopped once on the way, at Ardveck Castle on Loch Assynt, on the basis that this looked like a tidal island. The castle sits on a promontory in the loch where waves whipped up by the strong wind were bigger than any I'd seen in the sea on my last two trips to the Highlands. This is a fresh water loch but it could easily have been beside the sea as I walked in driving rain across a small beach and the narrow neck of land to the 'nearly island' that was once the 15th century seat of the MacLeods of Assynt.

Nestled under the hills that surround Loch Broom, Ullapool is a picturesque fishing village, popular tourist destination and departing point for the ferry to Stornaway. As fishing has declined tourism has grown, helped by various music festivals held throughout the year, but mainly by its superb position. Not only is Ullapool beautifully situated on the side of the loch, but it is the largest settlement for miles and the only place of any size on the coast from Mallaig to Thurso. The road from Inverness is good, hence the coaches come and American voices could be heard in the craft shops that stayed open late into the evening.

Lunch was fish and chips from The Seaforth Chippy, a busy establishment just off the front. The food was excellent but I wonder how much longer they will feel able to advertise as the 'UK's Best Chippy' as voted for by BBC Radio 4 listeners in November 2004. I ate sitting by the still loch, watched closely by a seagull hoping for a tasty morsel. When I did drop a chip he was too busy calling over the rest of Ullapool's resident gulls to get a bite. Throwing the last few chips to the birds, a reckless act that resulted in a good proportion of Scotland's gull population descending on Ullapool, I set off for the Summer Isles.

Despite intermittent rain again it was a spectacular drive on narrow roads past mysterious lochs and mountains. I'd read that the Summer Isles were outstanding and as I approached the little settlement of Altandhu a misty expanse of sea and islands opened up before me. When I returned in evening sunshine a few hours later this was one of the most magnificent views of all my travels. I climbed to the viewpoint at Cnoc Breac looking across to the roughly mile square Isle Ristol. With no idea how easy this is to walk to it was encouraging to see just a narrow strip of water between island and mainland. There were almost 2 hours to low tide, so signs looked good for a visit.

Leaving the car by Old Dornie Bay I walked down to the shore. A large area of seaweed covered rocks had to be negotiated to get to the crossing point, but with still plenty of time until low tide I wandered around the picturesque little bay. The crossing was still not dry and like Samalaman Island it was to be a long wait to see if the water would clear. With an hour to go I started to pick my way over the slippery rocks. The gap was still about 15 yards and a couple of feet deep. Half an hour before low tide the rain came back. A waterproof clad man standing on the rocks and staring at an island must have made a strange site to the three walkers who appeared behind me on the shore. Had they still been there half an hour later, they would have perhaps added to the various people around the coast who may have questioned my sanity.

Low tide was 6.00 but it was becoming plain that the crossing would not dry. Perhaps the strong wind had affected the tide. At 5.55 the wind suddenly dropped and a patch of blue sky appeared behind the island. Was this a sign? At Cei Ballast I'd decided that a 300 mile journey wasn't to be wasted for the sake of wet feet. Isle Ristol was 611 miles from home. Perhaps it is fortunate that no one was present to witness the pulling up of leggings, rolling up of trousers, run through knee deep water, dash across the beach, leap and triumphant punching of air, and immediate return journey. Another island had been conquered.

The next question was whether it would count as tidal. The island is owned by the Scottish Wildlife Trust and I'd read a warning not to walk to it due to the risk of getting stranded, but had been unable to find out any more. The tide today was rising to 4.7 metres, with the evening low at 1.3 metres. Subtracting 0.5 metres which was roughly the depth that came to my knees and assuming there'd been no effect from the strong wind, the tide would need to be 0.8 metres to be dry. Checking heights on Easytide for the 7 weeks after I visited, on 10 days the low was 0.8 or less. Whilst not accessible on most days, the number of days Isle Ristol can be walked to with dry feet is therefore well inside my once a month limit. On the list it goes!

The 400 acre island is uninhabited, however in the 19th century the British Fisheries Society built a curing station here and there was a small inn for the fishermen, but neither lasted long into the 1900s. Virtually nothing appears to have been published about Isle Ristol and information was hard to find. The Scottish Wildlife Trust show nothing on their website, which the lady on their switchboard thought was because its 'nigh on impossible to get to'. She however put me in touch with Mark Foxwell, Reserves Manager for Highlands and Islands. Mark agreed that he has one of the more enviable jobs and was able to tell me a little about the island.

It was donated to the Trust in 1993 and whilst not necessarily somewhere that they would have hunted down, it's a nice, unspoilt island which links with Ben Mor Coigach, the Trust's largest reserve. Probably Ristol's most notable feature is its juniper, which thrives here but has been largely lost on the mainland as it is badly affected by burning. There are the normal sea birds found in this part of Scotland but the island has no SSSI or other designations. To my comment that there's nothing remarkable there then, Mark's answer was 'Who knows? There may be things that people don't know about'. Other than some surveying of plants, including mapping the juniper, there have been no studies of the island's wildlife. It could easily harbour rare moths or other insects, but anything that is there lives with very little human interference.

Under the Scottish Access Code there is no restriction on people visiting Isle Ristol, other than of course the tide or need for a boat. There is still a pier on the island and Mark said that local boatmen may be willing to take people over. Mark has walked but usually arrives by water as he needs to stay longer than tides allow. He confirmed what I had found, that Ristol is not dry on every tide, but thought that on the lowest tides access on foot is possible for longer than an hour. Mark's suggestion was however that anyone walking over had a back up means to return.

Having stood in the rain waiting for the tide to fall, it was in bright sunshine that I enjoyed my sandwiches sitting on the quay looking across Old Dorney Bay to Isle Ristol. Keen to see more of this island group, thought by many to be one of the most beautiful of all Scotland's many archipelagos, I continued along the narrow road to the village of Achiltibuie. The views to Tannera More and the smaller islands were superb. I'd been recommended the Summer Isles Hotel which looks out across the bay, but with costs of travel mounting, had settled for a cosy B&B in Ullapool. Before driving back I stopped for a wander on the little beach at Badenscalli looking across to Horse Island, then climbed back to the viewpoint at Cnoc Breac. In the evening sunshine, with deep blue sea, Isle Ristol in the foreground, other islands beyond and distant mountains, this was perhaps the most beautiful place I'd yet found. My time on Ristol had been short, but I had experienced something of the splendour of the Summer Isles, a remote and little known part of Scotland.

I had intended to make an early start next morning but Birchgrove was the sort of friendly B&B where everyone talks – a welcoming family home where host Donna cooks breakfast and her charming daughter Hannah serves the guests around a shared table. Rather than the quiet and perhaps slightly strained atmosphere of some breakfast rooms, this relaxed arrangement inevitably led to conversation between guests. Like railway dining cars, people you meet in B&Bs invariably have an interesting story to tell. One couple were stopping just a night before catching the ferry to Stornaway and the other here for a few days from Aberdeen. We talked of the winter's snow, Highland scenery and of course islands. My plan was to return to Tain the way I'd come, but Donna said they use the longer route but quicker road via Garve and Dingwall. After all those single track roads I was glad of an easier drive, but still with great scenery.

It was a most enjoyable four mile walk across Morrich More to Innis Mhor. As instructed I left the car at the range entrance, climbed over the gate and followed tracks to the shore. It was a strange feeling being in this large, flat area, looked over by the empty control tower and an assortment of derelict concrete buildings. These were supposed to have been demolished after the war, but the farmers chose to keep the money they'd been paid for demolition and leave the buildings up. One was knocked down in 2006 after a long running campaign by local councillor Alan Torrance, but some locals and others with an interest in airfield history wanted them to stay. It seems that the latter view prevailed and the historic buildings remain, providing atmosphere and acting as a reminder of the aircrews who fought for our freedom.

Morrich More has been relatively unaffected by human activity and other than a few tracks and the evocative buildings, which are all some way from the shore, virtually the only signs of man's interference are the old military vehicles now used as bombing targets. As in recent years the forces have been actively engaged in various conflicts, the need for live weapons on the range has lessened. The army don't use it for firing, their only activity being training exercises to guide bombers into their targets. Even so I kept a close eye out for anything which might go bang.

Wildlife seems to have become used to the noise of the jets with birds, deer, foxes and otters thriving here. The otters live not by the shore but around a couple of ponds close to the control tower. Military activity directly affects only a small part of Morrich More and otherwise has preserved the biodiversity which otherwise may have been lost as it has in surrounding land. It is an SSSI, Ramsar site (wetland of international importance as designated by the 'Ramsar Convention') and a Special Area of

Conservation. The site comprises mainly salt marsh, sand dunes and woodland and has the largest expanse of coastal juniper in the UK.

Perhaps of greatest significance is a population of one of the world's rarest animals. Asked to name endangered mammals most people will probably say panda, tiger or rhino. Few will know that there is a creature living far closer to home, which with only 400 individuals in the wild is at even greater risk of extinction. This is not an insect, bird or even a tiny mammal. It's an animal that grows up to 80cm long, over a metre with the tail, and pound for pound considered to be one of the most impressive predators in the world – intelligent, fearless, patient, resourceful, agile and powerful. As recently as the 1950s they were believed to be man killers.

The once common Scottish wildcat is an ancient species that roamed alongside cave bears and woolly mammoths. Resembling a very muscular domestic tabby, but heavier, with thicker fur, wider jaw and thick ringed tail, this is no household moggie. Even when born in captivity they are completely untameable and will fight to the death to maintain freedom rather than submit to domestication. With superb camouflage, powerful thigh muscles enabling 30 mph sprinting and 18 razor sharp retractable claws with rotating wrists for gripping prey, the wildcat is a fearsome hunter.

Sadly this splendid creature is now critically endangered. Numbers dropped dramatically in Victorian times as gamekeepers slaughtered countless wildcats despite the fact that they take little game. Their favourite prey is rabbit and more enlightened farmers are realising that wildcats on their land can be an asset by reducing rabbit numbers. Sadly others have shot them mistaking them for feral cats (who can be legally killed), or laid snares for foxes that indiscriminately kill other creatures. Loss of habitat, human interference and most critically hybridisation caused by amorous encounters with feral domestic cats, has brought the Scottish wildcat to the brink of extinction. Only with human support can they be saved. The Scottish Wildcat Association (www.scottishwildcats.co.uk) leads the campaign to save Britain's most endangered and perhaps most remarkable mammal.

Billy Livingstone had given me a range map, with instructions to follow the tracks to Target 6, then cross the sands to the island. Passing the collection of armoured personnel carriers and a caravan that once belonged to the Royal Engineers (who if the military graffiti is to be believed 'Are Gay'), I came out on the extensive Whiteness Sands. From here it was another mile across salt marsh and firm sand to Innis Mhor. The island is basically a long and shifting sand dune, reinforced by marram grass. I'd wondered if it would pass my 'human activity' test, but found that there was once a two compartment enclosure depicted on the 1st edition of the 6 inch OS map in 1881, although not shown on current maps.

More obvious signs of activity were two army vehicles perched on the top of the dune. Like those on the mainland these are used as targets for the swooping RAF jets. As I reached the top of the island a spectacular vista opened up, with golden sands, blue sea and the distant peaks of the Sutherland Hills. This was a view that few see and a beach which is rarely trod by human feet.

I ate my lunch looking out over this beautiful beach, watching the tide gradually rise, but for once relaxed knowing there was still plenty of time to get off the island. Innis Mhor is a tidal island which is dry for longer than it's cut off. As with the Islands of Fleet, my deadline was car related, with an extra day's rental to be charged if I didn't get it back to Inverness by 5.00. I'd rather have spent a bit longer on the island, but at least there are worse places than Inverness to pass a few hours waiting for a train home.

As I started my leisurely stroll back I spotted something suspicious on the sand. Lying in the marram grass was a blue shell, marked 'DANGER'. Whether live or not, this looked new and wasn't to be touched, but was another hazard of tidal island travels. By now I'd been to over 30 tidal islands but Innis Mhor was different to all the others – a mile of sand dune, an unusual challenge to get there, but like so many others, a haven for wildlife in a beautiful setting. From here I was more than half way round the coast from St Michael's Mount and heading south. Islands on the east coast are few and far between and there was just one more to visit in Scotland. I left Morrich More to the sheep, wildcats and bombers, with a little sadness that this was to be my final trip to the Highlands of Scotland. I needed justification for further journeys north. Ideas for future books were forming.

# CHAPTER SEVENTEEN

# CRAMOND ISLAND

After remote islands in the west and north my final Scottish island was just five miles from Edinburgh. Cramond Island lies at the end of a causeway and is the only one of the islands in the Firth of Forth to be accessible on foot. Once again my day had started with matters of glue, a morning spent near Glasgow watching our adhesive run on a label making machine – and very well it ran too. A train to Edinburgh, another one to Dalmeny and a short walk down the hill, took me to the foot of the Forth Bridge at South Queensferry. In keeping with tradition workmen were busy painting the bridge, although its famous red paint is gradually being replaced with epoxy resin, which will last for 25 years and perhaps put an end to the famous expression to describe a never ending job. Completed in 1890 it was the world's first major steel bridge and ranks as one of the great feats of civilisation. The more modern road bridge behind would look impressive in its own right, but alongside the magnificent spans of the railway bridge, seems a mere functional crossing.

There's a regular bus from Edinburgh to what is still called the village of Cramond, but is now part of the city's suburbs, however with plenty of time until low tide I'd chosen to walk along the coast. A 4½ mile path runs through the Dalmeny Estate, mostly in woods but with good views to the Forth. First however, on what was quite a warm day, an ice cream seemed in order. Catching the end of the conversation between the person ahead of me in the queue and the lady serving, I heard that 'It wouldn't be Queensferry without a fight'. As I was to find, this is an area of contrasts; beautiful scenery but not always the most respectful of people.

At Hawes Pier the Maid of the Forth was just setting off to Inchcolm Island, known as 'Iona of the East' due to its early Christian connections.

The dramatic abbey complex comprises the best preserved monastic buildings in Scotland. As I travelled around the coast I'd seen many non-tidal islands and some had particularly tempted me to visit. Inchcolm was one such island and one (calm) day I too hope to board the Maid of the Forth and explore.

The walk took me past Longcraig Pier from where ferries used to run across the Forth, then through woods to Hound Point. Here what the map suggested might have been tidal islets were just rocks. Just off the shore is Hound Point Terminal where tankers from all over the world load with North Sea oil that has been refined at Grangemouth further up the river. Over the sandy beaches and extensive mudflats of Drum Sands, which attract many sea birds and form part of the Firth of Forth SSSI, was Cramond Island.

After another mile or so Barnbougle Castle could be glimpsed through the trees, then the path emerged from woodland onto Dalmeny Golf Course. A sign indicated that the path to Cramond Ferry ran across the course and urged caution, however I saw not one golfer. From here there were excellent views of the impressive Dalmeny House, family home to the Earls of Rosebery. It was built in 1817 to Tudor Gothic design and used as an auxiliary hospital during the First World War. From the golf course an unpaved path ran close to the shore. I stopped several times to photograph Cramond Island through gaps in the trees. Then my problems started.

The main path turned sharp right heading inland, but I needed to stay by the shore. A very overgrown path continued straight on, but soon became impassable, especially in shorts with brambles scratching bare legs. Instead I climbed down onto the beach aiming for the start of the causeway at Cramond, that was now just a few hundred yards away. Soon I was there, or at least 50 yards short, with just the River Almond to cross. Several signs had indicated a ferry, but there was none to be seen. I learned later that the ferry which had operated from the mid 1800s, stopped running in 2000 at the time of the foot and mouth outbreak. Even then however it could be a challenge to get across. First it was necessary to attract the ferryman's attention, noting that on Fridays, lunchtimes or inclement weather he couldn't be tempted out. Then to pass the test – no dogs, prams or bicycles permitted, and no picnics to be concealed about your person. All being well, he'd then scull you over.

It had been intended to re-start it, but the jetty was found to be unsafe. Since then there has been much wrangling, but no ferry. A chain ferry was suggested to replace the old rowing boat and plans were drawn up for a floating jetty. In 2007 the Earl of Rosebery told Edinburgh Evening News that he would support a ferry across the river, provided it was paid for and managed by another body. A year later the paper reported a likely cost of around £250,000 but that Edinburgh Council had said they would not be able to provide any funding. A footbridge has been proposed but the Earl of Rosebery objected on the grounds that it would 'attract an unsavoury crowd to his land'. Although reminiscent of the 'roughs' of Hilbre Island, as you will soon read, I can understand the Earl's concern. Hence walkers have to take a 3 mile detour inland. I considered wading, but with the mud soft and current fast, thought better of it. I preferred to arrive on the island alive and on foot, not washed up on the shore by the next tide.

Retracing steps along the beach, I followed the main track inland but this soon took me off my photocopied map. Having spent a small fortune on Ordnance Survey maps I thought I could do without one for this trip. At a crossroads I turned left, aiming to stay close to the river, but in a few hundred yards the track reached a dead end. Returning up the hill and by now distinctly warm, I met a couple with two young grandchildren. They'd been combing the beach and the children proudly showed me several pieces of driftwood with remarkable animal likenesses. The couple were from Dumfries and didn't know the way to Cramond, but although they thought the track was going the wrong way, there seemed no alternative.

Eventually the track passed two cottages, became a tiny lane, then came out on the busy A90. Here there was a bridge, but even better, a pub. There was no doubt where I'd be spending the next half hour! Refreshed by drink and cake, I crossed Cramond Brig, a picturesque 500 year old stone toll bridge over the Almond. As with the Forth bridges, the newer A90 road bridge is functional but far less aesthetically pleasing than the old one. From here it was a mile and a half walk along the river. Refreshed, in the shade and knowing where I was going, this was a lovely walk, the path running close to the dark river.

I'd expected to take no more than an hour and a half from Dalmeny, but with diversion and pub it had taken three. My plan to watch the tide drop and causeway clear was thwarted, the mile long route now dry and dotted with people. Leaving the pretty Cramond Quay, where yachts moored in the river and visitors milled about, I set out on the dead straight concrete walkway to the island. This covers a storm water overflow, with several drain covers visible at intervals, hence some say that it's not a true causeway. Most striking however is a line of concrete pyramids running just to the right of the path, all the way to the island. Known as 'Dragon's Teeth', these were erected in 1938 to prevent enemy vessels from slipping through the gap between the island and shore at high tide, thereby avoiding the booms and defences across the Forth. They do not, despite what a few people have suggested, provide a high tide route to the island for anyone able to leap from pinnacle to pinnacle! Two thirds of the way to the island the water pipe leaves to the left and the causeway narrows. From here, although it was almost low tide, the sea was only a few yards from the walkway, running up to the 'teeth'.

Cramond Island has an interesting military history, with many buildings remaining in various states of disrepair. The first structure seen on arrival is the emplacement for a 75mm gun and associated search light, which was installed in 1941 to protect the concrete barrier. Like all the extensive defences in the Firth of Forth, it wasn't fired in anger during the war, although search lights were active in spotting German mine laying planes. I left exploring the gun emplacement for later and headed up the hill to the highest point, which at 28 metres gives superb views across the Forth and back to Edinburgh. The castle and hill of Arthur's Seat behind it could easily be picked out, and even from here one could see that Edinburgh is a city of interesting buildings.

The first indication of the bad side of Cramond Island came when I tried to read the information board, but found that supporters of Heart of Midlothian Football Club had covered it with graffiti. Descending the other side of the hill I entered the small wooded area and found the remains of a stone farmstead that was inhabited until the 1930s. It appears on an Ordnance Survey map of 1853 but may be considerably older. The 1901 census shows three people listed as residents of the island; James Hogg (59) the head farmer, Peter Hogg (29) his nephew and assistant, and Margaret Gibb (21) the housekeeper. With rather limited scope for meeting other young people, Peter and Margaret took the simple option and married in 1903.

I'd noticed rubbish left by the path and more in the ruined cottage, but as I walked around the northern side of the island was quite taken aback at the state of the place. Everywhere were piles of discarded bottles and cans, remains of fires, broken glass, clothes and even sleeping bags. Every building was covered with graffiti, inside and out. I had read that the island is used for parties by punks and other groups of young people, but hadn't been prepared for this. I was used to unspoilt and beautiful islands. This was an island which should be beautiful, but had been defiled by the selfish actions of the few. Well I say the few, but this amount of mess wasn't from just a handful of people and as I was to find out, large numbers come here to 'party'.

The previous month five hundred people had attended a rave organised by a group of Edinburgh DJs who advertised it via the social networking sites Bebo and Facebook. They walked over the causeway at low tide but as evening came and hot sunshine turned to heavy rain, many had ignored advice to leave by eight o clock and found they couldn't get back. Several called 999 in panic and a rescue operation estimated at costing £10,000 was launched, involving the coastguard, RNLI, police and ambulances service. Around 170 partygoers were trapped on the island. Queensferry and Kinghorn lifeboats took off fifty youngsters, six of whom were treated for hypothermia, summer clothing proving woefully inadequate for a wet and windy Scottish night. Five more were rescued from the causeway after getting into difficulties as the water rose. When the tide went out at 1.30am more soaked revellers were led across the causeway, which had to be illuminated for safety, and at 7am a lifeboat returned to collect another sixty three people after the police decided that the party had become a public safety issue.

This was however far from an isolated instance. South Queensferry lifeboat station is often the busiest in Scotland, and apparently the crew call it the 'Cramond Ferry'. In May 2008 a heavily intoxicated couple were spotted entering the water at the island end of the causeway by a Queensferry Coastguard rescue patrol, who called the inshore lifeboat. The two were rescued but had it not been for the vigilance of the coastguard team their chance of survival in the cold Forth water would have been slim.

After 12 people had to be rescued in one incident in August 2009 and a further two teenagers had swam ashore, Tom Robertson, a lifeboat manager at South Queensferry was reported as saying with commendable patience; 'Our main concern is that increasingly people who are cut off by the tide are attempting to dash back to the shore. We recommend that anyone who finds themselves cut off stays on the island, rings 999 and asks for the coastguard. We do not want anyone to put themselves in danger'.

Of all Scotland's tidal islands, Cramond is the only one where tide times are posted by the causeway. There really is no excuse for anyone to need the services of the lifeboats. As I was finding however, some of the people who visit Cramond Island are very different to those who walk to other islands. What a shame that so little respect is shown for the sea and for this historic island.

The Cramond area is rich in history and archaeological excavations have shown evidence of habitation dating to around 8500 BC, making it the earliest known site of human settlement in Scotland. A stone burial cist uncovered in 1941 while military installations were being constructed, is evidence that prehistoric people came to the island too. Within the grounds of Cramond Kirk, the village church dating back to the 15th century, are the remains of a large Roman fort which would have guarded the land that they had managed to wrestle from the Iron Age inhabitants. Their stay however was short, being forced to retreat south to Hadrian's Wall after just 15 years. One can assume that some of the 500 men who worked on it would have ventured across to the island, although there is no evidence of Roman occupation here.

In medieval times there was a rabbit warren (cunningar) on the island to provide food. The rabbit population has died out and reappeared a number of times over the centuries and it's thought that they have been introduced rather than cross the sands naturally. There are none on the island now, which along with the lack of domestic grazing animals is allowing brambles, elderberry, bracken, willow and sycamore to cover much of the area. Almost 30% of the island's 26 acres are now covered with scrub or woodland.

Cramond was used for oyster fishing, with huge numbers being dredged in the 16th century, but by 1740 stocks were reported to have greatly declined, probably due to a combination of over-fishing and pollution. Kelp was once harvested from around the island's shores and throughout most of its history Cramond has been used for farming. Sheep were grazed here until the 1960s. It may also have served as a fishing outpost. There are remains of a jetty on the north west side, which was made from local stone and may be mediaeval in origin.

I am grateful to John Dods from whom I obtained a copy of his excellent little book *Cramond Island* (published by Cramond Heritage Trust) for much information on the remarkable history of the island. Dods tells the story of a legalised duel held on the low-lying flat area of the island in 1597. The protagonists were Adam Bruntsfield and James Carmichall, who in previous duels had killed all four of Bruntsfield's brothers and their father. With form strongly favouring Carmichall one might question the wisdom of the youngest and sole remaining brother taking on the man who had slain five of his family. Perhaps that provided sufficient motivation as Bruntsfield won the duel. There was no fairy tale ending however, as on being told of the news of his victory Bruntsfield's widowed mother promptly dropped dead.

Kirk Session Minutes of 1690 record in suitably discreet language, rumours that the island was serving, *'as an asylum for unfortunate females whose situation required a temporary retirement'*. The local midwife, her friends and family seem to have made a good living from running this 'service' in association with the island's residents. It was reported to the Session that *'a stranger gentlewoman was brought to bed in Robert Young's house on Cramond Island'* and the Youngs later admitted to getting eighteen pound Scots for their part in the venture at a time when the average annual wage for a farm worker was just twelve pounds.

In the late 18<sup>th</sup> and early 19<sup>th</sup> centuries there was a quarry on the island from which whinstone was taken mainly for use in the floors of ovens. The large flooded hole left by the operations was filled in by the army during the Second World War. In the late 18<sup>th</sup> century the Earl of Rosebery attempted to acquire the island from the Duke of Queensbury, stating his intention to *'ornament with plantations an object standing in conspicuous view from Barnbougle Castle'*. His offer of £600 was accepted but before the transfer could be completed the entire Estate was sold to Lord Glenorchy. He attempted to purchase Cramond Island from the new owner, but the price had risen to £2100, however Lord Roseberry eventually managed to secure the island in the mid 19<sup>th</sup> century and it has remained part of the Dalmeny Estate ever since.

From the mid 1800s to the Second World War Cramond Island was a holiday destination, with cottages let to visitors. Water was obtained from a well and groceries either collected from a Mrs Fee who lived in the nearest house in Cramond, or brought over the sands by horse drawn vehicles. Holiday makers swam from the island's beaches, played tennis on its grass court, sailed model boats on the old quarry and even shot salmon jumping a sand bar as they headed for the River Almond.

Much of Cramond Island's more recent history is related to its military use and remnants of a variety of installations can still be seen, albeit all heavily covered in graffiti. Most are in the north east corner, which was occupied by the army in the First World War. In the next war the whole island was taken over by the military. It is still possible to enter most of the shelters, stores and gun emplacements, plus two engine rooms that once provided power to all the island's military installations, although in many the floors were covered in broken glass and in some the odour not what one might call pleasant.

On the northern coast low concrete stumps protruding from the undergrowth are all that remain of the barracks that once housed the island's garrison. On the north west corner of the island is the ruin of a small stone building, known as the Duck House. This was built as a shelter for shooting parties from Dalmeny Estate while they waited for ducks to fly by. The tiny single roomed building once housed up to five people as holiday accommodation.

All these buildings are of historic value but covered with graffiti inside and out, some more explicable than others:

Heart of Midlothian
Island of Punks
Animal Lib
Rolf Harris
Terry & the Idiots
Bottom Feeders
Ersecore not Hardcore

I believe that the last two are local punk bands. Hearts are of course one of Edinburgh's top two football clubs (but whilst their supporters had left much graffiti on the island, I saw none from their rivals Hibs). Punks appear to have claimed the island for themselves, with their graffiti everywhere. Quite where our favourite Australian entertainer fits into all this I'm not sure.

Some people might argue that this is youthful expression adding to the island's history, but whilst I would agree that in the right place graffiti can be an art form, a beautiful island is most certainly not such a place. Generally speaking I'm pretty tolerant of young people having a good time (I too was once young and not always well behaved), but the state of Cramond Island goes far beyond acceptability – piles of rubbish, historic buildings covered with graffiti, broken glass and a complete lack of respect for the island, its wildlife and others who wish to visit. Somewhat sad that after so much beauty around the country's coast, my final Scottish island should have been spoiled, I walked back across the causeway angry at the selfishness of such behaviour.

Lasagne and chips at the Cramond Inn improved my mood a little, so rather than spend the rest of the evening in Edinburgh I went back to the causeway to watch the tide come in. Twenty minutes after the advertised final crossing time a young couple with baby in pushchair appeared at the island end. The tide was rising fast and water now touching both sides of the causeway, although still with a foot or two to rise until it was covered. As the couple reached the mainland a lady passed them, walking quickly towards the island and waving. Two lads at the other end waved back and ambled towards her. Words were said when they met halfway. It was fortunate that today the causeway wasn't covered until almost an hour after the advertised time otherwise the lifeboatmen from South Queensferry would have had another mission for their 'ferry'.

As I stood by the causeway two groups of young people started shouting at each other on the beach. A bottle was thrown smashing on the promenade. I shall not repeat the words that accompanied it, but suffice to say that if the glass had removed what the assailant hoped it would cut off, this particular young man would not have been passing on his anti-social genes to future generations. With the sands covered by sea and Cramond Island at peace, I wandered up the hill to find a bus. Already at the stop were some of the youngsters I'd seen on the beach, their 'colourful' language punctuating the cool evening air. How sad I thought that these are not youngsters trapped on rough estates, but those able to spend time on a beautiful coast.

Having almost completed this chapter I went back and looked through my photos again and realised that perhaps I have been a little harsh. There is much of beauty about Cramond Island. Its setting just a few miles from a large city, but with superb views across the Forth in all directions. Its little wood, colourful scrub, small hill and more remote feeling northern side. Its slightly mysterious buildings in various states of disrepair. Cramond Island hasn't been ruined by the party goers and graffiti writers. It is still a lovely place but it's a pity that some visitors are so selfish. We are fortunate that volunteers from Cramond Heritage Trust and Cramond Boat Club regularly give up their time to clean up the island. I was told that I'd visited at an unfortunate time shortly after a rave. Some groups apparently tidy up after themselves, others sadly don't.

On returning to Essex I contacted the Forth Estuary Forum, a voluntary partnership of organisations with an interest in the wellbeing of the Forth and its coastal communities. Chris Cuts the Forum Manager put me in touch with John Dods who proved to be a most useful source of information and with Mark Hamilton, author of *Cramond Island Management Plan*. This report had been commissioned by Edinburgh and Lothians Greenspace Trust and Dalmeny Estates, and having confirmed that both were happy for me to see it, Mark kindly sent me a copy.

The 58 page document includes a thorough survey of the island, its habitats, plants and wildlife. A total of 109 plants were recorded in 2009, none of which however are particularly rare. Lothian Wildlife Information Centre list 59 bird species, of which 27 are land birds and the other 32 more or less confined to the water or inter-tidal flats surrounding the island. The survey found 10 breeding species, including linnet and song thrush which are both on the Amber List for Birds of Conservation Concern. The survey found no sign of other protected animals such as bat, otter, badger or water vole.

The Plan aims to perpetuate the island's current appeal by preserving and enhancing the range of natural habitats present and by protecting historic buildings and features. It hopes to involve local groups such as Scouts and hence promote a sense of stewardship. The report outlines a five year work programme and sets out the following objectives:

*To protect and enhance the habitat and wildlife value of the site. This will be achieved through a combination of woodland management works, management of ruderal vegetation, and through native woodland expansion onto areas of low conservation interest.*

*To improve recreational provision band amenity and thus enhance the site for public use. This will be achieved by minor improvements to the path corridors on the Island, by opening up views, by removal of graffiti, and by removal of rubbish. (Improvement of the causeway which would be of significant benefit is outside the scope of the Plan).*

*To preserve and protect historic buildings and features and to keep them in a condition that does not present a hazard to the general public. This will be achieved by removal of graffiti and infilling of a safety hazard.*

*To involve Scouts groups in practical management tasks. This will be achieved through the design of a work programme that can be implemented by voluntary labour while providing a range of practical and educational opportunities.*

Thoroughly laudable although these objectives are, whilst undeniably they will improve the island for both people and wildlife, I could not help but feel that they don't directly address what seemed to me to be the biggest problem facing Cramond Island – the lack of respect that some visitors show for it. I put this to Mark Hamilton who agreed that anti-social behaviour is a problem, but said that as the island is not publicly owned, is accessible, but remote from any controlling presence, to control overnight parties would be 'very problematic'. He agreed that education, more active management and involvement of local people may reduce the problem, but cautioned that this could lead to the island having a higher profile and potentially exacerbating the situation.

Of all our tidal islands Cramond faces unique problems. Here it is not the effect on our climate of mankind across the world that threatens the island by erosion, but the action of a minority of local people who show no respect and spoil it for others. It is good that there is a Management Plan and it must be hoped that with the improvements this will bring to the island and with greater involvement of local people, stewardship will prevail.

Now though it was time to think ahead, and to Lindisfarne an island I'd been looking forward to visiting from the very start and where behaviour would surely be more genteel.

# CHAPTER EIGHTEEN

# THE HOLY ISLAND OF LINDISFARNE

Almost everyone who I told that I was writing a book about tidal islands mentioned Holy Island. This and St Michael's Mount seem to be the only tidal islands that everyone knows about and all those who had been there told me how much I would like it. I wasn't to be disappointed.

I nearly didn't get there though. The easiest way to visit with just two days away was to get the sleeper to Edinburgh, then take a train south to Berwick-upon-Tweed. With the sleeper due to arrive in Edinburgh at 7.15, I set my alarm for 7.05. Ten minutes later I felt the train draw to a halt and pulled up the blind. We were at Carlisle. A broken down freight train had blocked the line between Wigan and Preston, but I was assured we'd still arrive in time to catch the 9.00 to Berwick. Indeed we would had the train not stopped at Carstairs for 45 minutes. According to a train driver who was getting a lift back to Edinburgh in the lounge car, the man (the 'shunter') whose job it is to split the Glasgow and Edinburgh portions and attach another engine to the Edinburgh train, had gone home. Another man had to be sent by taxi from Edinburgh.

It took ScotRail just a week to reply to my letter. There was no comment on my suggestion that the delay had been compounded by the 'shunter' going home and they gave the wrong location for the freight train failure (Carstairs), but included the usual apologies and generous compensation vouchers. ScotRail really do give the impression that they care about their passengers.

We arrived in the Scottish capital at 9.33, three minutes after the last train to Berwick that would have connected with the Holy Island bus – a service that outside the main season runs on just Wednesdays and Saturdays, with a complicated timetable varying according to tides. The next train to Berwick didn't leave until 11.00. It was looking as if I wouldn't be able to cross until the evening low tide. In a moment's inspiration I rang my wife. Could she find a Berwick taxi firm on the internet and see if they'd meet the train and could get me over the causeway before the advertised shutting time of 12.15? The first company said no. The second, A2B Taxis were most helpful and would be waiting for my 11.39 arrival.

George, the company's owner, was outside the station as promised. The firm is the semi-official island taxi and shown on the Lindisfarne website. We arrived at the causeway with ten minutes to spare. George said it would be safe for me to walk over, so dropped me at the mainland end.

A sign warns of danger and not to proceed when water reaches the causeway. Close to the mainland end is a refuge – a little wooden hut on stilts. Steps lead up to what looks like a garden shed, but over the years has saved many lives. A popular tourist destination, with around 500,000 visitors a year, Holy Island has more tales of people trapped by the tide than any other island. Tide tables are clearly displayed and all over the island village were signs with a photo of a partly submerged car warning – THIS COULD BE YOU – CONSULT TIDE TABLES. But still people try to beat the sea.

The Seahouses lifeboat is called out about once a month to rescue those who become trapped in their cars or who make it to the refuge. Each call-out costs around £2,000. There have been dramatic rescues with people clinging to almost submerged cars and winched to safety minutes before the sea would have washed them away. A helicopter call-out costs the tax payer upwards of £4,000. A few months before my visit eight holidaymakers were rescued after attempting to cross an hour and a half after the safe time, and their three ruined vehicles retrieved when the sea had receded. Earlier in the year the lifeboat had been diverted from a school visit and launched to rescue a couple from Nottingham who'd abandoned their vehicle and called for help from the refuge box. RNLI volunteer Lifeboats Operations Manager Ian Clayton commented, 'I am dismayed that despite the clear signage and all the publicity we are still being called to rescue people from the causeway' and pointed out that people fail to appreciate that they are driving into the North Sea, not crossing a quiet country ford.

There have been calls for barriers, but these are opposed by islanders as they would inhibit the short timescale to get on and off the island. Suggestions of raising the causeway to provide a permanent link are fiercely resisted by those who live on Holy Island and cherish the magical qualities that come from it being cut off from the rest of the world.

As I walked, a silvery patch on the road in the distance gave me some concern. Had I been right to take George's word that it was safe to walk over? Cars were still crossing but I immediately quickened my pace. Soon it was clear that the silvery area was indeed water. It seemed that the sea had reached the causeway. After all my care at previous islands it looked as if having taken local advice I was going to get wet feet. Reaching the water however I found that it was no more than a couple of inches deep and was standing water, rather than incoming sea. That was about three inches below the northern edge of the causeway and rising fast. I could cross safely but with probably no more than 15 minutes to spare. As I continued on the two mile walk towards the village cars still passed me for half an hour or so, but with wet wheels and increasingly larger splashes on their body work. Then all was quiet and the road that runs alongside the sea and salt marshes deserted until the tide receded once more.

The most direct way to the village in the island's south west corner is across the sands. The Pilgrim's Path, an ancient 11th century route, crosses the sands forming the start of two long distance paths; St Oswald's Way to Heavenfield on Hadrian's Wall and St Cuthbert's Way to Melrose. It should however only be attempted with care. The route which is marked by wooden poles is covered for up to four hours longer per tide cycle than the causeway. Anyone straying from the poles risks getting stuck in quicksand or soft mud.

Two horse riders were out on the sands as I walked across the causeway, but safely loaded their mounts into a horsebox before the sea arrived. Earlier in the year a couple had brought their former racehorses down from Hawick and got stuck in the mud after one bolted. One animal was quickly freed, but a dramatic rescue operation launched to assist the other. Coastguards, lifeboat volunteers, fire-fighters, the RSPCA, a vet and members of the public worked for three hours to try to free the stricken creature. The vet too got stuck in the mud and had to be pulled out. Two hours after the alarm had been raised the horse was still stuck fast. With the tide rising and serious fears that the animal was going to drown, a second lifeboat and a Sea King helicopter from RAF Boulmer were summoned. Finally, with the sea now swirling around the horse, the winchman and helpers managed to get a lifting strap underneath it. Dangling ungainly forty foot above the water it was flown to a field on the mainland where the vet administered a sedative to help with the shock. Later the horse was reported to be eating and none the worse for its experience.

There's limited accommodation on Holy Island but I made a good choice with the Lindisfarne Hotel. Host Sean was most welcoming and recommended a 'stottie' for lunch in their café. This round flat loaf is a Geordie speciality although he thought my choice of bacon with brie was perhaps a bit posher than local tradition – Geordies Sean said, might slap a bit of cheddar in it.

His wife Jackie had said when I booked that one night wasn't enough to see Holy Island, and I was soon to find that an afternoon was inadequate to do justice to the castle, priory and village, let alone the rest of the island. I'd planned to walk off next morning, but with the rather strange bus timetable from Beal on the mainland (two buses every two hours, but running six minutes apart), would have had to leave straight after breakfast. Hence I called George and arranged for A2B Taxis to pick me up just before the tide covered the causeway at 12.40.

The castle is in the south east corner of the island, standing on a crag almost a mile from the village. The view of it across the harbour is the iconic Holy Island picture and one of our few famous tidal island sights. A courtesy bus runs from the village, but for those able the dramatic approach on foot alongside the sea is one not to be missed. The castle is owned by the National Trust and opening hours vary according to the tide. Today it was to shut at 3.00 and I arrived only just in time for the last entry half an hour earlier. It's fortunate that there are only a few rooms to see as much of my limited time was spent talking to the guides and enjoying the superb views from the battery.

The man checking tickets told me that he's employed by the Trust and part of a rota of four people who spend five or so nights on the island in charge of the castle. Although they don't stay in it, the castle is their responsibility for the duration. The lady based in the Ship Room was a volunteer who came from Norfolk. Interested in my book, she told me that as a student she'd walked to Scolt Head Island, but had to wear wellies. I was yet to find out whether this would qualify as a tidal island.

The castle was originally an Elizabethan fort protecting the harbour, with the island occupying a key position near the unruly Scottish border. Although the accession of James VI of Scotland to the English throne in 1603 united the countries, the castle kept a garrison for over 300 years. In 1901, eight years after the soldiers moved out, Edward Hudson the founder of *Country Life,* discovered the now derelict castle. Realising its potential he commissioned his friend Sir Edwin Lutyens to convert it into a home. Lutyens created the austere but beautiful interiors, linked by dramatic corridors, galleries and stairs. This is a castle where the main appeal is from the building and its setting, and into which the mostly plain furniture preferred by Lutyens fits well. Particularly notable are the entrance hall with columns and arches, which mimics the Norman nave of Durham Cathedral, and the Ship Room with its vaulted ceiling to take the weight of canons on the battery above.

Behind the castle are lime kilns, which were built in the 1860s and last used in 1900. They are well preserved and visitors can walk through the tunnels – just the sort of place that we'd have loved to play in as children. We did come to Holy Island during a family holiday at Berwick, but I recall just the long walk to and from the bus at Beal. I often wonder if now in middle age, I'd be walking along coasts if our childhood holidays had been spent sitting around swimming pools in the Mediterranean. My wife and I came to the island briefly many years ago and this time I recall two things – the castle being closed and me reversing into a wooden fencepost in the car park. No damage was done to the car and the pole was merely flattened, but amusement was provided to sundry onlookers. The short tramway which once carried lime to the kilns is now a grassy embankment and all that remains of the jetty are a few timbers standing upright near the castle. These provide foreground interest in many photos of the castle, but few who admire the dramatic setting would imagine the industry that once carried on around the famous building.

A couple of hundred yards from the castle is a lovely walled garden. It's set some distance from the main building as the low lying area between used to flood, although this seems to have been a Northumbrian tradition, with many large houses in the county having walled gardens in sheltered spots some way from the house. There were once plans to turn the low lying area into a moat, with a bridge to the garden. It was designed by Gertrude Jekyll, the foremost garden designer of her time. In May 1906 Jekyll took the train north, accompanied by a cantankerous raven called Black Jack and a large bag of peppermint bull's-eyes. A large woman, she must have made quite a sight as she was gingerly hoisted into a small boat and rowed over to Holy Island. Her garden was designed with flowers to give the best colour in July, plus espalier fruit trees (trained against a wall), vegetables and herbs.

In 2002 the National Trust started a project to restore the garden, following the original Jekyll plans, although some of her plants have been lost to history. 'Heritage' vegetables now grow, with varieties of runner bean, tomato, parsnip, beetroot and onions dating from 1880 to 1911. I have a particular liking for walled gardens and Gertrude Jekyll's Holy Island garden, with the dramatic backdrop of the castle and North Sea waves behind, was one of my tidal island gems.

From here I headed for the island's almost deserted east coast. The vast majority of visitors stay around the village or make it as far as the castle, but few venture to what is probably the most beautiful part of Lindisfarne. The North Sea is often dull and grey, but today it was sparkling blue, with waves crashing over offshore rocks. Each wave trailed a line of fine white spray, looking I thought to those of us who might appreciate a 1970s football metaphor, like Ralph Coates in full flight. A few miles across the sea were the Farne Islands. This was the sort of sea where those boarding the little boats taking visitors out to see puffins needed to be issued with buckets – a day to be visiting an island with 'no boat required'.

Visible for some distance is a white stone pyramid at Emmanuel Head. This is a 'daymark', a navigational point maintained by Trinity House, which was built in the early 19th century and may have been the first of its kind in Britain. From here as I turned west the pebble beaches of the east coast gave way to sandy bays backed with dunes. Somewhere here are the remains of a short lived coal mine, which closed after the seam ran under the sea and the passages were inundated. Also under the dunes are the remains of a medieval village, which was the first settlement on the island.

There was once a nine hole golf course here but now the dunes are a nature reserve. A sign warns of quicksands and unexploded ordnance, the latter as the northern part of the island was part of the former Goswick Sands bombing range. Another warns of piri-piri burr an invasive non-native plant which sticks to clothing and animals. The Natural England sign advised that the plant has a negative impact on native wildlife and asked visitors to check their clothing and pets for burrs to prevent it being spread to other sites.

A path back across the centre of the island gave another excellent, but less well known view to the castle over The Lough, a small lake which attracts a good variety of birds. Further exploration would have to wait for tomorrow, as on Sean's recommendation I'd booked dinner at The Crown and Anchor. With few places to eat and nowhere serving meals after 8.00, visitors are advised to reserve somewhere in good time. After an excellent meal I went for a wander around the now almost deserted village, but after several circuits and with it too dark to stray far, returned to my hotel to enjoy watching Spurs get thoroughly beaten! (Sadly us West Ham fans all too often have to resort to watching our rivals lose for footballing enjoyment).

Before breakfast I walked to another island. Eighty yards or so off Lindisfarne is St Cuthbert's Island, which at low tide can be walked to over rocks and sand. Yesterday afternoon I'd looked across to it surrounded by sea and now I was the lone person standing on this little islet. The only others who seemed to be up early were a couple of cockle pickers on the rocks nearby. This tiny island, not far from the priory, was for a short time home to St Cuthbert of Lindisfarne.

Many tidal islands have religious connections, but none more so than Lindisfarne, which is intimately linked to the history of Christianity in Britain. In AD635 St Aiden was summoned from Iona by King Oswald of Northumbria and with his Irish missionaries set out to convert the northern Anglo-Saxons. St Aiden founded the first monastery on the island and established Christianity in Northumbria, but it was St Cuthbert, Prior of Lindisfarne, who became the most celebrated of its holy men. A Northumbrian himself, Cuthbert became Prior of Melrose, ministering to the people who lived in the hills and surrounding country. Moving to Lindisfarne in the 670s, his reform of monastic rule to bring it more into line with Roman practices caused bitterness among the monks. After a while he decided to retire and was granted permission to live out his life as a hermit, initially on what became known as St Cuthbert's Island, then on Inner Farne Island.

In the centre of the islet stands a tall wooden cross inside the low walls of a late medieval chapel. This was probably constructed on the site of an earlier chapel that was built in the time of St Cuthbert. A small circular mound north west of the chapel may be the remains of the saint's house. On a rock at the side of the island a plaque reads:

> *Mightier the thunders of many waters,*
> *Mightier than the waves of the sea,*
> *The Lord on high is mighty.*

> *Psalm 93.4*

> *God is always greater than all of our troubles  M.B.*

After several years of austere life on Farne, Cuthbert was persuaded to return to a more active role in the church and became Bishop of Lindisfarne. His life back on the island was however short lived, as after less than two years Cuthbert felt death approaching and returned to Farne to die. He was buried on Lindisfarne where his grave soon became a place of pilgrimage. Many miracles of healing were said to have occurred, and his status as a saint was further enhanced when after eleven years the coffin was opened. Rather than a skeleton, inside was Cuthbert's complete and undecayed body. His body was enshrined before the high altar of the church, to where even more pilgrims flocked to pray.

Viking raids on the monastery a hundred years later killed many of the inhabitants and forced the monks to flee to safety on the mainland, taking St Cuthbert's relics with them. After various temporary resting places his body was eventually taken to Durham and enshrined in the cathedral where it still rests. Monks from Durham returned to Lindisfarne in the 12th century, building a magnificent church over the spot where they believed he had originally been buried. The priory's fortunes were badly affected by border warfare, but a small community survived here until 1537. The extensive ruins which stand today are of the priory that was built in 1150 for the Benedictine order in the style of Durham Cathedral.

After bacon and eggs back at the hotel I set out to complete my exploration of Holy Island. First stop was the priory, which is owned by English Heritage and considered to be one of the most important centres of Christianity in Anglo-Saxon England. Both the monastic buildings and priory can be viewed, although all are now ruins. The church tower collapsed in the 18th century, but remarkably the stunning rainbow arch vault survived. Set against the backdrop of the castle and North Sea this is another iconic tidal island view. Unusually, the priory was fortified, battlements, towers and a barbican being built in the 14th century in response to war with the Scots and defensive arrow slits can still be seen.

The trouble with ruins is that they don't take long to look round. An inspection and few photos of the priory, a walk round the monastic buildings, most of which are now just footings, and general admiring of the view, took me no more than twenty minutes. Another five in the visitor centre and I was on my way. I felt a bit like a tourist 'doing' Holy Island, but there was no point in lingering for the sake of it. Being an English Heritage member I didn't feel the need to stay for sufficient time to justify the entry fee. In any case, although the priory may be the most famous building on the island and centre of its religious past, it is just a part of what makes Holy Island so special – the churches, priory, castle, village, history, but also the less visited shores that I'd walked along yesterday, plus the serene atmosphere of the whole island.

Next stop on my morning tour was the parish church of St Mary the Virgin, the island's Anglican church, which holds three services a day catering for both the local community and visitors. It was built on the exact spot where the original monastery stood and parts of the Saxon building survive in the wall containing the chancel arch. Most of this historic and attractive church date from the 12th and 13th centuries. It became Anglican after the Reformation, but fell into disuse until restored in 1860. The first thing to catch the eye on entering is an imposing statue known as 'The Journey' depicting the monks of Lindisfarne carrying St Cuthbert's body on the first stage of its journey to Durham. Sculpted from 35 pieces of elm wood and carved mainly with a chain-saw, its depiction seems more real than colder stone statues. A bronze copy stands in the Millennium Square in Durham, marking the finish of St Cuthbert's journey.

South of the church and accessed by the path that runs above St Cuthbert's

Island, is an area of high ridge known as the Heugh, with good views over the priory, harbour and towards the castle – another fine spot for photography, on which is one of our most photogenic islands. Again I could clearly see the Farne Islands and although today the sea was calmer, it was still a day more suited to visiting tidal islands. Indeed any day when the sea doesn't resemble the proverbial millpond is in my experience one to be walking rather than sailing to islands. Looking back, on the mainland was Bamburgh Castle, standing dramatically on a volcanic outcrop overlooking the North Sea. At the eastern end of the Heugh are the remains of Osborne's Fort, which was built to defend the harbour in 1670 and on top of the cliff are an old coastguard lookout, a modern light and the island's war memorial.

Yesterday I'd decided that half a day wasn't long enough to properly explore Holy Island. Today I realised that 24 hours is still too short. With less than two hours until the taxi was booked, there were still more walks to do, the village to see in daylight and another museum. I had to do what my wife hates when we go away – plan my time. The village and its historic buildings were interesting, but what I enjoy most is walking in beautiful settings, hence I set off back to the castle and the north coast. This time I headed to Castle Point, a grass and shingle promontory at the south west corner of the island. In yet another idyllic island scene, under a blue sky a flock of sheep sat serenely on green grass beneath the rocky castle, while a fishing boat sailed by on a dark sea.

After an hour's wandering I was back in the village, taking a quick look in the handful of mostly tourist related shops. Picking up a copy of *Walks on Holy Island* by Chrissie Anderson in the Island Store, I wished that I'd been staying another night. Chatting to the owner about my book I asked whether he thought I should use Holy Island or Lindisfarne as the chapter title. The former he said is mostly used by locals, but suggested that I went for the official name of The Holy Island of Lindisfarne.

Before picking up my rucksack from the hotel I took a quick look in the island's Roman Catholic Church, St Aidan's. Much newer than St Mary's, this small wooden building was refurbished in 2007. It's not part of the main tourist trail and as the sole visitor in this simple building I felt closer to God than in the more ornate, historic, but busier priory or parish church. The church forms part of the community of St Vincent di Paul who provide an island holiday centre largely intended for children who might otherwise not have a holiday.

Time did not allow me to visit St Cuthbert's Centre the island's United Reformed Church. That a village of 150 souls has three active churches illustrates the numbers who come here, not just as tourists, but to experience the spiritual side of the island. There are several locations for retreats and many pilgrimages visit here. Yesterday as I was walking from the causeway to the village I had a call from one of our glue customers. Hearing where I was he told me that whilst not being a religious person, Holy Island is one of just two places where he feels a spiritual presence. The other, the Isle of Iona, off Mull, the birthplace of Christianity in Scotland has many similarities to Lindisfarne. His feeling is I think common on Holy Island, although perhaps defying convention, I still felt that the most special part of the island was not the religious buildings but the more rugged North Sea shores.

As I walked back into the village, coming the other way was almost a procession of people. At first I thought there must be some kind of event, but then realised – it was the mass exodus to the car park for visitors to leave the island before the causeway was covered. With most of the tourists gone the village was suddenly quieter. This is the time to see Holy Island – to stay over the tide or better still for a night or two.

There is one more site on the island that I'd like to have seen, but time had run out. The Lindisfarne Heritage Centre has been developed by the island community and contains interactive exhibits illustrating the history, wildlife and people of Holy Island. Centrepiece of the exhibition is an atmospheric inner-sanctum dedicated to one of England's most important books, the Lindisfarne Gospels. Made up of more than 250 leaves of beautifully decorated vellum, these contain the Gospels of Matthew, Mark, Luke and John. Written in Latin by Eadfrith, Bishop of Lindisfarne who died in 721, a translation into Old-English was added in the 10th century, making this the earliest surviving version of any form of the English language. The book is kept at the British Library in London, but a facsimile edition and an interactive version with turning pages have been donated back to Lindisfarne – the gospel's birthplace.

I'd arrange for the taxi to pick me up outside the post office, but with five minutes to spare had time for a quick look at the Lindisfarne Gospels Garden. This beautiful little garden is a reconstruction of Newcastle City Council's silver medal winning entry to the 2003 Chelsea Flower Show. Based on the 7$^{th}$ century gospels, it features a Celtic cross representing heaven and earth, a water feature, circular flower beds and rockeries designed to look like the intricate lettering of the manuscripts. With an arch depicting the priory's rainbow arch, the garden is a place for quiet contemplation on probably our most spiritual tidal island.

A couple of hours after being driven over the causeway I caught a last glimpse of Holy Island as my train headed south. With the tide high the island would have been quiet and at its best in afternoon sunshine. I told Sean at the Lindisfarne Hotel that I would come back and next time I'd bring the family. With its history, iconic buildings, serenity and beauty The Holy Island of Lindisfarne is one island that everyone should try to visit – but please not all at once and *mind that tide.*

# CHAPTER NINETEEN

# ST MARY'S ISLAND

One of the smallest of our tidal islands, but perhaps one of the most interesting, St Mary's Island is situated a couple of miles from the North Tyneside town of Whitley Bay. The half hour Metro ride from Newcastle took me through Wallsend, where station signs are in both English and Latin to assist any of Hadrian's soldiers who may have missed the order to return to Rome, and Tynemouth, where the vast Grade II listed Victorian station that was once the gateway to the seaside is now crumbling and on English Heritage's at risk list. Whitley Bay's fine station is in far better condition and the whole town I found surprisingly well appointed. So often seaside resorts close to cities are badly run down, but Whitley Bay was a pleasing little town, with a lovely sandy beach. The friendliness of the staff at the York Hotel was typical of everyone I spoke to during my visit.

There is no bay, the name having been changed from Whitley in 1902 thanks to a William Oliver, although he knew nothing of it. Mr Oliver had died while visiting Polton near Edinburgh and his family arranged for his coffin to be returned by train in time for the funeral. As the mourners waited at St Paul's church a telegraph message arrived from the Station Master at Whitby in Yorkshire, saying that the coffin had mistakenly been sent there. It was 8.45 in the evening by the time it eventually arrived at Whitley and the funeral took place by lamplight. Both the Railway Company and the Post Office had for some time been asking for the town's name to be changed to avoid such confusion, and after this distressing

*Eilean Ighe*

*Sandaig Islands & Knoydart*

*Sandaig Islands & Isle of Skye*

*Eilean Donan*

*Isle Ristol*

*Cramond Island*

*Castle - Holy Island*

*Refuge - Holy Island Causeway*

*St Mary's Island*

*Skippers Island 'Causeway'*

*Beach Huts – Mersea Island*

*Manor House – Osea Island*

*Brent Geese - Northey Island*

*Chiswick Eyot*

*Burrow (Rat) Island*

*Sea Tractor - Burgh Island*

disruption of a burial the Council finally agreed. A competition to choose a new name was run by a local newspaper and Whitley Bay was by a narrow margin the favoured choice.

It's a pleasant two mile walk along the coast to St Mary's Island (there's a bus most of the way if required), with the expanse of the North Sea to the right and a wide greensward with pitch & putt golf course to the left. For once there was no need for a map as I headed for the island and its 120 foot lighthouse. A short man-made stone causeway links St Mary's to the shore and is covered for three to four hours each tide. Today there were no constraints of trains, buses, or hire cars, so arriving when the tide was low I had ample time to explore this tiny island.

St Mary's Island is owned by North Tyneside Council who, responding to an outburst of popular feeling from local people, launched an appeal to buy it from Trinity House when the lighthouse was decommissioned in 1984. Many of the people who had worked to help make the appeal successful founded the Friends of St Mary's Island, which aims to raise funds to help maintain, promote and safeguard the island. Their greatest expenditure has been a contribution of £8,000 towards the cost of a ramp to improve access, which coincidentally was the entire cost of building the lighthouse and keeper's cottages in 1899. It is clearly cherished by the people of Whitley Bay and it was good to see many families and young children on and around the island. The Friends' attractive logo is a composite of drawings and suggestions from pupils of Whitley Lodge First School.

Members of the Friends are entitled to half price lighthouse admission, but having left my card behind I paid the full £2.30. After St Michael's Mount, Piel Island and Lindisfarne, this was only the fourth tidal island where I'd actually spent money on the island. The excellent guidebook which I bought in the island's shop is aptly named '137 Steps'. All but 20 of these steps are on a stone spiral staircase running from the base of the lighthouse. Years ago I'd have scurried up as the children were doing today, but for some reason with advancing years I've developed if not a fear, a dislike of heights. This was perhaps understandable on the perilous cliffs of Ynys Lochtyn, but barring a slip the only risk here was the quite ludicrous one of the staircase suddenly becoming detached from the wall after being firmly fixed for more than a hundred years. The thought did cross my mind, however ensuring that I stared at the wall and didn't look down, I reached the top having been overtaken by only four or five young children.

As on a plane, with no view immediately downwards, once at the top vertigo was no problem. Instead I could enjoy the views, with the Cheviot Hills clearly seen to the north. I spoke to the mother of two girls of about three and five who'd made it to the top. As we looked out at the sea the youngest slipped on a step by the window, but falling less than a foot, there were few tears. Her mother and I said at exactly the same time 'better here than on the way up'.

Lights have been kept on the island for many centuries, a chapel dedicated to St. Helen in 1090 carrying an endowment of five shillings a week to keep a light in the tower to warn sailors of rocks. There were however many wrecks around the island and many lives lost. The saddest was perhaps the *Lovely Nelly* from Seaham that was driven onto the rocks on New Year's Day 1861. The women of Cullercoats pulled the lifeboat over the headland and all the crew were saved except for the little cabin boy, Tommy, who was too scared to jump from the rigging. Thirty years later the *Gothenburg City* from Montreal struck the rocks to the north of the island. Her 44 crew were rescued and the 476 cattle she was carrying taken off by Tyne ferries. In an attempt to refloat the ship most of her cargo was thrown overboard, but whilst this failed (the vessel's remains can still be seen at low tide), locals gratefully collected discarded pit props and coal as they washed up on the beach.

The lighthouse was built to replace a light at Tynemouth five miles further south, as this was frequently obscured by smoke from steamships and industry on the River Tyne. It was decided that the new light should be situated away from the river mouth and St Mary's Island chosen as a suitable site. Three quarters of a million bricks were used to construct the tower, while the two keeper's cottages were made from Heworth stone. A covered passage between the cottages and tower was at that time a novelty, allowing keepers to reach the lighthouse, as a newspaper of the day stated 'in comfort and security however furiously the elements may rage outside'. Building took almost two years and in a ceremony at dusk on 31st August 1898 the lamp was lit for the first time by two little girls, Miss Miller and Miss Wilson, daughter and niece of the builder, Mr J. Livingstone Miller of Tynemouth.

The first two keepers, Messrs Roberts and Monk, transferred from Tynemouth Light which closed the day before St Mary's opened. Essential qualifications for keepers included a good head for heights, tolerance of others in confined spaces, a liking for solitude, and less obviously, possession of either a good set of teeth or none at all. On a similar theme of no half measures, they were required to be either clean shaven or to wear a full beard.

The Principal Keeper and his Assistant Keeper lived with their families in the two cottages, which have now been knocked into one to form the Visitor Centre. In winter an extra keeper was taken on to cover the longer nights. Their day started at dawn when the light was put out and the curtains closed. The paraffin lamp was then taken apart and its vaporiser removed for cleaning, with a spare one installed so the lamp was ready for immediate use. Lenses were washed and polished as were the 137 steps and brass handrail. Everything was expected to be spotless and Trinity House staff paid periodic visits to inspect the light and buildings. At sunset the lamp was primed. Every hour until dawn a keeper had to wind the clockwork motor that powered the mechanism which rotated the lens as it revolved around the lamp floating on a bath of mercury. Every three hours night and day a weather log had to be completed, so some keepers stayed up the tower for the duration of their shift. Most had hobbies to fill the time – woodwork, jigsaws, ships in bottles were typical, but one keeper even worked on parts of his motorbike.

Although St Mary's was one of our less remote lighthouses, life wasn't easy for the keepers and their families. Until 1948 fresh water had to be collected from the flat roofs of the cottages and filtered, or if supplies dried up in summer, brought over in barrels. Initially toilets were just earth privies, then Elsans, which were converted to water closets in 1954. There were no bathrooms, washing being done in a tub, or a tin bath in front of a fire. Electricity didn't reach the island until 1957. Before then light was from paraffin lamps and heating and cooking either by coal or driftwood fires.

In 1977 the oil lamp was replaced with an electric lamp and two years later a full power light installed which could be seen at 17 miles. Operation of this was automated, hence keepers were not needed. The unmanned light continued in operation until 1984, when a Trinity House review decided that it was no longer required. Technological advances and in particular ship's radar, had made navigation at sea far safer and most of the lighthouses that were retained around our coast are now not so much for warning as guiding lights. Despite a 3,500 name petition from local residents, the light went out for the last time on 30th November 1984.

The keepers' cottages have been converted to a small exhibition area, meeting room and shop selling a range of items mainly aimed at the family visitor. As I arrived one most friendly and entertaining gentleman was holding a little group of girls spellbound as he told them a long and involved story of the mermaid's eggs that are collected from the rocks each day. None were however tempted to buy any of the five pence glass balls and one slightly older girl turned to her Mum saying quietly but with still perhaps a little doubt in her voice, 'They're not real are they?'

Outside is a small garden which was started by the Friends in 1998. Horned poppies, thrift and silene thrive in the salty and windy conditions. The island, its surrounding rocks and adjacent shoreline are a nature reserve. A huge variety of birds are attracted by the pools and crevices which provide plenty of limpets, crabs, mussels, winkles and small fish, and the sandy beach with its supply of shrimps, lugworms and sand hoppers. St Mary's and its surrounds are used by significant numbers of turnstone and purple sandpiper, both of which have Amber Conservation Status indicating concern over declining numbers. Turnstone spend the winter here before returning to their arctic breeding grounds and can be spotted turning over small stones or fronds of seaweed as they search for food. A bird hide behind the lighthouse looks out over the rocks and gives particularly good sightings when strong easterly winds bring birds migrating along the North Sea closer to the shore.

I took a walk amongst the rock pools which were probably the best I'd seen since Worm's Head; deep, colourful and teaming with life. Small fish darted away as I approached, then standing still I watched crawling crabs and the more brave little fishes venture out from beds of seaweed. Children with nets and buckets busily investigated, with shouts of excitement when a creature had been trapped. Three girls rushed up to one of the visitor centre staff with a good sized crab, the youngest making sure that the lady knew it was her who had caught it. She identified it as a shore crab, telling them it was a boy as its tail was pointed. The girls rushed off to the shop saying 'let's tell the man'. The staff working here are employed by the council and clearly enjoyed their jobs. My notebook records, 'What a lovely place and what lovely people work here'.

I walked over the rocks almost as far as the concrete pillar which stands in the sea east of the island and was built as a rangefinder for coastal defence guns at Tynemouth Priory, then explored the area to the north known as Smugglers Creek. It seems that tidal islands were particularly favoured for the running of illicit goods and St Mary's has its associated tales of violence and death. In 1722, Anthony Mitchell, Surveyor of Customs, was found dead near the creek, with many locals pointing the finger at two villains who smuggled brandy. Seventeen years later another body was hanging close to the island. The landlord of the inn at Old Hartley a mile up the coast had been murdered and Michael Curry a local glass worker, found guilty and hanged in Newcastle. As was then the custom, his body was strung from a gibbet within sight of his crime, at a spot just inland from the causeway end. Now known as Curry's Point, a small plaque commemorates the gruesome event.

There is a tale about two drinkers, one of whom challenged his friend half a gallon of beer that he would not go up to the corpse and say 'How are you Curry?' Full of Dutch courage the friend set off across the fields to the point where the body hung, but unbeknown to him his challenger had taken a short cut, arrived before him and hidden behind the body. When his friend called out 'How are you Curry?' a deep hollow voice replied 'Very well'. Sober with fright the poor man took to his heels across the fields. Whether he found out the true source of the voice is not recorded, and nor do we know whether he was put off the demon drink, or downed his prize to try to forget the experience.

The island's early history appears less traumatic. It is probable that St Mary's was home to hermits in the early days of Christianity, although these holy men would have left after the Viking invasions. The chapel was probably built by Tynemouth Priory and monks lived here until about 1800, although they didn't own it. In the 1580s the island was owned by Thomas Bates, Queen Elizabeth's Surveyor for Northumberland, who may have burned kelp and made salt here. For many years it was also known as Bates Island.

A cottage was built on the island in 1855 by George Ewen a fisherman from Aberdeen, probably using some of the stone from the old chapel. He rented salmon fishing rights on the island, fish being caught with stake nets which were kept in a hut on the island. The thatched cottage was to provide shelter for the fishermen, but after ten years was turned into an inn, The Freemason Arms, known locally as 'The Square and Compass'. During work to extend the cottage human bones were found. These were probably the remains of Russian soldiers who had been isolated on St Mary's Island after developing cholera on a voyage south to fight Napoleon in 1799. Those who eventually died were buried on the island. It is said Ewan kept one of the skeletons in the cellar and would show it to customers for a small sum.

In 1894 a dispute arose between George Ewen and a farmer Joseph Patterson, who let a field on the mainland to the army for use as a rifle range. Ewen claimed that a right of way used by visitors to the inn was blocked and that there would be danger from bullets flying over the island. Patterson accused Ewen of damaging his property and of opening the inn on a Sunday. The following year the Ewen family were evicted, with bailiffs taking all their furniture over the rocks and leaving it on the headland. The family's pig evaded capture for six hours, but was eventually bundled into a cart and taken to the mainland. After spending several winter nights under the shelter of a tarpaulin, the family found lodgings in Whitley Bay, where they received a good deal of sympathy, having made St Mary's a popular place for visitors during their forty year occupation. Eventually Mr Ewen opened a butchers shop, although history doesn't record whether use was made of the pig!

Some of our islands were invaded by foreign forces many years ago. St Mary's Island was attacked more recently. On the 28th October 1973 thirty members of the 'St Mary's Island Liberation Front' stormed over the causeway wearing para-military uniforms and waving 'machine guns'. The keeper was told to 'declare U.D.I or be hanged' and the attackers announced their intentions to 'build a brewery and blast the lighthouse to the moon'. Independence was however short lived. Cold wind and steady rain dampened the 'storm-troopers' spirits and after four hours the 'soldiers', students raising funds for Newcastle Rag, returned to the mainland. The event nearly didn't get off the ground, as the invaders misjudged the tide (or perhaps were tardy in leaving their beds or the college bar), and the last soldiers had to wade across with water up to their thighs, but plenty was raised from the watching crowds.

Despite its small size, St Mary's has a lively history and is a most attractive island. With 80,000 people a year climbing the lighthouse, it is also one of our most visited tidal islands. By now the sun was out so before it disappeared behind more large clouds I returned to the causeway, taking repeats of earlier photos in the better light. Three hours later, after an excellent and remarkably cheap meal at an Italian restaurant in Whitley Bay, I was walking back to the island once more. The sun was setting, casting orange rays on the white lighthouse, presenting a 'photo opportunity'. Unfortunately by the time I reached the causeway the sun had set, but as the light faded I wandered around the rocks, taking pictures of the island and its iconic tower reflected in the pools. I chatted for a while to a lady with an expensive camera, who said she'd been here for three hours waiting to get a particular photo of the lighthouse reflection. Neither my camera or patience matched hers, but with interesting light and the tightly packed buildings, the atmosphere of St Mary's was one of the easier islands to capture.

Next morning I took my customary walk down to the sea for a last look at the island. With the sky blue and the sun bright I would have happily made the walk along the cliffs for a third time, but more mundane matters called. Today I had to leave the islands and return to my real job, with a customer to visit in Middlesbrough and long train ride home. With so few islands on the east coast, this was my final trip to the north, so it was with a little extra sadness that I boarded the Metro and switched my attentions to matters of glue.

# CHAPTER TWENTY

# SKIPPERS ISLAND & HORSEY ISLAND

With few islands on our east coast, my next true tidal islands were as far south as Essex. Three 'nearly tidal' islands however merit mention.

The first, Spurn Point descending 3½ miles from the Yorkshire coast into the Humber estuary, is not an island, but a narrow spit, just 50 yards wide in places. The history, geography and wildlife of this nature reserve could fill a book itself, but I mention it as winter storms occasionally breach the shingle, creating a temporary island. If it were not for the lifeboat station at the far end (the only one permanently manned in Britain), nature may be allowed to take its course. Such is the power of the waves and currents, that the new island created would be unlikely to survive many years before being swallowed by the sea.

The second, Read's Island, just west of the Humber Bridge and visible from the M62, is an RSPB reserve notable for its population of avocets. The island and its surrounding channels are constantly changing. Whilst it used to be possible to walk to it over soft mud and cattle were once led across, it's now permanently surrounded by water. The fast Humber tides are rapidly eroding the island and 40% of its area has been lost in the last ten years. Its saline lagoons no longer hold water, which has resulted in a reduction of the avocet population from 200 to 50 pairs. Fallow deer live on the island, which once had a single cottage.

Sources gave conflicting information about the third, Scolt Head Island on the north Norfolk coast, so a visit was the only way to check. Taking the train to Norwich, then on to Cromer, I picked up a car and drove the 35 miles along the winding coast road to the little village of Burnham Deepdale. Progress had been quicker on the narrow Scottish roads where slow drivers pull over to let you pass. In Norfolk however as soon as one driver turned off from the head of a queue, another took over its duties of keeping the procession at 20 miles an hour. It was like a pursuit cycling race and any minute I expected us to burst into life and race to the sea.

Swan Books managed to get me a copy of the quite rare 1952 National Trust publication *Blakeney Point and Scolt Head Island* (original price three shillings and sixpence) and the excellent *Island of Terns*, by Bob Chestney, the island's warden from 1950 to 1986. He talked about walking to and from the island and mentions an old cart track that was once used by fishermen, although also relates stories of people getting stranded or stuck in mud. An internet guide to the Norfolk coast path suggested crossing at Burnham Overy Staithe harbour, walking the three mile length of the island, and returning to the mainland along the path shown on the OS map at the westerly end. On other websites however I found warnings that it is highly dangerous to try to cross the mud. The lady in a small information centre in the village told me that they certainly don't recommend people to cross – it's necessary to wade, very muddy and only last week two people had been trapped there.

I opted to try the marked path from Burnham Deepdale first, but after a few hundred yards met a barrier of a narrow, muddy creek, with a channel of water perhaps ten yards wide. The depth was hard to judge but must have been at least a couple of feet. How much further one would sink into the mud only trying would tell. As had become my usual practice, I stopped to consider options. Perhaps I could wade, however the area of salt marsh beyond (an unnamed island itself) was not Scolt Head Island. I would have to walk another mile across the marsh, then cross a second channel; this one a few hundred yards wide, part mud and part water. Getting wet and muddy I was prepared for, returning at least an hour later to find the first channel full would have been rather less advisable.

Turning back I drove to Burnham Overy Staithe, at the other end of the island, from where a ferry runs in summer months. Like several Norfolk coastal villages, the harbour is a couple of miles from the sea, protected by barrier marshes, spits or islands. Following the Pedlar's Way (the Norfolk coast path) to Burnham Beach, then climbing onto the grassy dunes of

Gun Hill, I was no more than a couple of hundred yards from Scolt Head, but half of this width was water. Scolt Head Island would fail not only the 'dry feet' test, but probably the entire dry me. People do walk there, but in suitable attire and at some risk. Others swim, the channels being a popular 'wild swimming' location, provided the tides are safe.

Scolt Head Island formed around 1000 years ago, its method of formation probably similar to other islands of this type. Prepare for a geography lesson:-

Originally an offshore shingle bar or ridge, it was pushed landwards by storm waves caused by northerly winds, assisted by east to west longshore drift. During a severe storm the ridge finally arrived in shallow water and when it abated a section remained exposed above normal high tides. This allowed wind and tide borne seeds to germinate, soon establishing an embryo dune system, which in turn stabilised the sands, increasing the height to above even the highest storm tides. As more sand and shingle were carried northwards, the island grew in both length and breadth. Northerly winds curled the western tip towards the south, creating a lateral ridge, a process which has been repeated several times. Between the laterals are bays or 'bights', where the base consists of sand. Mud sediment built up, creating mudflats. As the height of these increased they eventually reached a level where plants could slowly colonise, creating the first stage of salt marsh. Criss-crossed with countless drainage ditches meandering to the main channel, these are a feature of which I was to see many fine examples, both around Scolt Head and on the coast of Essex.

Scolt Head was acquired by the National Trust in 1923 to nurture its ecosystem and population of sea birds. Ownership is now shared with Norfolk Wildlife Trust and the island managed by English Nature. Considerable numbers of birds come here, with internationally important populations of over-wintering geese. The ternery on the western side of the island, which is closed to visitors in the breeding season, can hold up to a quarter of the UK's population of nesting sandwich terns. When Bob Chetsney took over as warden 300 pairs nested here and when he left there were up to 5,000, the increase in numbers a tribute to his hard work and ideas ahead of his time.

Bob's father, who was warden before him, had tried to convince Scolt's management committee of the need to reduce human disturbance, but with the island relying on the generosity of visitors for its financial support, they were reluctant to limit access. People expected to be able walk through the breeding colony and examine the eggs and young on the ground. Bob limited disturbance by meeting each boat and conducting visitors on a tour through a limited nesting area, but keeping them away from the main ternery to which unauthorised access was barred. He tells a story that graphically illustrates the affect of disturbance on nesting birds.

One cold and wet June day three ladies arrived on the ferry, saying that they had come to see the nesting terns. Bob told them that in such weather it was not a good day to visit a colony just as they are hatching young. The ladies were insistent saying that they had come from Norwich and were National Trust members. Bob told them that no bird lover would dream of disturbing birds with very small chicks in such weather, but it made no difference to their attitude. He reluctantly agreed to take them into the ternery, but first made them take off their coats, explaining that as the tern chicks would have no protection from the rain when their parents were disturbed, why should they. Still they were adamant that they should see the nests. As they walked the parent birds rose from the nests leaving the fluffy newly hatched chicks with no shelter. Then they saw older youngsters who had scurried away to hide, but running through wet grass become wet, cold and bedraggled. Bob writes, 'It was heart-rending to see these pathetic little creatures, looking like wet sponges covered in sand, on their backs and kicking their little legs in the air. They were making weak little calls. With great concern the ladies asked why they were in this sorry state'. Bob explained that it was a result of their disturbance in putting the parent birds to flight, as their only protection against the weather is their parents brooding them. As they continued to walk they came across several more chicks that were past the point of no return. By the end the ladies were in tears. As they put their coats on Bob remarked that now they know what a wet tern chick feels like. The next day he went back and witnessed the tragic result of their visit and vowed that such an occurrence would never happen again.

Scolt Head Island could easily fill a chapter of its own, but having decided that it doesn't meet my tidal island definition, it is time to move on. However first I must retell one more of Bob Chestney's stories.

Bob spent long hours on the reserve and armed with binoculars prided himself on knowing everything that happened on the island. Challenged during their annual excursion to Scolt to prove this by a committee member who claimed he had visited a few days earlier without being noticed, Bob responded as follows:

'Now just let me think. Oh yes, it was last Thursday. You walked down the cart road with a friend. You both went to the Hut and tried the door. It was locked. From there you walked to the north beach. Continuing you reached the water's edge and 'tested' the water. You looked around. There was not a person in sight. Thereupon you both undressed and ran into the sea, and frolicked in the water for about ten minutes. You then left the sea, picked up your clothes, walked to the foot of the highest dune and, while the young lady remained, you ran to the top of the high dune – presumably to check who was about. Returning to her you stretched out nude in the sun, then you… shall I go on?'

With the rest of the committee roaring with laughter the suitably embarrassed member conceded that Bob had made his point!

And so to Essex, my home county and a coast I know well. A low lying coastline, with few cliffs but much mud; a mass of inlets and salt marsh, this is ideal tidal island country. With its five estuaries and many creeks, Essex has probably the longest coastline (around 350 miles) of any English county, although Cornwall makes the same claim. What is however certain is that the 30 to 40 islands along its fragmented length is the highest number in England. Only in Scotland is there such a density of islands.

All the Essex islands are close to the shore and many have little water around them at low tide, so defining which qualify as tidal for my purposes was not easy. Canvey Island would once have counted, as low tide access was by stepping stones across the mud, but now two bridges link it to the mainland. Similarly Foulness could once only be reached by the highly dangerous Broomway over Maplin Sands, but is now bridged, as are Two Tree, Potton and Havengore. Ramsey and Bramble Islands have become part of the mainland, whilst the likes of Rushley and Hogmarsh can only be accessed on foot by wading through deep mud. Wallasea Island, an RSPB reserve opposite Burnham-on-Crouch, is cut off only on the very highest of tides, usually just a few times each year, so qualifies as only one of my nearly tidal islands. A little about each of these islands can be read in *Essex Coast Walk*. Six Essex islands appeared to meet my definition; Osea, Northey, Horsey, Skippers, Ray and Mersea. There is an excellent book covering all the county's islands and I would like to thank Ian Yearsley for allowing me to use information from his *Islands of Essex*.

Skippers and Horsey Islands are in Hamford Water, a large basin between Harwich and Walton-on-the-Naze, extending four miles inland and largely filled with islands, tidal creeks, mudflats and salt marsh. It could be described as a riverless estuary, being fed by just three small brooks and is sometimes referred to as 'Walton Backwaters'. The creeks and islands were the setting for Arthur Ransome's *Secret Water*, Skippers Island being Mastadon Island in the book. This quiet and remote area is managed by English Nature and Essex Wildlife Trust. As one of the last remaining areas of its type worldwide, Hamford Water is a hugely important site, and of international importance for its populations of wildfowl and waders that feed here in winter, and of national importance for its resident breeding birds.

## Skippers Island

An Essex Wildlife Trust reserve, Skippers Island can only be visited by arrangement, hence I was put in contact with the warden, Ray Marsh, who has been looking after the island for 51 years. He said that it's no longer safe for people to walk to Skippers without a guide as they have to be shown the safe route, something which I can certainly verify having crossed the mud with him. He also has to inform the farmer through whose yard the private road to the crossing point passes. Ray told me that it was getting too much for him to regularly take visitors out to the island, so had informed the Trust that he'd take occasional parties of twenty. I rang Essex Wildlife and put my name on the list. It was 6 months before a trip was arranged and when the day came I was the only customer.

In order to have time to explore and for Ray to do some work on the island, we arranged to go over by boat and walk back. It took only a couple of minutes to cross the channel and I managed to stay in the *Seastrike* all the way, unlike a lady in her sixties who on one trip fell into the water, then announced that as she was in it may as well have a swim and proceeded to swim around the creek.

First Ray took me into the 'Lodge', a little wooden building on the waterside. To be more precise it is three little buildings joined together, one of which used to be a garage that was floated over the water and is now a bedroom. Ray had already been over early in the morning and lit the wood burning stove to give us some warmth. The Lodge used to be let out by the Trust, but although it was making good money, 'Health & Safety' means that's no longer possible. Ray and his wife often stay the night here though, with their homely little sitting room looking out across the ever changing creek. They even had a couple of tomato plants growing inside the big window. I didn't notice a television, but with a large and varied bird population, seals swimming by and the occasional fox crossing, nature provides live entertainment. As we talked Ray spotted a marsh harrier hovering over the rough grass outside, then right by the window a greater whitethroat, one of a pair that he'd seen around for a few days looking for a nest site. For 13 years they'd often watched the same fox, identified by a damaged tail, waiting opposite the causeway until the tide fell, then later on the island side until the waters dropped again and he could walk home.

The island is now purely a nature reserve, but used to be farmed. Since the last crop of wheat was grown in 1918 what were once arable fields have reverted to salt marsh, rough grass, scrub and woodland. Cattle were kept here until around 1900 when two drowned crossing the causeway. The farmer used to tie a bull behind a cart so the cows would follow, but two got stuck in the mud. More horses were brought from the farm to try to pull them out, but their efforts were to no avail, and the cows drowned. Other than an attempt to keep cattle during World War Two, which had to be abandoned as they had a tendency to wander off into the mud, after that only sheep were grazed. The last flock however all drowned in the Great East Coast Flood of 1953, when the island was under water for three days, and all that could be seen the tops of two elm trees. These are now long gone, victims of Dutch elm disease, although suckers still come up, but seem to succumb too once they reach a reasonable size. Once grazing stopped the scrub grew, hawthorn and blackthorn seeds being spread by the birds.

For many years Skippers Island was owned by Fred Williams, who was concerned that if sold it would be turned into a holiday camp, so arranged that on his death it be leased in perpetuity to what was then Essex Naturalists' Trust. Whilst visitors used to come here regularly, the Trust now mostly discourages access in order to limit disturbance to the birds who choose to nest on islands, as they are quieter than much of the mainland coast. Even school trips came over, but one can imagine today's teachers having heart attacks at the 'risk assessments' required. Ray told me that the causeway is deliberately kept difficult to cross in order to dissuade casual visitors and there are 'No Landing' signs to stop boats. However a while ago he and his wife noticed three oyster catcher eggs in a nest as they left the island, but found it was empty when they returned the next day. Those despicable people, egg collectors, had obviously been over. Ray said he sees hare coursing on the mainland opposite the island, which too is of course illegal. Does it not tell us something about those who gain pleasure from cruelty to wildlife that they think they are above the law?

I left Ray to get on with cutting the grass on the maze of paths that run through the woods, a job that he does to create firebreaks as they've had problems with fires in the past, and set off to explore Skippers Island. The island is in three distinct sections, almost like a trefoil, and totalling 233 acres is larger than it appears from the shore. It used to be possible to walk all around the sea wall, but the sea has breached a section to the east, creating salt marsh and making it hard to reach the further area of woodland. Wave action is continuing to erode the saltings and Ray fears that one day it will all be gone. Not being agricultural land the sea walls, which were originally built by Napoleonic prisoners, are not repaired, unlike nearby Horsey which is maintained as sheep and horses are kept. With perhaps a note of sadness Ray said the island will eventually flood, but until then the 999 year lease will ensure that it remains in the care of the Trust.

With few visitors there are no paths on the wall and walking not easy; a choice between long grass on the wall or muddy areas below it. I walked almost to the breach, looking over the water the short distance to Horsey Island, then back through the woods and to the Lodge where Ray invited me in to eat my lunch. It was still a bit early and with the sun coming out I preferred the opportunity to sit by the sea, with the sound of the birds in my ears and feel of the breeze on my face. I'd hoped to see seals, which often lay on an upturned boat near the island at high tide, although their main colony is on Garnhams Island nearby.

Skipper's Island and Hamford Water support one of Britain's rarest coastal plants, sea hogs fennel, which highlights an excellent example of the interdependence of species and the potential catastrophic effect upon them from climate change. A large and attractive plant, growing up to five feet tall, with feathery leaves and yellow flowers, sea hogs fennel is the exclusive foodplant of the fisher's estuarine moth. This attractive moth, quite large and pale orange-brown in colour, is entirely reliant on the sea hogs fennel, where its caterpillars live, remaining hidden until they emerge in September as adult moths. Virtually the only UK populations are around Hamford Water, and there is concern that rising sea levels will force out the sea hogs fennel, which whilst growing in coastal areas, is not salt water tolerant. To safeguard both the sea hogs fennel and the fisher's estuarine moth, Essex Biodiversity Project are working with Essex Wildlife Trust, encouraging it to grow on higher land, away from the rising sea.

I ate my lunch looking down Hamford Water towards Landermere Quay, which was once a popular location for smugglers. It is said that barges using the quay would drop off their captain on the island with any contraband they may have been smuggling, leaving him to wait out of sight until the vessel had been cleared by customs, after which the captain and illicit goods would be picked up. Hence, so the story goes, the island became known as Skippers Island. A more probable if less romantic explanation is that it was named after the Skipper family who lived in nearby Kirby-le-Soken, or a John Skipper who rented the island in 1758. It has also been called Holmes Island and was marked with both names on a British Army map of 1805, when the area was being surveyed for an anticipated invasion by Napoleon.

After fully exploring the network of grassy paths and the several other wooden buildings on the island, I returned to the Lodge where Ray invited me in once more as we waited for the tide to drop. He'd offered to row me back but understood that I needed to walk for book purposes. We talked more of wildlife, Ray telling me that smaller birds like bullfinch, yellowhammer and skylark are far less common now, he thinks due to predation from the barn owls, sparrow hawks, marsh harriers and long-eared owls who all live here. A pair of cormorants dived repeatedly into the water by the still covered causeway and we agreed it was unusual to see two together.

There are no badgers on the island, but as well as occasional visiting foxes, the mammal population includes some muntjac deer which appeared in mysterious circumstances. A gentleman with a keen interest in deer asked the Trust if he could release some on the island, but they said no due to the damage they cause to young trees. Soon after however Ray started seeing muntjac, a creature never before known to live on the island. Was it just coincidence that some swam or walked over just after someone had asked to introduce them?

On the opposite bank is a small concrete building which was used to store diesel in World War Two. When enemy aircraft were approaching burners were lit along the sea wall as decoys, hoping that bombs would be dropped harmlessly here rather than on towns, particularly the port of Harwich which was a prime target. Ray said that the Home Guard used Skippers Island to practise, but unlike much of the Essex coast there don't appear to be any relics of defences on the island.

With the water falling rapidly more mud was appearing. This wasn't the type I'd walked over to other islands, but soft and glutinous – the sort that looked ready to gobble up a man. Ray told me that not long ago someone living by Hamford Water had gone out to his boat and got stuck waist deep in the mud. Unable to extricate himself he shouted for help, but his wife hearing the noise simply commented that they hadn't moved to such a quiet spot to hear people shouting. Only when he called her name did she realise that it was her husband in trouble. With the tide rising a helicopter pulled the very relieved man from the mud, but had his wife not eventually responded to the shouts he would have surely drowned.

By the crossing point is what looked like an old raft. This is actually two Bailey bridges which had been used in the war for crossing the Rhine. Linked together with boards placed on top and an outboard motor attached, they were used to bring a tractor over to the island. Even people were carried this way, with groups of 20 to 30 visitors standing on the boards under strict instructions to keep still, however with today's more exacting safety standards the raft hasn't moved for 30 years.

After considerable delay caused by a padlock problem, about which I shall spare Ray's embarrassment by saying no more, we walked down to the waters edge. By now a veteran of tidal islands, I'd walked across causeways, sand, mud, rocks and even climbed down cliffs, but had experienced nothing like the Skipper's Island crossing. Once a farm track, it's now a mix of short lengths of wobbly stepping stones, mud and wooden walkways, then bits of salt marsh linked by a couple of narrow plank bridges over narrow muddy channels. Ray had said I must wear wellingtons and although there was no water to cross, I was to find that they were indeed essential.

A good sense of balance is necessary if one wishes to avoid the mud. I asked Ray how deep it was, and to the left he said just to ankles, but to the right, waist deep. Halfway across the stepping stones disappeared, but Ray assured me they were still there under the mud. 'Follow my footsteps' he said, and watching intently as he felt for each stone I placed my boot into the rapidly filling prints behind him. Knowing that one false step on the slippery and moving stones could mean ending up waist deep in mud does tend to concentrate the mind. A small boat part way across gave us hand holds for a couple of yards, then we moved to another section where the stones whilst still slippery, at least weren't hidden several inches below the brown ooze. The sign by the shore saying 'No Path' isn't just to put off potential visitors. I have read and given many warnings on my travels, but anyone attempting to walk to Skippers Island without expert guidance would be foolhardy in the extreme.

## Horsey Island

Horsey Island is privately owned and unauthorised visitors are not permitted. I'd been told that it's owned by a Joe Backhouse who keeps sheep and horses there, but several people had suggested that he didn't take kindly to visitors. Unable however to make prior contact with Mr Backhouse, I caught the train to Kirby Cross and walked the mile to the sea through Kirby-le-Soken, then another to the causeway, hoping that any welcome would be friendly. On a warm but slightly misty early autumn day, I'd eaten my lunch sitting on the sea wall close to Kirby Quay, a notorious smugglers haunt and one of my favourite places on the Essex coast. With the tide down and Hamford Water an expanse of mud, bird life abounded. A group of ten greylag geese stood not far away on the mud, watching me uneasily for some time before eventually deciding that human company wasn't appreciated and flying off into the distance.

By the start of the two thirds of a mile long Island Road causeway to

Horsey Island is a concrete World War Two pillbox and small wooden jetty. A car was parked by the lane but there was no sign of its owners. There was no 'Private' sign so off I went on the 'road' through the mud to Horsey Island – a route that is generally passable two hours either side of low tide, but highly dangerous to the ill-informed or foolhardy traveller.

Other than the mud covered route to Skippers Island, the causeway was probably in the worst condition of any I walked. Although the base was mostly firm underfoot, much of it was covered with pot holes, puddles and pools, often across the full width and ten or twenty yards long. Off the causeway the mud was too soft to walk – I quickly found that a detour around the pools was far from safe. Although poles mark the track in parts, attempting to cross in dark or mist and losing the narrow causeway could easily be fatal. Wellies would have kept my feet dry, but walking boots were quickly swamped. This was the only causeway I shared with shoals of little fishes. Part way across I looked up and saw a lady walking quickly towards me. The moment of truth was approaching. Her purposeful stride suggested I was about to be turned back.

Mrs Backhouse was charming. How interesting she thought my book was and yes I could walk round the island. What was my name? She'd phone her husband to let him know I was coming, but had to hurry to collect their car from the end of the causeway. Joe Backhouse met me on his quad bike. His greeting – 'No one with the initial P is allowed on the island'. A smile and shake of the hand confirmed that yes I could stay. He suggested that I walked round the sea wall which is more interesting than the house. Joe told me that his parents had moved to Horsey in the 1930s and he'd been brought up on the island. His response to my question about access was however very clear – 'It's private'.

Horsey Island is by some way the largest island in Hamford Water and has been linked to the mainland by a causeway since at least the late 18th century. The most obvious and likely derivation of its name is because it was used as an enclosure for horses, although it has been suggested that 'horse' may have been a corruption of 'Norse' and that it was used as a base for Viking attacks on Essex.

To readers of Arthur Ransome's *Secret Water* Horsey is 'Swallow Island', the causeway 'The Red Sea' and the landing area at Kirby-le-Soken 'Witch's

Quay'. Ransome spent a lot of time around the Backwaters and it's thought that his inspiration for *Secret Water* came from a meeting with the Busk family who were camping on Horsey in September 1938. The story revolves around a group of children who were set the task of exploring and mapping the low-lying islands, mudflats and creeks, and of course got into the usual adventures and scrapes. The Busks were also engaged in map-making and Ransome even inserted their yacht *Lapwing* into the fictional story. Interestingly comparison of modern charts with those made in the 1930s show many changes to the Backwaters, but that the landscape on the 1930s maps is very similar to that in *Secret Water*.

The island has been used for grazing for centuries and sheep and horses are still kept on the 300 acre working livestock farm. It is however for racehorse breeding that Horsey is probably best known. Horsey Island Stud was established in 1935 by Nancy and Jasper Backhouse and bred top class Pure Bred Arabians. Their three children who were brought up on the island all followed their parents' trade, Mary marrying Angus Bancroft and setting up Water Farm Arabians near Ipswich, Hannah marrying Robert Skepper and starting Heritage Coast Stud at Woodbridge and Joseph taking over the mantle of Horsey Island Stud.

The short, sheep cropped grass on the sea walls made for easy walking as I headed anti-clockwise around the island. To the right was Hedge-end Island. This was once part of Horsey but became separated during the 'Black Monday Floods' in November 1897, which affected other islands in the Backwaters transforming them from grazing land to marsh. Horsey was flooded again in the 'Great Tide' of 1953, however unlike much of the east coast, the walls did not give in but were overtopped.

At the north of the island is a shingle beach, from where I could see across to the cranes of Harwich and Felixstowe Docks. Although looking quite natural the beach is man-made. Horsey Island is one of a number of experimental sites on the Essex coast where sediment dredged from Harwich Harbour has been deposited in an attempt to reverse salt marsh erosion. In 1998 20,000 cubic metres of mud was sprayed from a dredger on a spring tide, with sunken barges (15 if I counted correctly) placed to reduce wave attack and allow the tide to disperse the sediment. After 9 months considerable salt marsh growth had occurred, and the process was repeated in 2001, raising the height in order to encourage further plant growth. The experiment appears to have been successful, but ongoing monitoring is required. Horsey Island provides protection against wave action for much of Hamford Water and if it were to further erode away the whole nature of these fragile backwaters could be changed.

The island is part of Hamford Water National Nature Reserve, a designated SSSI and RAMSAR internationally important wetland area for birds. Many species over-winter here and in spring huge numbers of lapwing, avocets, redshanks and oyster catchers arrive to claim their nesting sites.

With the sun breaking through it had become quite a hot afternoon, so I changed into the shorts I'd brought for such an eventuality. Perhaps I should have made the change before crossing the causeway, but I hung my very muddy jeans over the back of my rucksack. One advantage of tidal island walking is that most are remote with few people to see one's strange attire.

Joe had told me that it was a fair walk round the island, which is about 1½ miles from end to end but has the typical Essex irregular coastline, and having completed the longer half I decided to head back across the middle to the causeway. Not wishing to disturb the Backhouses, I found a way through the fields to the track that runs to the collection of buildings in the island's centre. All that I disturbed was a peacock who seemed as surprised to see me as I was him.

Back at the causeway I sat on the jetty to eat a cake I'd bought in Kirby Cross and reflect on Horsey Island, an island I felt honoured to be able to visit. Although casual visitors are not permitted, Mrs Backhouse had told me that they had recently started letting out the island's 19th century cottage. Available through Holiday Lettings, but not in the bird breeding season, this is true 'get away from it all' accommodation. Much of the Essex coast is remote, but even with the tide low Horsey Island, in the middle of Hamford Water, had a real cut off feel. When a true island, it must seem even more isolated, but the ideal place for those seeking peace, birds, or perhaps a family adventure.

Across the mud I saw Mrs Backhouse return and drive very slowly over the causeway, weaving around the deepest holes and giving me a cheery wave as she passed the jetty. Letting information for the cottage describes the crossing as 'very bumpy', but suitable for all but the smallest cars. I think however that I'd take up their offer to drive people over. A friend of ours who lived in Kirby Cross told me that years ago the Backhouses used to have a combined boat / road vehicle, similar to that I'd seen at St Michael's Mount. It was apparently quite an event when they drove it into Frinton to visit the bank.

With low tide now past, for my return journey the water had fallen a little and the puddles were not quite so large. The little fishes had moved off the causeway and small shoals swam in pools alongside. Nevertheless with jeans removed this time it was my legs that splattered with mud as I negotiated the crossing. It was a strange feeling walking alone on this narrow track across the huge expanse of mud, watched just by the many birds for whom the mudflats provide a rich larder.

Back on the mainland I continued on what becomes Island Lane, then followed the main road into Walton-on-the-Naze, a typical Essex seaside town. Lively in the summer, it was very quiet on an autumn afternoon as I sat by the pier eating fish and chips, looking out across a flat and still slightly misty North Sea. No one seemed to notice a rather muddy walker climb the hill to the station with mud covered trousers trailing behind him.

# CHAPTER TWENTY ONE

# MERSEA ISLAND

Nine miles from Colchester, sitting between the mouths of the rivers Colne and Blackwater, Mersea is the seventh largest English island. It is the UK's most easterly inhabited island and its population exceeds by a long way the total of all our 42 other tidal islands. Mersea however only just qualifies, its causeway, the Strood, being impassable for only around an hour on larger tides. Local tables show that for just over half of tides the Strood is expected to be covered, for a quarter it may be covered depending on weather and currents, and for the remaining one in five it remains dry. There has been talk of having it raised, but this would be expensive and although some locals would be pleased to do away with its inconvenience, most of the older residents value their island status.

With a mile walk to Upminster station, three trains and a bus, it took me three hours to get to the causeway. A journey not helped by the Victorians running the railway a couple of miles from Colchester and Mersea buses departing from the centre, requiring a wait for the shuttle train to Colchester Town. The island has a good service though, running every half hour, an improvement on that 100 years ago when Berry's open top 'Motor Bus' made the journey three times each day.

Preferring to arrive on foot I alighted at the Peldon Rose, a 15th century coaching inn half a mile inland. Walking down the hill, the obligatory warning sign, 'Danger When Water Covers Footway', was far milder for than many of our tidal islands. The Strood is not usually covered to a great depth and the risks less than approaching the likes of Cramond, Sully or Holy Islands, however care is still necessary.

The tide was almost at its lowest and just the famous Essex mud could be seen in Strood Channel as I crossed the half mile causeway. With a regular succession of cars passing in both directions, this was so different to the other islands I'd visited. I was used to quiet and often solitude so an island with cars, shops and almost 7,000 people was quite a contrast. However, as I was to find, most of Mersea is rural, with its own beauty and quietness, and the commercial waterfront area has much character and interest.

The Strood is the country's only remaining Anglo Saxon causeway, analysis of timbers exposed during excavations for a new pipeline in 1978 dating it at around AD 700. The Romans had also built a causeway when they lived on the island, but it's not known if this was on the same site. A Roman soldier, visible only from the waist up, is said to haunt the Strood and occasionally be seen marching across to the mainland. Now a fenced road (the B1025), vehicles drive over seemingly oblivious that they are crossing the sea. There are even yellow lines, with signs indicating no parking in summer months, but it didn't seem quite right that cars could park here at all, and with no warnings that the sea covers the road, the uninitiated driver could return to an unpleasant surprise.

Immediately after the causeway the road splits, the left fork to East Mersea, the quiet and mostly agricultural end of the island, and the right to West Mersea, where all but around 250 of its population live. As I was to find, to modify that famous football cliché, it's an island of two halves. The size of the island meant it would be difficult to fully explore on foot in a day, especially in November with dark coming not much after 4.00. Hence I'd decided that today would be spent at the western end and I'd come back another time to walk the island's perimeter, a walk I'd been told was well worthwhile.

Soon after the fork I took the path which leaves to the right, running on the sea wall alongside salt marsh. Like much of the Essex coast Mersea has important bird populations, particularly waders. A little egret stood close to the path and a couple of shelduck pottered about on the mud. A little further on a flock of brent geese took off from a field, flew around me noisily, landing again once I'd passed. I always feel guilty for disturbing birds but they never seem to listen when I tell them I mean no harm.

The sea wall path was quite muddy and walking not easy, particularly as I was wearing trainers, my walking boots having rubbed a blister due to careless wearing of a sock with a large hole in the heel. I slid and slipped towards West Mersea town, several times almost falling into the mud and was fortunate that when I did topple from the wall it was down a grassy bank and I was able to remain upright. Having survived all those rocky islands around the country it would have been a shame to have had to call out the helicopter to pull me out of the mud so close to home.

After a couple of miles I passed my first Essex caravan site before arriving at West Mersea's working waterfront, where commercial fishing and recreational yachting exist side by side. A hundred years ago 200 fishing smacks were based here, but as with so many ports, the island's fishing fleet has steadily declined, however Mersea's most famous industry, oyster farming, still thrives.

It was the Romans who first cultivated oysters here, initially harvesting them from the wild and apparently declaring that they were 'the only good thing to come out of Britain'. They found that the warm summer sea temperatures and abundance of nourishment from the surrounding marshes, combined with beds of shell, made an ideal place for the oysters to fatten. In the 10th century hundreds of men and boys were involved in the oyster farming industry and the 'West Mersea Native' oyster is still sold to restaurants throughout the UK and abroad. It is said that if you eat an oyster in London it's more than likely to have come from Mersea. Families have been involved in the industry for generations. The Hawards have been growing oysters in the shallow creeks leading from the River Blackwater to the west of Mersea Island since 1792 when William Haward sailed to Billingsgate to deliver his crop, and have nurtured the same stretch of Salcott Creek for the last 100 years. Sadly, apart from those which are sold on the island or eaten at their own seafood bar, The Company Shed, they now leave Mersea by road.

The oyster fishery is officially opened each year on the first Friday of September, when the Mayor of Colchester, the Town Clerk, and the Town Sergeant, in their full civic regalia, are taken on an oyster dredger into Pyefleet Channel. A flotilla of small boats carrying invited guests follows and oaths are sworn, pledging devotion to the monarch. The Mayor dredges and consumes the first oyster of the season, then proceeds with his guests to an oyster lunch. Personally I can't think of much worse to eat than a raw mollusc, so should Mr. or Mrs. Mayor be thinking of inviting me, any chance of cod & chips?

The oyster fisheries were badly damaged in the very cold winter of 1963, when the creeks froze and literally millions were killed. New stock had to be introduced to prevent the industry from folding, but the shortage of oysters led to high prices and it was a long time before the trade recovered. The oyster beds had also been devastated in the floods of 1953, huge numbers being suffocated by silt and mud when the water eventually receded.

Being higher than other Essex islands and much of the mainland coastline, Mersea was less affected by the floods than other more low-lying areas. However many houseboats and yachts broke from their moorings, the yacht *Ruddy Drake,* being blown all the way to Holland. With the Strood covered to a depth of seven feet and the water extending half a mile inland to the Peldon Rose, for some time it was a 'real' island. Some houses were under three feet of water and 20 people forced to leave their homes, but there was no loss of life and most of the agricultural land was unaffected. It is fortunate that operation of the aptly named 'King Canute' flood rescue plan was not essential, as the official holding the keys to the filing cabinets holding the plans lived off the island and was unable to reach it to activate them!

Whilst Mersea is an increasingly popular visitor destination, it's far from a traditional holiday resort. The waterfront is a working one, with boatyards, sail makers, yacht clubs, fishing boats and of course the oyster sheds, but not one amusement arcade or bucket and spade shop. The island has extensive beaches, which as I was to find, are very different depending on the state of the tide. The view from the west of Mersea is typical Essex coast. Close by are two small islands, Cobmarsh Island and Packing Shed Island, the latter named after the shed which is thought to date from the 1870s for packing and storing oysters. Beyond these is the head of Old Hall Marshes peninsula, an important RSPB reserve and one of the most remote areas of coast in England.

There are plenty of pubs, cafes and restaurants along the waterfront, but I headed into the town for lunch at the Art Café. I have to confess that my choice wasn't made purely on culinary grounds, but because the Art Café sells local books and I hoped to persuade them to stock *Essex Coast Walk.* I am pleased to report double success; an excellent bacon baguette and agreement to give the book a try.

Opposite the café is the attractive parish church of St. Peter and St. Paul, my next port of call. The Kingdom of the East Saxons was evangelised by St. Cedd, who built the historic church of St. Peter on the Wall near Bradwell, having been invited to Essex to spread the Christian faith by King Sigbert. With lower sea levels it was once possible to cross the Blackwater estuary on horseback and it's thought probable that Cedd and his monks established the first church on Mersea, dedicating it to St Peter. In the 11th century, under the rule of King Edward the Confessor, a small Benedictine Priory was established on the island and it is likely that the current church's tower dates from that time. The nave and chancel were probably built in the 14th century and the south chapel in the 15th. Various additions and replacements have been made in the last 100 years. The most recent of these, a simple but attractive memorial window commemorating the 'Fisherman and Oystermen of Mersea Island' was installed in 2005. After so many islands where Christianity was confined to their history, it was good to find that on Mersea as of course on Lindisfarne, the church is still an active part of community life.

Much has been written of the island's history and space allows me to include only the most important buildings and stories. Should you wish to read more detail I can recommend Elsie M. Karbacz's *A Short History of Mersea*, to which I am grateful for some of the information in this chapter.

The island has its own museum, but this opens only in the summer, so after a quick wander round the town (or village as some prefer to call it), I returned to the sea, walking a mile or so along the beach to the end of the built up area. With the tide down this was typical Essex beach; sand, shingle and shells at the top, a couple of hundred yards of mud, then calm sea beyond. Walking just above the mud and so far from the water, it was strange to see a sign warning boat users of bathers, but in summer this is a popular beach and many visitors enjoy a swim when the tide is high. At the top of the beach is a long line of beach huts, mostly newly painted and all in tasteful pastel colours. Beach huts generally resemble garden sheds, but with their little balustrades these reminded me of large dolls houses.

Four miles away across the Blackwater estuary (or 44 miles by road) is the slightly mysterious hulk of the now decommissioned Bradwell Nuclear Power Station and south of this Sales Point, which with its shell beaches is one of my favourites Essex spots. For many years views of the Blackwater, the largest estuary between the Thames and the Wash, were dominated by laid-up shipping. The river was full in the 1930s as the world recession reduced trade and after the war damaged or life-expired vessels gathered here, awaiting decisions about their future. Some stayed for a few weeks, others for years. Locals still remember the *Samlong*, the ship with a hole in its side from action off Juno Beach in the Normandy Landings, and the *Helena Modjeska* which was salvaged from The Goodwin Sands and kept in the river with her two halves alongside each other. The last vessel to be laid-up here was the former Radio Caroline ship, *Ross Revenge* in 1995. The ships provided employment for locals as on most there was just a watchman left onboard. Much of the work taking off crews, turning over engines and bringing supplies was carried out by Clarke & Carter of West Mersea. There was occasional excitement, the *Port Melbourne* catching fire in the 1930s, the *Protokllitos* having an engine fire in 1983, the *Michalakis* running aground opposite the Esplanade on West Mersea and the river freezing in the winter of 1962/3, when helicopters had to be used to reach the ships.

Turning left where a long sewage pipe runs across the beach, I followed a lane inland, passing more of the ubiquitous Essex caravan. This led to Dawes Lane, a typical rural Essex road, running in a straight line between flat fields, with no fences or hedges to interrupt the views. Just before Smith's Hall a footpath crossed the road, but I was glad not to have come this way, the signpost to the left pointing straight across a ploughed field and the sign to the right indicating that one should walk over a newly sown cornfield. Neither way was there any semblance of a path, the farmer having failed in his duty to maintain it, something that happens all too often and is part of the reason why I like to walk on coasts or National Parks where ploughing is less likely.

Beyond the cornfield was the next landmark on my tour, the island's best known Roman relic, West Mersea Barrow. This Romano-British barrow is believed to date from around AD 100. Originally 60 foot high and 300 feet in diameter, but now considerably smaller and covered with trees, this is still an impressive mound. Excavation in 1912 found a small burial chamber built of Roman bricks and containing a lead casket about two feet square. Inside this was a green glass urn holding the cremated remains of an adult. A Roman burial and British mound are an unusual combination and many stories have been suggested in explanation. Perhaps the most romantic is that the remains were those of the daughter of a Roman leader who fell in love with a British nobleman and on her death was buried according to local custom. The more likely explanation however is that it was erected in honour of a local chieftain, or other important or wealthy person. The casket and urn can be seen in Colchester Museum.

The barrow is on private land and surrounded by an iron fence, although it can be visited on occasional open days. A locked gate stops anyone approaching the entrance to the passage that was dug out when the barrow was excavated, however I managed to get a quick look by walking into the derelict farm next door. A padlocked metal gate bars entry to the tomb, but I was at least able to take a few photos of the entrance.

Being close to the Roman garrison and once capital city of Colchester (or Camulodunum as it was then known), Mersea was well used by the Romans. It's thought that the island was a retirement retreat for veteran legion officers and traces of their villas and mosaic pavements have been found here.

Another relic from these times is the 'Wheel Tomb' in West Mersea, a small hexagonal room connected to a larger encircling wall by six other walls, and from above resembling a spoked wheel. The structure is made of tile on foundations of mortar and ragstone, but with no sign of a doorway or floor. It has been suggested that it is not in fact a tomb, but the remains of a Roman lighthouse, a theory supported by its location being close to Pharos Lane, Pharos being Greek for lighthouse. Identification as a tomb is however generally accepted based on parallels with similar examples in Italy and Germany, and we can be fairly sure that this was a family mausoleum, which would have contained memorial busts and cremated remains preserved in decorated urns. It's likely that the tomb's owners lived in a villa that was excavated nearby and found to contain several splendid mosaic floors, one of which still lies under the churchyard.

From the barrow it was just a short walk back to the causeway, completing my circuit of West Mersea. The sun was falling over Strood Channel, its light shining into the few patches of water on a sea of the mud, providing an atmospheric end to an enjoyable day on one of the unique Essex islands.

It was the middle of May when I returned to walk around the island. I'd waited until spring weather and more importantly for the muddy paths to dry out, which made for a most enjoyable walk around the 13½ mile Mersea perimeter. Starting in the town with an excellent late breakfast in the Art Café, I chose to go anti-clockwise so I'd be walking by the North Sea at high tide.

Although the island's south coast has few permanent buildings after the town of West Mersea, caravans and chalets are plentiful, and the quiet sea shore very different when the summer visitors arrive. Today however most were empty, although there was some life at the Youth Camp where green tents stood in a neat line and half a dozen youngsters played a half-hearted game of football. A sign pointed inland to Mersea Island Vineyard where 10 acres of vines produce 20,000 bottles of wine a year. The business opened in 1985, but according to local legend the Romans were first to grow grapes on the islands gently sloping south facing fields.

A mile or so east is the 12th century partly moated St Edmund King and Martyr Church, which perhaps I should have visited, but with quite a long walk today had decided to stick to the coast. The church's most famous rector was Reverend Sabine Baring-Gould, best known for writing the hymns *Onward Christian Soldiers* and *Now the Day is Over*. Amongst his remarkable 1,200 publications was the novel *Mehalah – a story of the salt marsh,* an evocative tale of love and anguish, set around Mersea and published in 1880.

According to Saxon Chronicles, Vikings wintered on Mersea and it's thought that the area around the church was the camp of Hasten, a chieftain who led raids across England, battling with Saxons led by Alfred the Great.

After a large caravan park (the population of East Mersea increases considerably during summer months) the map shows the footpath splitting with the choice to head inland or along the beach. However only the former was signposted and with the tide high the latter would have required swimming. With the Strood covered only for a short time today my access to and from the island hadn't been affected by tides, which was fortunate as they create havoc with the bus timetable. Instead the sea had conspired to make my walk longer. A succession of large signs directed the walker around Fen Farm and its caravan park. Either they didn't want walkers accidentally entering their property or were being particularly helpful.

Following a lane I entered Cudmore Grove Country Park, an area rich in bird, wild flower and insect life, which covers the south east corner of the island. Here are the only cliffs on Mersea and some of the few in Essex. In the Pleistocene deposits left by the Thames which used to flow past here, have been found bones of bears, wolves, monkeys and straight tusked elephants who lived here 300,000 years ago.

Between the wars Cudmore Grove was part of an eighteen hole golf course, but it became a wartime defence site and never re-opened. The several concrete bunkers are reminders that Mersea was not always so peaceful and that it lost 19 men in World War Two. The 50 men who died in the First World War represented 5% of the island's male population, but at only marginally above the national average, illustrates the scale of the country's loss.

Although only cut off for short periods, in many ways Mersea mirrors more isolated communities. The island was once said to be known for 'idiocy, incest and venereal disease', possibly a consequence of many poor families living in small houses. Brothers and sisters often had to share beds and sometimes babies resulted. Some say that Mersea was saved by new blood coming to the island in World War Two when 2,000 troops were stationed here.

The island became a restricted area in 1940, with beaches mined and the army requisitioning a large part of the esplanade where a coastal battery was set up. At East Mersea a 'Q' site decoy was constructed from wood and canvas to confuse enemy bombers into believing it was Brightlingsea where there was a shipyard building small naval craft. In late 1942 No. 1 Motor Boat Training Company was formed on the island to train recruits in the art of seamanship and patrol inshore waters in a variety of requisitioned craft. The company remained on Mersea until just prior to D-Day, when it left for the Isle of Wight and thence the invasion beaches. Also in preparation for the Normandy Landings, in conditions of great secrecy, part of the famous Mulberry Harbour was assembled at East Mersea. The first bombs fell on the island in June 1940 and considerable damage was caused by a raid in November that year, but the island escaped most of the ravages of the Blitz.

With RAF Bradwell Bay just across the water, aircraft regularly flew over Mersea and on one occasion a Mosquito developed engine trouble crossing the estuary. The plane struck trees and burst into flames at the back of The Fox public house, the impact detaching one of the engines which hit a cottage and came to rest against the living room wall. A Mrs Hoy who lived next door went out to investigate and found one of the aircraft's fuel tanks in her garden, her baby's pram burning and the weatherboard on her cottage alight. Despite the risk of explosion she fought the fire until the fire brigade arrived, but apparently she and her husband were rather put out at receiving only £30 compensation from the RAF.

At the easterly tip of Mersea a short spit protrudes into the Colne estuary. With the tide high it was almost cut off but I crossed the few yards of dry shingle to explore, finding a lovely shell beach. On the opposite banks of the Colne are the village of Point Clear, which anyone who has read *Essex Coast Walk* will know wasn't my favourite place, and Brightlingsea, an attractive small port and yachting centre and scene of major demonstrations against live animal exports in the 1990s.

After the spit the path turns sharp left, following the Colne for a mile or so. I stopped for a rest, sitting by a little channel where the summer ferry from Brightlingsea lands, the distant rumble of guns from Fingringhoe Ranges failing to spoil a peaceful scene. Soon the Colne was behind me as I started along Pyefleet Channel, the grassy sea wall making ideal walking. Indeed it was perfect for walking; sun shining but neither too hot or cold, enough wind to be cooling but not trouble my hat, soft grass underfoot and none of the mud I'd splashed through on my first visit to Mersea. Having often been caught out by the first sunny walk of the spring I'd applied sun cream, although according to a writer in the 1907 '*Building Trade Journal*' maybe on Mersea this isn't necessary. He '*was struck by the freshness of the complexions of the women – not browned and sunburnt – but fresh and bonny – a mute testimony to the ozonic qualities of the air*'.

The sheds of Colchester Oyster Fishery were the last buildings for some miles, as the path took me past rapidly draining marshes, then alongside the channel. I scanned the water for the seals that can often be seen here, but like my visits to Skippers and Horsey Islands, none were around today. To my left the large green fields of the well drained Reeveshall Marsh were home to cows, sheep and birds, but no people were to be seen. I'd often been the sole human on an island, but here on the north bank of Mersea it seemed that despite its 7,000 inhabitants, the island was just mine.

A mile or so from the Strood a sign indicated that the sea wall had been breached, but that there was permissive access along the edge of the fields provided by the farmer as part of the 'Higher Level Stewardship Scheme', which aims to create new habitats for small mammals, invertebrates and birds. By the road another sign advised:

**PRIVATE MARSH – KEEP OUT**
**SAMPHIRE PICKERS WILL BE PROSECUTED**

Marsh samphire is one of our last uncultivated foods, but gathering it is a tricky business. Firstly it grows on inaccessible marshes, with the best plants said to be those covered on every tide, and secondly you need a permit. As the sign suggests, anyone caught collecting it without a permit is liable to a fine, although apparently throughout East Anglia many pickers regard the rules as an infringement of their traditional shore rights and flout them. The plant, which was once used for making soda based glass (hence its other name, glasswort), is said to be a delicacy resembling asparagus and is often served with fish.

Crossing the main road, I retraced my November steps on the now dry sea wall along Strood Channel opposite Ray Island, coming out once more by the fishing boats and yachts of West Mersea's working waterfront. Just before heading back into the town, I found St Peter's Well, which for a thousand years was the main source of fresh water on the island and 'never known to run dry'. It was reconstructed true to the original as a millennium project.

I had greatly enjoyed my walk around Mersea, probably as much as any section of the Essex coast. Indeed the island's shoreline could easily be described as a microcosm of the whole of the county's coastline, with its mud and salt marshes, birds and flowers, yachts and fishing boats, caravans, beaches and of course sea. A delightful walk and a beautiful island.

# CHAPTER TWENTY TWO

# RAY ISLAND

One of the lesser known Essex islands, Ray Island can be reached by a path from the mainland end of the Strood causeway to Mersea. It is however unlike most of my other tidal islands, in that there's no expanse of sand or mud, no causeway or rocks to cross, but instead a path over salt marsh that floods on higher tides. The island is owned by the National Trust, but jointly managed with Essex Wildlife Trust, whose warden David Nichols kindly offered to accompany me. Living on nearby Mersea, and having been warden for 30 years, David probably knows more than anyone about Ray Island, or The Ray as many locals call it (the O.S. map gives both names). He keeps a small herd of rare breed soay sheep on the island and comes out here several times a week to check on them.

Again I alighted from the bus at The Peldon Rose, but this time went inside, looking for a quick lunch. Expecting to find just a handful of customers, I was rather surprised to find the place packed with diners. More restaurant than pub, and more smoked salmon than bacon sandwich, it is no longer a traditional Essex hostelry and has moved a long way from its coaching inn origins. Nevertheless I was not too disappointed at having to order a full lunch. My scampi and chips was excellent, if not the cheapest.

We'd arranged to meet at 2.00 by the end of the Strood and David arrived just as I was changing into wellies. He'd told me that access to the island was not difficult, but probably muddy, which indeed it was. The path is covered on every tide, with a depth of 4 – 5 feet on spring tides, giving Ray Island its tidal status. It crosses several single plank wooden bridges without hand rails, which David warned can be slippery when wet.

He told me that the majority of visitors arrive by boat, most often from

Mersea or Bradwell across the Blackwater, and had offered to take me over by water. However of course I chose to walk on the mile long path over the marshes. Once a drovers' track, this crosses Bonner's Saltings, an area of salt marsh owned by a wildfowlers club. Shooting is not permitted on Ray Island but David said that it has been allowed through the official club on Bonner's Saltings, partly to control poaching and partly to allow the traditional local custom of the ordinary working man bagging a couple of ducks for the pot. He said this has little effect on bird numbers, although I'm not sure the ducks would see things in quite the same way.

Neither a public footpath nor permissive track, land access to Ray Island depends on the goodwill of the wildfowlers. Other than the warden the agreement officially allows only authorised Essex Wildlife Trust members to cross the land for research and recording purposes from March to August inclusive, and some intending visitors have been turned back. Anyone wishing to visit would be best advised to contact the Trust.

A sign warns that the path floods at high tide, but there are no dire warnings. David said that there used to be a DANGER sign, but it was removed as its presence implied that it wasn't safe to walk to the island, hence the Trust could have been sued if anyone came to harm. What a ridiculous situation. The path winds its way across the saltings, with views to Mersea Island. Several wooden bridges cross muddy channels, the largest two of which were constructed by British Telecom executives on a team building weekend. The track was once wide enough to take a horse and cart, or to drive sheep, some hundred of which were kept on the island during World War Two and in summer had to be taken to a pond the other side of the road for water. There was once a wide gate on one of the bridges, but one owner narrowed the pathway to restrict access.

Seeing footprints in the mud David was concerned that youngsters may have been onto the island, as there have been problems with people causing damage, lighting fires or scaring the sheep, although this usually occurs in the summer. The sort of people who fail to treat an island with the respect it deserves aren't generally the sort to go walking across muddy salt marsh on cold winter days. Plus he thinks the troublemakers generally arrive by boat. In any case we found nothing of concern.

A final bridge separates Bonner's Saltings from Ray Island and is marked by a National Trust sign. Soon we were on slightly higher land, with salt marsh giving way to rough grass, then scrub; first blackthorn then well established hawthorn with little grassy glades. The blackthorn has grown up in the last 80 years but the grasslands are unimproved, looking the same now as they would have done when Saxons or Romans came here. The many humps are the long established ant hills of the yellow meadow ant. The most skilled nest builder of the 50 species of British ants, these little chaps can dig more than a metre underground, but other than for mating flights are rarely seen on the surface.

David didn't know if we'd see the sheep, as although they are always pleased to see him, they don't like strangers. The herd numbered just six, some having recently been moved to Thorndon Country Park near Brentwood, to help control vegetation in the woods. As David scattered brussel sprout peelings and stale bread on the grass the soays started to appear; first the rams, then the more cautious ewes, deciding that lunch of recycled greens was worth the risk of venturing close to a strange man with rucksack. Personally I'd have been more wary of the sprouts. Originating from the St Kilda group of islands, soay are as close as we have to wild sheep. The secluded and quiet Ray seems to suit them and they breed well here, some of the herd having been born on the island and others acquired from various sources. They have a fenced enclosure, but it's usually left open on one side, the gap only being covered when the sheep have to be injected or tagged. For the rest of the time they are free to roam anywhere on the island and although they could walk off along the path, they don't seem to want to leave their isolated little home.

David had carried a small plastic drum to the island, which was to be a feeder for pheasants. He'd made a small hole at the bottom for the birds to peck grain and hung it from a branch to try to stop the sheep stealing it. The last feeder they'd managed to knock over and eat the contents. With the cold winter the island's female pheasants weren't in the best condition, so wouldn't breed well, and David hoped that a bit of supplementary wheat would help. The moorhens could use it too, and the sheep and rabbits would find any remnants of grain on the ground.

Close to the northern shore is a small fresh water pond, which for most of the year provides water for the soays and wildlife. Today it was almost full, but in summer it dries to mud and David sometimes has to carry water out for the sheep. It's not an easy task to lug heavy containers over a mile of marsh. The pond is man-made, but its age and origin are unknown. At its side is the skeleton of a weeping willow tree, which had been planted here many years ago, but was drinking a great deal of the pond's water. As a non-native species David got permission to ring bark the tree, killing it in order to preserve the water. Not far from the pond is a water-filled hollow, which may once have been the island's well.

Another hollow close to the pond is a World War Two bomb crater. The island was used for wartime bombing practice by the RAF and the crater is generally thought to originate from this. However, David knows a man on Mersea who recalls seeing a German plane dropping bombs which may have been aimed at Mersea's water tower, but one of which landed on Ray Island. With a metal detector David has found many bomb fragments, but whether they were friendly British or nasty German ones, we don't know. The Americans also practiced bombing here, dummy shells being dropped around a target on the saltings to the north west of the island. Wooden stakes marking the target area still protrude from the marsh.

On the northern shore of the island, bordering Ray Channel, is what David calls the picnic area; a grassy shoreline with a shingle beach where visitors moor their boats in summer. For at least 150 years The Ray has been popular as a picnicking place for locals and boating people, and on a summer's day there are sometimes over 100 visitors on the island. In winter however only a few hardy souls venture over the marshes and on many days the sheep see no human visitors. Part of the bank is eroding badly but there is little that can be done to stop it. Like so many of our tidal islands Ray is constantly changing, but rising sea levels will accelerate change. First the marshes will flood leaving just the central area, but rising to only a few feet above the highest tides, this too would soon erode away.

Ray Island is an alluvial deposit; a sandy cap left on top of clay after the Ice Age. From the Strood the mound of the central scrub area stands out above the marsh and appears to be the extent of the island. In fact it is almost ¾ mile long but only about 100 yards wide, with a long marshy peninsula extending to the west. As we walked along the shore a huge flock of brent geese took off from the mudflats and with more further down the channel there must have been well over a thousand around the island. Like me,

David felt a little guilty disturbing them, with each flight using vital energy as they try to build reserves for their long migration to Siberia.

As we walked across the salt marsh a bird flew up just yards ahead of us. David immediately identified it as a jack snipe, telling me it was quite a rare spot. Smaller than snipe and with a shorter bill, these secretive birds tend to crouch down when approached, relying on excellent camouflage and only flying off at the last moment. They usually fly low, quickly dropping again. This one did exactly that, its flight more like the flutter of a moth, making it easy to identify. Jack snipe over-winter in the UK, living on wetlands where they eat insects, worms and snails. I was pleased to have seen an interesting bird and to be able add it to the relatively short list of those I can easily recognise.

Ray Island is an SSSI, with large numbers of wildfowl and waders over-wintering. Redshank, oystercatcher and shelduck breed here, and all the common finches can be seen throughout the year, but especially winter when large flocks feed on the seed heads of sea aster. Birds of prey, including short-eared and long-eared owls, barn owls, merlin and hen harrier are commonly seen. Golden samphire, lax-flowered sea lavender and sea rush add colour to the salt marsh, and much of the higher marsh is covered with sea purslane.

It's not easy to walk to the tip of the island and we stopped at a point which David pointed out showed one of the rare features of Ray; the natural transition from sea to mud, to salt marsh, to higher salt marsh, to rough grass, to scrub and to wood. Half of all of this type of feature found in Essex is on Ray Island, where unlike most of the county's coast, there is no sea wall. The landscape is however constantly changing, with areas that were once grass slowly reverting to salt marsh.

Whilst management is now mainly limited to conservation and access, as David showed me, there is much evidence of man's use of the island from at least Saxon times to World War Two. With its proximity to Mersea and being close to Colchester, the Romans would almost certainly have visited the island, although there seems to be no evidence of habitation. Norsemen over-wintered on Mersea and it is quite possible that they came to Ray too. The National Trust commissioned an archaeological survey and David brought archaeologists out here, but found that as is their way, they look interested, say little and never give a firm opinion. What appears at first to be a double sea wall across the western end of the island may well have been a Viking defence earthwork, protecting Ray from Saxons who could have attacked across what is now Bonner's Saltings, but was then probably grassland. David has found bricks and pottery shards on the island, which he's had dated to $14^{th} - 16^{th}$ centuries, but their origin is not known.

Several ditches run across the island, one through the pond, showing that they were dug before this was made. Other ditches and cuts run along the southern side, and although most have become filled in, walking along them we could feel the softer ground underfoot where they had silted up. Some of the ditches were probably related to agriculture, as the area beyond the central mound was once arable land. The ridge and furrows of the old field system can still be seen, but as the land level dropped (southern England is slowly sinking) the area reverted to salt marsh. I was to see similar patterns on Northey Island further round the Essex coast, but there agricultural land was lost when the sea walls breached. David thinks that livestock may have been kept at one end of the island and crops grown at the other. Stakes running part way across Ray Channel, which he had carbon dated to mid $17^{th}$ century, could have been fencing to keep the animals from venturing into the crops area.

Archaeologists say that some of the ditches are relatively recent, having too sharp a profile to be 'of an age'. They may have been dug by the army, but no one seems to know, Ray's ditches being another little island mystery. Also unexplained is a small pond or crater on the opposite side of the island to the main pond. This was full of water but dries in summer. It has been suggested that it is another bomb crater, but as one edge is straight, this seems unlikely.

As we walked David spotted something on the grass and handed it to me as a souvenir of Ray Island – a fox's skull. I said I'd give it to my youngest son, although wasn't sure if his reaction would be yuk or wow. It was in fact both, his initial disgust tempered when he realised it would make an interesting exhibit for 'Show and Tell'. The next day he returned from school saying the teacher had said yuk, but the other children had crowded round to see the skull, complete with fox's teeth. It now resides by his bed under the name of 'Dead Fred', next to a bird's skull I found on Piel Island ('Dead Barry').

Like Mersea, the island is associated with Baring Gould, Mahula and her mother living here in his Victorian melodrama. He writes about a house on the island, although there was none at that time, or no evidence of anyone having lived here since Viking times, and even their presence is a mixture of conjecture and legend.

The island has close links to Mersea and David told me he'd read in the Essex Records Office that in the late 17th century it was part of a marriage settlement between the daughter of a Reverend Andrew from Fyfield and a John Loy of Coggleshall. Ray Island was then part of the estate of Bocking Hall on Mersea and was rented to a John Sengar for the annual sum of 21 shillings.

The Ray was the National Trust's first purchase on the Essex coast. It was bought in 1970 partly due to its association with Baring Gould, but mainly to protect it from possible development. The previous owner, a businessman from Colchester, had said he wanted to run it as a nature reserve, but then announced that he would need somewhere for the warden to live. When he applied for permission to build two bungalows locals smelt the proverbial rat, and feared his 'nature reserve' was really a plan for development. The National Trust stepped in, buying the island for £20,000 and giving the previous owner a tidy profit on the £1,800 he'd paid five years earlier.

As the island hasn't been inhabited in modern times, with no residents to trace I found the second best thing – a next door neighbour. Gerald Grimes was brought up at Strood Villa towards the end of World War Two, but now lives in Frome, Somerset. He told me how it was a very different place then, with only one other house on Strood Road and very little passing traffic. He had a small dinghy and sailed Strood and Pyefleet channels. To his family Ray Island was like something out of Swallows and Amazons and they often camped out on the island. It was a great place to be then but he hasn't been back as he hates the development of the area with speed boats etc. Perhaps he should come back to visit on a winter's day with just the island's birds and soays for company.

Like much of the Essex coast, Ray Island has its tales of ghosts, the most famous being the Roman soldier who walks across the Strood visible only from the waist upwards. Gerald never did see him, but said that sea frets made people's legs vanish at a distance, which probably explained why only the top half of the Centurion can be seen. He thought that other ghost stories might be explained by overhead power lines which arced with a blue light on misty nights. On one occasion however he did see a real ghost on the Pyefleet Marshes, but chose not to enlighten me with what was a 'long story' – or did he mean 'tall'? David told me a story about a group of children who many years ago went blackberry picking on the island. They separated, each going their own way, and while they were picking one girl suddenly heard horse's hooves as if the animals were charging across the island. In fright she ran to the beach, to find all the other children doing the same. They had all heard the running hooves, yet there were no horses on the island. Horses were grazed here before World War Two – were these their ghosts that the children heard?

As we walked back across Bonner's Saltings David told me how the tide moves over the marsh very quickly, and a little boat in a channel can suddenly find itself in the sea, with land seeming a long way off. Whilst the approach to other tidal islands changes dramatically with the incoming sea, they are usually separated from land by sand or mud, whereas here we were walking over an area shown on the map as marsh, but definitely land not sea. The map suggests that Bonner's Saltings is also an island, but as it regularly floods the marsh cannot count as either a true or tidal island. The bridges that cross the channels would have disqualified Ray from my tidal island criteria if they were not regularly covered by sea, but The Ray is cut off often enough to qualify as a tidal. Thanks to David I had not only seen its beauty, but gained an insight into the history, wildlife and mysteries of this unique island.

# CHAPTER TWENTY THREE

# OSEA ISLAND

In my youth I was ejected from West Ham football ground, escorted from a golf course, thrown out of numerous lessons and our family once even asked to leave a bed & breakfast (the owner didn't like my young brother complaining about the food). Today I could add to the list – I was told to leave an island. Hence my visit to the beautiful but most mysterious Osea Island, was shorter than planned.

The day had started so well, three trains and two buses taking me to the village of Goldhanger on the Blackwater estuary. All bang on time and the rural buses friendly as ever, with their helpful drivers and scattering of almost exclusively retired passengers (only I was of working and indeed fare paying age). Headingham Omnibus's number 91 picked me up in Kelvedon for a pleasant ride through rural Essex, passing Tiptree's famous jam museum (apparently marginally more interesting than it sounds), then dropped me in the village of Toleshant D'Arcy. I'd asked for the Red Lion, as indicated on the timetable, but the driver told me that it hadn't been called this for some years and was now an Indian restaurant. He showed me exactly where to catch the 95, which arrived as promised in precisely 25 minutes, calling at Goldhanger on its way to Maldon.

Goldhanger is an attractive village with an 11th century church. I can recommend the Chequers pub where my wife and I had enjoyed an excellent lunch earlier in the year, but with a tide to catch today there was no time to stop. From the village centre it's a short walk down Fish Street and along a footpath to the sea. I say sea, but with the tide low Goldhanger Creek was just Essex mud. However the weatherman had been correct and early morning mist was just giving way to sunshine, as I set out on the 2½ mile sea wall walk to the Osea causeway.

The winding mile long man-made causeway dates back to Roman times. I had been unable to find consistent information on for how long it is passable, sources varying from an hour a day to three hours each side of low tide. The commonest seem to say 2 hours either side of the tide, but the fast tides and length of walk dictated caution. Hence I planned to arrive 2 hours before low tide so as to judge the likely safe crossing period. As I approached a van was driving to the island, looking quite out of place seemingly on a sea of mud and splashing through occasional patches of water. Whether these were just puddles or meant I'd be getting wet feet it wasn't possible to tell. Deciding that the sign prohibiting unauthorised vehicles from crossing didn't mean walkers were barred, I set off to the island. The causeway was hard, made-up although not tarmaced, and its many pot holes and puddles would give a bumpy ride, but caused no problems to the pedestrian. Other than a short length of water close to the island, there was just mud either side, which as I found when stepping aside to let the returning van pass, was very soft. The sign had warned drivers not to leave the causeway in order to pass other vehicles (there are passing places), advice which if ignored could have disastrous consequences

So I arrived on Osea with dry, if slightly muddy feet. To the right of the road an English Nature sign instructed:

*Please help protect this area. Follow the Countryside Code and in particular stay on the beach and avoid salt marshes and sea walls which are fragile habitats thus protecting plants and wildlife. Please take away all your litter.*

A wooden sign below it said PRIVATE, but its position suggested this may refer to only the immediate area on the right. With conflicting instructions, I continued to give myself the benefit of the doubt and set out along the road which runs on the northern side of the island. After a while a grassy track on the left led to a landing point which appeared to be well maintained so I guessed was still used, although now there was just mud and salt marsh around it. Further down the estuary was the grey hulk of Bradwell nuclear power station, a landmark from much of the Essex coast.

The lane turned right, heading across the island. A rabbit popped out of the hedge, took a quick look at me and scampered away into a field, but there was no sign of any people. Soon the road opened out into 'the village', a handful of houses, but again deserted. Passing a long driveway saying 'Captain's House' I continued along the road, not knowing where it would take me. On the left two donkeys in a field ran to greet me and on the right pheasants screeched as they watched me pass, but still there were no humans. A sign indicated that as the road curved right it led only to the Manor House, but hoping it would take me to the southern shore of the island I carried on. Approaching the house a chicken ran out to say hello, but still no people. This was an eerie place.

On reaching the Manor House a view of the sea opened up and beyond on the far bank of the Blackwater, the waterfronts of Maylandsea and St Lawrence. Bearing left I walked down to the beach and what a lovely spot this was. A colourful shingle beach above blue sea and in the distance a Thames sailing barge ambling by with its characteristic rusty red sails. Bright sunshine and truly not a cloud in the sky. An old ruined wooden pier on the pebbles, added interest but without detracting from the scene. Behind was the beautiful Manor House with its neatly cut lawns and attractive pond.

I wandered around on the beach for a while enjoying the beauty and sunshine, then heard a lady call. So Osea isn't the Marie Celeste island, it does have people. 'Can I help you?' she asked, to which I replied 'No I think I'm OK thanks'. She seemed somewhat displeased to see me and even if my response wasn't quite as expected, she soon persisted. This is a private island I was told. What am I doing here? Expressing surprise that it was private, I explained about the book and that I was visiting all the tidal islands around the UK. I mentioned *Essex Coast Walk*, but whilst this usually elicits interest, there was none here. Instead she got on her phone, calling 'Nigel' who she said was in charge of the company who owned the island. Hearing only one side of the conversation I'm not sure what he said, but maybe there was some confusion as she told him I was writing about 'tidal waves'. Next she phoned Mark, the Estate Manager, arranging to take me up the road to him. It wasn't quite arm behind your back stuff, but it was very clear I wasn't wanted here.

As we walked I tried to make conversation, hoping to get some information on the island – and they do say you should try to bond with your captors. Anyway she was having nothing of it. Did she live on the island? – 'I spend a lot of time here'. Did she work on the island? – 'I spend a lot of time here'. She wouldn't tell me if anyone lived in the Manor House, what it was used for, or if there were permanent residents on the island. It wasn't for her to say.

Mark the Estate Officer was however quite charming. Getting into his Land Rover I expected to be driven off the island as the lady had implied, possibly after a few hours interrogation in a windowless cell. However we stopped at the office, where with no sign of any thumb screws he copied the contact details for Nigel Frieda, chairman of Matrix Studio Complex, the island's owners. He told me that the company had bought Osea from English Nature about five years ago. Checking I was OK to walk back, he bade me farewell and off I went, a free man. With the sun still shining I stopped by the causeway to eat my lunch sitting on the beach. A car drove slowly towards the island, a man driving and the passenger a young lady of Asian appearance with a headscarf. A few minutes later it left the island, without the passenger. As I wandered around looking for an Osea shell to bring back for my wife, the lady from the Manor House drove by, this time her passenger a young man also of Asian appearance. Were these comings and goings related to the secret of the Manor House? The lady looked surprised and none too pleased to see me. Winding down the window she said she thought that Mark was going to drive me off the island. I explained that I'd been happy to walk and after waiting a short while simply to make the point that I wasn't going to jump to her instructions, set off over the causeway, leaving this secret island behind.

Back on the mainland I turned left, heading up river towards Maldon, rather than back to Goldhanger, where buses are few and far between. Whilst still very pleasant, the walk this way is less enjoyable than around the creeks from Goldhanger, the path being paved and Essex caravans lining the shore. From here things started to go wrong again. I'd mislaid my map of this section of coast, so was relying on some pages printed off the internet, however found that I'd managed to forget the sheet that covered Maldon. Hence I wasn't quite sure of the quickest route, knowing from my Essex Coast Walk that it's further than it looks. Near Heybridge Basin I went inland, thinking it would cut off a corner and on finding a bus stop with a bus due soon, decided to wait for a ride into town. Fifty minutes later I was still waiting. It was freezing cold, almost dark and I had no idea if the bus would arrive. I didn't fancy walking on the coast path in the dark and didn't know the way by road, but just as I started to phone the customer service number on the stop, a bus appeared. Not the 73 to Maldon that I'd been waiting for, but the return service towards Chelmsford. The driver told me that the outward service hadn't come because 'the driver got lost!' This one however was calling at Hatfield Peverel where I knew I could catch a train.

There's only one train an hour and I'd no idea when it ran, but seeing two people hurrying down the road towards the station, I too made good pace and on arriving saw it was due in one minute. Stepping onto the platform I saw train lights just down the track. My luck was changing – or so I thought. Then I realised the train was stationary. A waiting passenger announced that he worked for Marconi and with this insider information knew the signals often failed, so this was the cause. I didn't like to tell him that the signal was at the other end of the platform, not by the train. As the twenty or so passengers waited in the cold I walked to the end of the platform. From here I could see that the lights were not of the London train, but of a freight train, with its diesel engine ticking over quietly. A note on the booking office door advised that there were no staff 'Due to illness', so we all waited for the inevitable computerised announcement. 'We apologise for...' The freight train had broken down and we should walk over the bridge to the opposite platform. Over we went and just as the last passenger had carried his bike across the steps, with a roar the diesel engine burst into life and trundled through the station, pulling its long line of container wagons. By now we'd past the tutting stage and passengers were looking at each other ready to smile as the inevitable announcement came – '... proceed to platform one...' Once more across the bridge we all went, resuming our positions on the original platform, in the way of British travellers taking in their stride disrupted journeys and instructions from a remote computer. The recorded announcer was now in full spate, updating us every 60 seconds to add a further minute to the expected length of the delay, as a succession of non-stop trains passed through. Eventually ours arrived, but with a now missed connection in Romford, buses and trains had conspired to make it a three hour journey home from Maldon. It had been a frustrating but nevertheless enjoyable, interesting and intriguing day.

Arriving home I wrote three letters:

Dear First Buses – Please tell me why I had to wait for 50 minutes in the cold for a bus.

Dear English Nature – Please tell me why you sold Osea Island.
Dear Mr Frieda – Please tell me the secret of Osea Island.

Shane Mills, Senior Customer Service Agent for First Group replied promptly, thanking me very much indeed for my letter, saying that he was really concerned to hear about my unsatisfactory experience, and into what was clearly a standard, and mostly irrelevant letter inserted the paragraph: *'I'm really sorry to hear that the driver of this service had got lost – this must have been both extremely frustrating and also very inconvenient indeed. The particular driver concerned has been identified with the assistance of your feedback and appropriate action taken with a view to preventing any recurrence of this nature'*. What Mr Mills probably meant to say was – *Thank you for complaining – people like you keep me in a job. I shall not spare you the usual platitudes and excuses. The driver concerned has been given a kick up the arse, and a map.*

Natural England, the new name for English Nature also replied promptly, Conservation Adviser Carol Reid telling me that Osea had never been owned or leased by English Nature, but that the foreshore and grassland at the eastern and western ends of the island lie within the Blackwater Estuary SSSI, are part of the Special Protection Area for Wild Birds (under the EC Birds Directive) and a wetland of international importance under the Ramsar convention. It seemed rather odd as the Estate Manager had told me that English Nature had sold Osea and Ian Yearsley's book (1999 edition) stated that they owned two thirds of the island. I contacted Ian and his recollection was that the then residents of the Manor House had told him it that most of the island was owned by English Nature.

Seeking clarification of recent ownership I emailed Maldon Tourist Information Centre, where Kathy Brewster was most helpful. She found a press article by local historian Robert Long, which said that for some time Osea had been owned by a local eccentric, the improbably named Major Allnutt. He sold the island in 1969 to the Cole family, from whom Cambridge University purchased it in 1980. Kathy told me that it is now owned once more by the Cole family, although this conflicted with the information I'd been given from the Estate Manager that the owner was Matrix Studio Complex. Osea is certainly an island of mystery.

Further research confirmed that David and Hilary Cole had put Osea on the market in 2000, because they wished to retire without the effort required to run the island. The asking price was £6 million and there were rumours locally that David and Victoria Beckham were interested in buying it. David Cole said that the island had been in his family for almost 30 years, his father having purchased it in 1966, sold it in 1979 and bought it back again in 1986. Digging deeper I found that Nigel Frieda had bought Osea in 2004, for the sum of £5.4 million (the Coles apparently paid £70,000 in the 1960s). This date correlated with the information I was given on the island, but whether there was another owner between 2000 and 2004, and why some say it was English Nature, I haven't been able to ascertain.

Mr Frieda didn't reply. I left it a month then wrote again asking some more specific questions about access to the island and saying I'd like to give him the opportunity to answer them. Again he chose not to reply.

However I soon found the secret of Osea Island – it is home to The Causeway Retreat, a 'Drug and alcohol addiction treatment rehab and detox clinic'. This is however no ordinary clinic, but one dedicated to helping those who demand and are able to pay for an extremely high standard of care and accommodation. It serves the rich and famous – arguably perhaps those who are least deserving of such help.

Anonymity is obviously very important to The Causeway and whilst one would not expect them to divulge names of clients (or guests as they prefer to call them), a number of press articles claim that some well known celebrities have been treated here. Amy Winehouse was said to have come to Osea after collapsing following an overdose of drink and drugs, although apparently declined to stay long, and locals say that Kate Moss also came to Osea for treatment. At an alleged cost of £60,000 for a six week stay in the Manor House (or a mere £30,000 in one of the village homes, some of which date back to the 16th century), The Causeway has apparently provided rehabilitation for fallen members of some of the country's aristocratic families.

Nicholas Knatchbull, the great grandson of Lord Mountbatten, godson of Prince Charles and a friend of Prince William at Eton, was said to have been sent here by his parents Lord and Lady Brabourne after becoming addicted to ketamine (a horse tranquiliser) and MDMA (the key ingredient of ecstasy). Count Gottfried von Bismarck, the great great grandson of Germany's Iron Chancellor and who in 1986 was widely blamed for the death of Olivia Channon, daughter of Mrs Thatcher's cabinet minister Paul Channon, was reported to have spent 6 weeks on the island. An alcoholic and heavy cocaine user, The Causeway failed to save von Bismarck, who in July 2007, shortly after his reported stay, was found dead after overdosing on heroin.

Somewhat up market from your standard NHS clinic, The Causeway Retreat advertises helicopter transfers to the island, a 20 minute flight from London. Facilities for 'guests' include personal training, gym, sauna, cinema, library, 200 year old billiard table, swimming pool, croquet and even a recording studio. Those staying in the Manor House have king or queen sized four-poster beds with bedding from the likes of Harrods, Jasper Conran and Ralph Lauren.

It's not however only those with addictions who attend The Causeway. A broad range of psychiatric disorders and mental health issues such as stress, clinical depression and 'executive burnout' are also treated here. Most of the last of these are apparently female and from the world of investment banking and law, with the effect of the recession leading to a 60% increase in the number of such corporate executives enrolling. I wonder what they could do for the hard working owner of a not very profitable glue factory?

I may not have the qualifications of The Causeway's therapists, but I shall nevertheless pass on my advice to stressed business people for no charge whatsoever; simply take some time to walk on Britain's coast. Walk the coast path, visit some islands, forget about work and if you are so inclined, write a book or two. Actually perhaps I should be charging £30,000 for my advice as it seems half way to meeting The Causeway's stated philosophy:

*'We believe that any person suffering from problems affecting their mental health will stand the best chance of sustained recovery if they receive excellent and innovative medical care and attention combined with a tranquil, beautiful and natural environment and the best in complementary care and nutrition'*

What the company doesn't say is that such opportunities are available for the very few and at the expense of denying access for the rest of us to a tranquil, beautiful and natural environment – Osea Island. I had asked Mr Frieda if he considered this to be appropriate, or if he had considered opening the island on at least a few days each year, but clearly he didn't feel it appropriate to reply.

The Causeway Retreat was not the first such enterprise on Osea. In 1903, around 100 years before Mr Frieda's clinic opened, the island was purchased to be used for another remarkable institution, a 'Home for Inebriates'. This was founded by Frederick Charrington of the famous brewing family, after he witnessed a drunken man punch his wife because she asked him for money to provide food for their children. Some accounts add to the tale that as the drunken husband slammed the bar door, Frederick saw above it the sign 'Charrington Ales', and recoiled in horror. So shocked was he at witnessing the effect of the family's products that Charrington sold his brewery shares, spending much of the £1 million proceeds on encouraging people to give up alcohol. He selected Osea, as a secluded and self contained island, with no public house, for his 'House for gentlemen suffering from the baneful and insidious effects of alcohol'.

Initially the idea worked well, with those who we might now refer to less colourfully as alcoholics, unable to feed their craving. However local boat owners soon saw the hardened drinkers as an easy opportunity for profit. Liquor was smuggled onto the island, bottles being hidden beneath bushes or tied to buoys under cover of darkness, and boats hired out to enable the 'inmates' to row across to the inns of Maldon. There were tales of men stealing boats to cross to the mainland at night, where they would get hopelessly drunk, before attempting to row back, some missing the island in the dark and never being seen again. Charrington did his best to try to keep his charges' minds off the demon drink, even setting up a small zoo, with emus, kangaroos, cockatoos and seals. Unfortunately and probably inevitably, the drinkers' lack of desire to abstain meant that the scheme was doomed to failure.

The Manor House, opposite which I had been challenged, was originally built by Charrington for his temperance colony and the pond in front of it had once housed his seals. Whether he would approve of its current use one can only speculate. He had plans to develop the island into a popular seaside resort, of course with stringent restrictions preventing the sale of any intoxicating drink, it being his belief that temperance was necessary to health. However with the onset of the First World War the island was taken over by the Admiralty and appropriately for Osea, used as a secret base.

Designated HMS Osea, the island was used for the construction and testing of motor torpedo boats. These were designed by Sir John Thorneycroft, who had raced high speed launches at Monaco in 1913, and wrote to the Admiralty proposing a design for boats up to 55 feet in length, to carry two torpedoes which would be launched over the stern whilst travelling at 30 knots. The fast boats were able to skim over some obstacles and move rapidly on their targets, fire torpedoes, then retire before being detected. They were developed too late to see much active service in the war, but were employed successfully in Russia in 1919, destroying warships in a raid on Kronstadt harbour, an operation that earned two officers the Victoria Cross. While the boats were being built around 1,000 Naval personnel lived on Osea, with several large workshops, factory buildings and accommodation blocks having been constructed. The pier was extended and a railway built on the island, rails from which it is said can still be seen on the beach. Unfortunately my exploration having been cut short, I was unable to confirm this.

Osea's less recent history was not so remarkable and it appears to lack the legends or religious activity connected with so many of our tidal islands. It has however been inhabited for 5,000 years, with evidence found of Neolithic villages. The island was occupied by the Romans, who built the causeway and used it as a major pottery production centre. There have been many archaeological finds and a number of 'red hills' show that they made salt here, a practice which is still carried out in nearby Maldon. It is recorded in the Domesday Book as having a well stocked fishery and enough pasture for 60 sheep. Agriculture has always been Osea's main activity and it's still used for sheep farming. Through the Middle Ages the island was owned by various noble families, including the Earl of Essex, although it seems that they went about their business quietly, unusually amongst the islands, Osea having its most interesting period in relatively recent history.

By the 18th century Osea Island had become well known for wildfowling, with people travelling some distance for the 'pleasure' of shooting birds. In his 1727 *Tour Through the Whole Island of Great Britain* Daniel Defoe wrote that Osea was well known to Londoners 'for the infinite number of wildfowl – duck, mallard, teal and widgeon', but warned that gentlemen 'often return with an Essex ague (fever) on their backs, which they find a heavier load than the fowls they have shot'. He was referring to marsh fever, an illness once common amongst those living on or visiting the marshes of Essex and Kent, and which we now know to be malaria, spread by the many mosquitoes living on the coastal wetlands.

After the Second World War a scheme was put forward to turn Osea into a holiday camp. Commercial development had boosted the economies of Canvey and Mersea and it was thought that a camp with chalets, beach huts, a dance hall, cinema and shops could do the same for Osea. There was however local opposition, James Wentworth Day the East Anglian writer and short time 1950s television 'personality' (he was dropped from the BBC after stating that all homosexuals should be hanged), speaking out in Osea's defence. It appears however that it was lack of funds rather than Wentworth Day's words – 'You might as well put a holiday camp on Holy Island or start a funfair on Runnymede', that meant the ambitious project was never started.

Osea continued to be used for agriculture, Cambridge University carrying out experimental farming and breeding of rare sheep, but life on the island continued little changed until opening of The Causeway Retreat. Like most islands, it had always been privately owned with access varying according to the owner's wishes. Now it is private, in both usages of the word – ownership and visitors not welcome.

What a shame that enjoyment of this beautiful, historic, but mysterious island is now restricted to a few wealthy clients in need of treatment for problems that some would say are largely brought on by their lifestyle. Should not such a beautiful island be for all rather than just those who have had the best opportunities in life but chosen to scorn them?

## Post Script:

In November 2010 the company that ran The Causeway Retreat was prosecuted by Care Quality Commission for carrying on an unregistered service in breach of Section 11 of the Care Standards Act 2000. The company was fined £8,000, plus £30,000 costs and The Causeway Retreat closed down. Describing the company as 'this atrocious organisation' District Judge Cooper said that they had been 'scandalously negligent, if not downright misleading and fraudulent' adding that its standards would 'shame a Third World country'.

From 2011 the island's manor house and cottages are available to let as part of the new 'Osea Island Resort' (www.oseaisland.co.uk). The sporting and outdoor activities that previously were available only to those paying a fortune to receive what we now know were 'dubious' treatments, can now be enjoyed at reasonable prices. The island remains private with access not permitted to casual visitors, but at least those wishing to enjoy its wildlife, beauty and tranquillity can stay for a holiday or short break.

# CHAPTER TWENTY FOUR

# **NORTHEY ISLAND**

Today it was back to the Blackwater and my final Essex island. Close to Osea Island and a mile's walk from the town of Maldon, Northey Island is somewhat more welcoming than its larger neighbour. Owned by the National Trust, visitors require a permit, but a simple phone call to the warden 24 hours in advance is all that's needed to arrange a visit. So on a cold February morning I set out once more for the Essex coast.

It was an easy journey from Upminster. Train to Chelmsford, where there are excellent interchange facilities for the bus to Maldon, an attractive town with old streets, inns and towers clustered on the hill, and a picturesque quay on the Blackwater. My first port of call was the Tourist Information Centre to deliver copies of *Essex Coast Walk* and seek literature on Northey Island (they had none). Next it was to a baker's to buy lunch, then a walk down the hill to Hythe Quay from where Thames Barges once carried cargoes to London and now take tourists on trips around the Essex estuaries. A kiosk by the quay tempted me with chips, which I enjoyed with my cheese roll, sitting on a very cold stone sea wall looking out across the muddy river. Plenty of gulls stood on the mud, but unusually didn't seem to notice my chips, and a few smaller birds which I think were knot or sanderling, wandered around by the water's edge. When a gust of wind blew my plastic fork off the wall I joined the birds for a minute, climbing down onto the mud to retrieve it.

It was a pleasant walk along the promenade, which for a winter's day was quite busy, although I seemed to be the only person who was not either over retirement age, or accompanied by a pram. Once on the rather muddy sea wall I was however alone, walking alongside typical Essex salt marsh. Northey Island causeway is marked by two tall yellow posts indicating underground cables, but looked very different to the day I'd walked by on my Essex Coast Walk. Then the tide was high and Northey a remote island, but today the short causeway cut across a sea of mud. Like Osea, it's thought that the original causeway was built by the Romans, and the current road, lined with seaweed covered rocks, is hard and potholed, but easy walking. As I crossed, the busy Maldon High Street seemed miles away, the only sound a cacophony of 'cronking' calls from a huge flock of brent geese on the mudflats.

A lane runs along the east side of the island, ending at Northey House and Cottage, the latter home to wardens Martin and Bo Palmer. I'd arranged to call to show my National Trust card (non members have to pay £2.00) and pick up a leaflet (£1.50) which describes the trail round the island. It's a most unusual house, however I couldn't find the front door. What looked as if it was once the main door had no knocker or bell, and walking further round the house I suddenly realised that I was being watched by half a dozen faces eating lunch inside. For a moment, with my experience on Osea a few weeks earlier, I felt like an impostor, but then Martin appeared. And what a contrast. A most friendly welcome and interesting chat with him and Bo, who enthused about the island's beauty and birds. The couple had been here eight years and as Bo said 'Wonderful job, isn't it'. They told me that there are more birds in winter and Bo thought the flock of brent geese, which had now moved to one of the island's meadows, must be a thousand strong.

I wanted to clarify visiting arrangements and Martin said that people can come any day, provided they call the day before so he can check the tide times, as for two hours either side of high tide the causeway is covered by up to 2 metres of fast flowing water. The phone number is on the National Trust website and although this says that access is also dependent on weather, over-wintering wildfowl and ground nesting birds, Martin said that these don't normally prevent visiting. Every two years, usually in September, there's an open day and last year 1,200 people came over in 5 hours. He agreed with me that there wouldn't have been many birds hanging around that day. I was far happier to be the sole visitor and armed with my leaflet, set out to follow the trail around Northey Island.

The island is made up of two distinct areas. Around 80 acres to the south (causeway end) is typical Essex flat green meadows, grazed by cattle in summer and a high tide retreat for waders and wildfowl in winter. This however covers not much more than a quarter of the island's area, the rest being salt marsh, interspersed with little channels and which is covered by the highest spring tides. The trail follows the inner sea wall which divides the two areas. The outer wall which once protected the whole island has been breached in many places, but a length can still be walked opposite Southey Creek. What is now marsh with rare and beautiful plants, was once agricultural land. The straight lines of the old ridges and furrows can still be seen, but it is over a hundred years since the land was last farmed. Serious flooding occurred in 1708 and in the 'Black Monday' floods of 1897 the defences were breached in a number of places, sea water lying on the island for over a year.

We have to go back over a thousand years to Northey's main claim to fame – its role in the Battle of Maldon, an event which arguably might have changed the whole course of British history.

At the end of the tenth century England was ruled by King Aethelred 2nd, now more commonly known as Ethelred the Unready, from the Saxon 'unraed' meaning 'ill advised' or 'no counsel'. His reign coincided with a period of regular raiding parties from Scandinavia, the ravaging and pillaging Vikings. Ethelred had no military or diplomatic answer to the raids, so simply raised a tax called Danegeld to pay them off.

In August 991 a large body of raiders appeared on the English coast and having successfully plundered Ipswich, made their way to the Blackwater estuary and the important strategic settlement of Maldon. Rather than land on defended territory or risk the narrow channel to Maldon, the Vikings camped on Northey Island, with the town in their sights. A defending force was quickly gathered, led by Earl Bryhtnoth, a large and charismatic man who although in his sixties, was a strong and skilful fighter, greatly respected by his fellow soldiers.

While the tide was high the Vikings shouted across the water demands for gold and silver in exchange for leaving, but Bryhtnoth refused. With the Saxons lined up at the end of the causeway and the Vikings entrenched on the island, the two sides continued to trade insults. Then as the waters fell the raiders began to stream out along the causeway, but the narrow strip was easily held. With the causeway defended and the thick mud either side impassable to a heavily armed warrior, the English held a virtually unassailable position. No doubt realising this, the Viking leaders made the rather cheeky request to be allowed to cross unhindered, in order that a fair fight could ensue on the mainland. In one of the less inspired military decisions of our history, but in keeping with a very British sense of fair play, Bryhtnoth agreed to their request.

With surrender not an option so far from home, the Vikings were ferocious fighters and a fearsome battle took place. The invading forces were considerably the larger and despite heroic efforts by the English, the battle was lost when Bryhtnoth himself was killed and many of his men took flight. The Vikings however had suffered heavy losses and rather than continue further inland, they returned to their ships, sailing to another base on the Isle of Sheppey. Eventually King Ethelred paid them 5 tons of silver to leave England, but of course having been once successful they returned many more times to seek fortune.

As for Bryhtnoth, the English took his body to Ely Cathedral for burial, but not before the Vikings had cut off his head as a trophy, a wax ball being made to take its place. In 1769 his bones were examined and his height estimated at 6 feet 9 inches, which at a time when the average height was considerably less than it is today, would have made Bryhtnoth an extremely tall man.

One can speculate as to what would have happened had Bryhtnoth not treated war as if it were a game of cricket and refused the Viking demands for a 'fair fight'. Given the difficulty in crossing from Northey Island, it is probable that neither side would have been defeated. The Vikings would most probably have eventually withdrawn, but not until Bryhtnoth had been able to gather forces of far greater strength. Any battle on the Essex coast would then have been far from a foregone conclusion and the invaders may have been defeated or returned home. Perhaps a more prepared, confident and braver England would have withstood another invader 75 years later – William the Conqueror – and how different our history would then have been.

The story of the battle was recorded in an epic poem of over 300 verses, which was apparently written by one of the Saxon survivors. This became one of the most important early works in English literature. Unfortunately in 1731 the original manuscript was almost completely destroyed by a fire at the Cotton Library, a private collection by Sir Robert Bruce Cotton M.P. that formed the nucleus of the British Library. A sizeable excerpt has however survived, thanks to a John Elphinston who had made a copy some years before.

As I walked round the island I tried to imagine the scene with longboats, warriors, swords, axes and arrows, but it was just too different from the peaceful views along the Blackwater and the delicate colours of the saltings. Northey is now an island devoted to birds, butterflies and salt marsh plants. The grass is kept short to attract brent geese, aiming to dissuade them from landing on mainland farmland where they may trample crops, a policy known as the 'goose field' scheme, which has been successfully introduced at other nature reserves on the Essex coast.

Turning south, I headed away from the views of Osea Island further down the Blackwater, looking once more to the mainland and the remote Dengie peninsula. Until relatively recently the path ran next to the sea, but in 1992 this section of sea wall was deliberately breached in a process known as 'managed retreat' or 'coastal realignment'. Water was allowed to flood the area between the outer and inner sea walls, with the tide bringing in seeds and the land reverting to salt marsh. Although not as established as the areas abandoned a century ago, the new marsh developed quickly and one wouldn't suspect that this natural coastline was formed by man's intervention less than 20 years ago. The process has been successfully repeated at a number of other sites, allowing us to recreate the declining but important salt marsh wildlife habitat (40% of Essex salt marsh has been lost in the last 25 years) and providing more viable sea defences. It is becoming increasingly difficult to bolster traditional sea walls and a natural coastline which can grow and adapt is the most sustainable defence against rising sea levels. The newly formed salt marsh and lagoons absorb the waves' energy, providing an effective barrier to the incoming tide, a haven for wildlife and in direct contrast to the alternative of ever higher concrete walls, creating an environment of beauty.

Closer to the causeway the island is threatened by another process, 'coastal squeeze'. This occurs where salt marsh is trapped by a fixed landward boundary, in this case the sea wall armoured with concrete. Unable to naturally migrate inland, the saltings are squeezed against the wall and erode away. This in turn increases pressure on the man-made sea wall, meaning that it has to be continually strengthened or risk the island flooding. A concrete wall is hardly a natural coastline in keeping with a wildlife reserve and the National Trust hope to remove the wall to allow the salt marsh to move inland. Careful planning is needed to ensure that Northey remains a special place for both people and wildlife, a process made more difficult by mankind's effect on our climate.

Back at the causeway my circuit of the island was complete, however with plenty of time before the tide was up I took another walk along the lane, looking across the slowly rising Blackwater to Heybridge on the left and to Northey's meadows on the right. In the middle of first meadow were the brent geese, a huge flock standing on the grass. I passed as quietly as I could, but was soon spotted and as one bird rose, the rest took off with him – a majestic sight and one that I was fortunate to catch with my camera. These dark bellied brent geese arrive at the estuaries of East Anglia and southern England in October, feed on vegetation here, then leave for the tundra of Siberia in March. Around 8,000 over-winter on the Blackwater, 5% of the world population.

Brent geese are one of five sea bird species found in internationally important numbers around Northey, the others being shelduck, dunlin, grey plover and black-tailed godwit. Also a common site on the island are short-eared owls, who can be spotted hunting in the daytime for voles and other small mammals. In the 19th century a huge colony of ravens lived here, but these are now long gone, the bird until recently only found in the western side of the UK, but now spreading back to the east.

I stopped at the hide looking out across the Blackwater, watching the brent geese who'd now settled on the mudflats and wishing I'd brought binoculars and a book to help recognise some of the other species closer to the island. Leaving the hide I saw a lone brent goose flying overhead. Was he a scout sent out to see if the nasty man had gone from their favourite Northey roost – a brave goose prepared to put his own neck at risk to find out if it was safe for the rest of the flock? Or did he just have no mates?

Almost back at the house I stopped to take a photo, but not wishing to intrude or interrupt the lunch party, stayed the right side of the Private sign. It is a most unusual house with an interesting story. In 1923 the island was bought by Sir Norman Angell, a writer, politician, member of the Executive Committee of the League of Nations and Nobel Prize winner. He devotes a chapter of his 1951 autobiography *After All* to life on Northey, a copy of which the ever helpful Swan Books managed to find for me. It came from the USA, having been discarded by Hood College Library in Maryland and still had its ticket inside the back cover. No one had ever borrowed it.

After being involved in the negotiation of peace treaties following the First World War, Sir Norman purchased a 30 foot yacht, a converted ship's lifeboat, with the intention of finding solitude by living on her during the summer months. He took it up and down the East Coast estuaries, sometimes sailing into the Blackwater. He did a little writing on the yacht and took on board an early version of a linguaphone to brush up on his German. On one occasion a passing fisherman, hearing loud German spoken on board, reported to the authorities that a spy was being hidden on the yacht.

Exploring one day Sir Norman came across Northey Island and on finding it was for sale, bought it. He soon fell in love with the island, building a house adjoining the old farm cottage. The house was completely to Sir Norman's design, with its five bedrooms each having running water, lavatory and central heating. The upper part of the house has the appearance of a tower, consisting of a single room with large windows on every side, giving panoramic views across the island and estuary. Much of the interior woodwork was made from a derelict sailing barge that was lying on Northey and other was cut from trees on the island. The house is now let for family holidays, making a comfortable, unusual and exciting retreat for up to ten people. A rare opportunity to stay on a small tidal island (unless of course one meets the criteria of well off and suffering from an addiction, in which case next door Osea may be more suitable).

Sir Norman found a fascination in brick laying and bought a barge load of over-burnt bricks of all shapes, sizes and colours, supplemented with lorry loads of stones from demolished buildings. Over a few summers he built two or three hundred yards of wall, in which instead of buttresses for strength, he constructed small circular towers which were just as effective and far more picturesque. The irregularity of the bricks gave a weathered appearance and Sir Norman notes that most visitors guessed that his walls dated from the late 16<sup>th</sup> century. I too had been deceived, finding the walls around the house and assuming they were several hundred years old.

In 1940 Northey was hit by German bombs and the cottage almost destroyed, although damage to the house limited to broken windows. Sir Norman suggests that the island was deliberately targeted, perhaps because the walls he had built may have given it a military aspect from the air, although others have suggested that it was simply an aircraft dropping its remaining bombs when returning from a raid on London.

Sir Norman employed a married couple (who he referred to as the bailiffs) to look after housekeeping and make Northey self supporting, keeping cows, ducks, chickens and pigs. Soon after taking possession of the island he purchased a fine old sow by the name of Betsy, who discovered that succulent little crabs could be found in the marsh ditches at low tide. On one occasion she found herself marooned by the incoming tide and had to make a swim for it. The poor pig lost her head entirely and was found swimming in circles some way from dry land. Sir Norman had to go out in his dingy and shoo her towards the beach, which she reached in a state of collapse. However Betsy learned from the experience and next time she was marooned simply swam home. When a little later her family of thirteen piglets arrived she soon taught them to swim, entering the water with great serenity and grunting for them to follow. One day, looking from the top room of the house, Sir Norman spotted what he thought to be a flock of ducks swimming on a flooded meadow, but on closer inspection with field glasses found it to be Betsy calmly swimming home with thirteen piglets following behind.

Sir Norman managed to get a telephone installed on the island, as although it needed a submarine cable, he thought the Post Office were glad to no longer have to deliver telegrams in person. Telegrams were then read by phone and on one occasion the son of the bailiff came running up to him saying that the Post Office had a telegram, but could not read it to his mother, only to Sir Norman himself. Going to the telephone he heard an austere female voice, who on confirming that he was indeed Sir Norman Angell read the message; 'Can sleep with you after theatre Friday night. Love, Rosalinde'. Although he knew Rosalinde (Fuller), as Sir Norman puts it 'these were not my relations with her'. It was only when they later met for tea and the rather delicate matter was discussed, that the explanation that the telegram was neither a proposition nor a joke came to light. Some time beforehand Sir Norman had suggested that they meet for lunch or supper and Rosalinde had sent the telegram to say she could 'sup' with him after the theatre. Sir Norman knew the then Postmaster General Hastings Lee-Smith and told him that he intended to sue for damages. He had to think of his reputation amongst his country neighbours and of the shocked spinster who read the telegram and would have discussed it in secret with *all* her friends. Furthermore he could do with a few thousand for the development of his farm. A day or two later Lee-Smith responded 'Nothing doing, my dear fellow. Reflections on a man's chastity are not actionable unless he is a clergyman. You are not a clergyman. Ergo, no action lies. Go to blazes.' One or both men may have been bluffing, but either way, no action was taken.

Sir Norman had bought the island from Vierville de Crespigny, a member of a well known local family, and a rather eccentric gentleman. He had been an officer in the war and it was commonly reported (although quite probably not true) that he'd shot more of his own men (for shirking) than the Germans had. It was rumoured that his family had helped de Crespigny to buy the island in order to keep him out of the way and avoid embarrassment. If this was the case it was not entirely successful. De Crespigny had a complex about Irish people and lived in constant fear of Northey being invaded by them. Hence he spent much of his time in a little hut on wheels with iron barred windows, which was moved to strategic positions around the island from where he could more effectively see off invaders. Trespassers were not welcome or indeed immune from being shot at (perhaps he'd have been more at home on present day Osea). How even a tiny island can develop its own patriotism was once illustrated to Angell when he remarked to a visitor who'd been born on Northey, that Major de Crespigny used to shoot at people who ventured onto the island. 'And quite right too' was her reply. After selling Northey, de Crespigny took a job as a game warden in Africa, where he met a sad end, being trampled to death by an elephant.

Returning to the shore, instead of turning left and following the lane back to the causeway, I first went right, walking a short distance along the sea wall to investigate *The Mistley*, one of the three wrecks known to lie on Northey. I am grateful to Janet Witheridge from the Nautical Archaeology Society, for her assistance in providing information on these vessels.

This 64 tonne Thames Barge was built at Harwich in 1891 for the splendidly named Samuel Horatio Horlock from the Essex village of Mistley on the Stour estuary. Built to carry wheat she could take a load of around 135 tonnes. In the Second World War she was requisitioned to help in the defence of Harwich, but in December 1940 dragged her anchor in a westerly gale and was driven onto the Shoebury sands where she sank. The wreck was raised, but declared unseaworthy and converted to a timber carrying lighter. *The Mistley* came to Northey Island as a gift from Sir Norman Angell's nephew to his wife Nora on the occasion of her 60<sup>th</sup> birthday. After breaking loose from her mooring in a storm she is now ending her days slowly rotting in Northey's mud, within sight of the Maldon's restored barges as they sail down the Blackwater. Close by are the even more decayed remains of another barge, *The Gillman*, which was deliberately beached on the island on a big spring tide in 1937. Somewhere in the middle of the salt marsh lies Northey's third wreck, a barge of unknown origin, which may have been the vessel that provided wood for the island's house.

The sea was still well clear of the causeway as I left Northey, but the mud was probably even more dangerous. In my travels around the coast I'd encountered plenty of mud, but this was Essex's finest. Here the danger looked not to be of the unwary walker getting stuck and needing rescuing, but that anyone foolish enough to step onto it might disappear altogether.

Before climbing back up the hill into Maldon I walked to the end of the promenade. Here a bronze figure stands sword aloft guarding the entrance to the town – Bryhtnoth, looking towards the battle site and perhaps wishing he'd been a little less accommodating to the Viking request.

Back in the town, before catching the bus back to Chelmsford there was one more thing I wanted to see. Halfway up the High Street is the tower of St Peter's church. The nave and chancel fell down in the 17<sup>th</sup> century, and the building attached was commissioned by Archdeacon Thomas Plume of Rochester to provide accommodation for his collection of 7,000 books which he bequeathed to the town of his birth. The Plume Library, one of the oldest reference libraries in the country, is still housed on the first floor, but the ground floor is now the Maeldune Heritage Centre. Displayed here is the Maldon Embroidery, a 42 foot work of art depicting a thousand years of the town's history. The first two panels show the Battle of Maldon and the other five cover its history for the thousand years to 1991. The embroidery was the work of eighty six ladies who met once a week and became known as the Thursday Ladies. They also had one honorary member, a dog named Charlie who sat with them as they worked and is recorded for posterity (or 'prosperity' as the Embroidery Guide says) on the seventh panel.

With very limited winter opening hours I was lucky to find the exhibition open and almost as pleased to see it as the lady at the desk was to have a visitor to turn up. She told me that I could make my own way around, or she could show me if I preferred, although warned that she did talk a lot. I opted for the former, but every so often she appeared, telling me tales of Bryhtnoth and the battle. The lady said that her daughter is a historian and had told her that Bryhtnoth's actions were not unusual, as this was how battles were fought in those days. Maybe so, but this situation with the invading army camped on a tidal island would have been far from usual. Perhaps Bryhtnoth felt that the Vikings had to be defeated if East Anglia was to be protected from further raids, but with the enemy unable to cross he could have waited until reinforcements were gathered. Although the battle was lost it could be said there was some victory in that Maldon was not taken, but whatever his reasons, Bryhtnoth himself paid the ultimate price for his decision to allow the Vikings over the causeway.

So I had completed my exploration of the Essex tidal islands. Memories of my earlier walk around the county's coastline, its remoteness and unexpected beauty were rekindled. Now I'd been on some of the islands that I'd walked past, looking across sea or mud and wondering what these little known and slightly mysterious islands were like. And now I know. They possess the same beauty as much of the Essex coast, with salt marshes, colourful beaches and bountiful wildlife. There is much of interest in their history, but also in their present, whether for the wildlife, plants, or people. Now it was time to move on.

# CHAPTER TWENTY FIVE

# CHISWICK EYOT

For the first 40 islands I'd headed towards the sea. For the 41st I travelled inland from my Essex home. For the first 40 islands I'd travelled by train, bus or car. Today I caught the London Underground to Hammersmith. Each of my islands is unique and of course by definition one cannot be more unique, but the location of Chiswick Eyot is very different to the other islands. It is by a considerable distance the furthest from the sea. The Thames is generally considered to end near to Shoeburyness and should a crow choose to fly in its traditional manner to Chiswick Eyot, a mile upstream from Hammersmith Bridge, it would have covered 45 miles.

Pronounced 'eight', Eyot is used in the names of a number of little islands that dot the Thames from London to Reading. To most people it is probably known just as a curious term during commentaries on the Oxford – Cambridge boat race, which passes Chiswick Eyot as the crews round the huge Surrey bend. As I was to find out, to one man however the island is a special place.

The noise of London's traffic was rather different to the quiet approach to most of the islands. Once on the Thames Path it was a pleasant walk in bright sunshine, albeit with the ever present roar of the A4 Great West Road. The narrow, tree covered Chiswick Eyot soon came into view close to the north bank of the river. There's low tide access at both ends, but I went for the far end as this required a shorter walk on what at high tide is the bed of the Thames – a mixture of shingle and mud.

Signs at Chiswick Draw Dock warned:

## DANGER
### Tidal Water & Strong Currents

## BEWARE
### Tide Cuts Off Island

The latter was illustrated by a rather dramatic depiction of a person with arms flailing falling between two pieces of land. I'd survived isolated islands all around our coastline and didn't intend getting stranded in the Thames.

Stepping stones cross the mud part way, then it's firm shingle to the island. What I hadn't expected was that the mud would be even worse actually on the island. Recent tides had been quite high, depositing mud on Chiswick Mall, the road alongside the river, and inundating the island. Every footstep squelched and several times I nearly came a cropper on the slippery mud.

This inhospitable island of mud and dense vegetation however probably qualifies as our smallest inhabited tidal island, albeit the Eyot's only resident staying here on an unofficial and probably temporary basis. Shortly before I visited, BBC London had run a piece about 'Mr Nick' (as he'd asked to be called), described as a 'Modern-day Robinson Crusoe', a homeless man who'd been living on the island for 6 months. The well spoken 67 year old, said that he was a qualified architect who'd been to Westminster School and previously lived in Wimbledon with his ex-wife. He keeps a bicycle on the Eyot and leaves at low tide to ride off to get provisions, returning of course before the swiftly rising waters cut off the route home. Once the tide rises Mr Nick is alone on his island, where he enjoys the simplicity of his new life. It's not perhaps everyone's idea of island life, but Mr Nick says that he 'has achieved freedom'. His comment that most people given the choice between living here or working in a bank or office, would choose the island, is maybe more open to debate.

At the western end of the island I found his 'home'- a sort of den in the bushes and a netting hammock strung from a tree. Mr Nick had said that with his new uncomplicated life he didn't have to lock any doors, although of course he had none to lock. Nevertheless I still felt that I was intruding as I walked between his hammock and the little shelter he'd made by bending back trees.

Alerted by the BBC, Hounslow Council who own the Eyot sent someone to investigate. That they failed to report any sign of Mr Nick's presence suggests perhaps that either those sent didn't fancy the mud, or maybe with sympathy for his island life thought that as he's doing no harm he should be allowed to stay.

Beyond Mr Nick's shelter there were no paths, just nettles and trees, mostly osier, a type of willow which was once harvested on the island for basket making. Underfoot was a thick bed of dead osier leaves, assorted rubbish deposited by the tide and beneath this slimy mud and Thames water. I was glad to have brought an old pair of walking boots out of retirement for this trip, although a dunking in warm river mud rekindled old odours as I eventually realised when wondering what was causing a strange smell on the train home!

It was a bright sunny day but few rays were penetrating the canopy of trees. I fought my way onwards through the vegetation, attempting to find the driest route and hoping that no nasty hazards lurked beneath the soggy mattress underfoot. Although the island is narrow, on neither side was the Thames visible. If it wasn't for the distant roar of the A4 it seemed I could have been in the steamy Borneo jungle. When a disturbed heron took off just yards from me I jumped. When a few yards further on a squawking green parakeet flew from a tree I thought that perhaps I'd taken a wrong turning! Descended from escaped captive birds, and a relatively recent addition to London's wildlife, there are now something like 40,000 wild parakeets in the South East, but this was not the birdlife I'd expected to see on a watery island.

I made it to the end of the Eyot and settled down to eat lunch on the concrete wall that surrounds the island. For half an hour I watched more traditional water birds going about their business by the river – gulls wheeling in the wind and swooping down to pick up tasty morsels from the mud, a lone heron statuesque by the water's edge, four cormorants drying their outstretched wings in the sun, a group of ducks repeatedly diving into the dark river, a pair of swans dipping their heads occasionally as they swam serenely by – and all this by an island just a mile from Hammersmith Bridge. If one is prepared to stop and be still it's not just on our quieter coasts that peacefulness and wildlife can be found. As I sat on the end of Chiswick Eyot, cut off from the rest of the busy city, I recalled David St

John Thomas's excellent latest book *Remote Britain*. He had asked for suggestions of the remotest place in London. I had found my entry.

*Nature Conservation in Hounslow* was an unlikely book title to provide me with information on the island, but David Pape's publication by London Ecology Unit proved most helpful. The copy that Swan Books managed to find had been withdrawn from St Mary's University College library.

An 1846 map shows the island as having an area of around 4 acres, but erosion accelerated by its position on the outside of a bend has reduced this to around 2½ acres. If it were not for the Old Chiswick Preservation Society persuading Brentford and Chiswick Council in the 1950s to halt erosion with balks of timber and barge loads of shingle, it may have disappeared completely. In 1978 Hounslow Council considered removing the entire island because debris from its eroding banks was becoming a nuisance to boat owners using the Thames. Fortunately this idea was abandoned and instead they built the concrete walls that now surround the Eyot. These accentuate the ship like profile of the island with the pointed ends offering least resistance to the strong tides. They appear to have largely stabilised erosion and its future seems secure. One cannot imagine that public opinion would now allow what is an historic island to disappear

The stream between the island and Chiswick Mall was once a fine fishery, with rent for its use paid in salmon. With increasing pollution the fish died out in the 1830s and although the river is cleaner now than for 150 years, recent attempts to reintroduce salmon have had disappointing results. It's thought that water quality will not be sufficient to allow significant numbers to breed until London's new sewer system is completed, which won't be until at least 2020. It was not only salmon who ventured this far up the river. In the early summer of 1895 a porpoise appeared above Chiswick Eyot and followed the ebb tide down river to Putney, where it stopped opposite a public house. Here two 'sportsmen' went out in a boat to shoot it, but succeeded only in hitting two spectators in the back!

The pollarded willows which cover most of the island were first planted around 1800 and cultivated for basket making. Willow baskets were in great demand to transport fruit and vegetables from the thriving local market gardening industry to the London markets and for eel and fish traps. New growth was cut back each year by the osier or withy cutters, who would wait until high tide to float their loads to the bank rather than carry it across the mud.

Ownership of Chiswick Eyot had in 1934 passed from the Ecclesiastical Commissioners to the local council, who when the last person granted a right to cut them went out of business a year later, had to pay to have the willows cut and burnt. Regular cutting ceased after the Second World War and the island began to grow wild. Local residents however took it upon themselves to pollard the trees and replant where necessary, partly to preserve their views of the annual Boat Race. In 1949 a licence was granted to the Old Chiswick Preservation Society to 'plant willows and do what they can to prevent erosion of the island' and to 'cut and sell withies to meet the costs'. The branches of the several types of willow are still cut every two or three years in early spring, leaving almost bare trunks, but the crowns soon bush out forming the close, low canopy.

Rather than fight my way back through the jungle, and not knowing what tropical creatures might be disturbed this time, I left from the downstream end of the island. Here another set of stepping stones cross the mud and the shallow channel that was still draining as the tide fell. It seemed strange walking along the Thames foreshore, that many look down to but few set foot on. A set of steps by the Black Lion took me back to the top of the wall and onto the Thames Path. Rather than return to noisy Hammersmith I headed further up the river.

Opposite the island are some of London's most exclusive addresses; Hammersmith Terrace and Chiswick Mall. The 18th century houses of Hammersmith Terrace include three with blue plaques noting famous previous residents – The typographer and antiquary Sir Emery Walker, the author and humorist Sir Alan Herbert and Edward Johnston a master calligrapher who invented the Johnston typeface for London Underground.

Whilst Hammersmith Terrace runs inland of the tall houses which block public view to the river, on Chiswick Mall a terrace of fine Georgian mansions are to the right of the road, with each house having a garden on the other side. These run down to the river bank and provide exclusive views of the northern side of the Eyot. Through a gap in the trees I could see what looked to be the remains of an old wooden jetty by the island, but locked gates and 'Private' signs deterred further investigation. The gardens must flood on the highest tides, as does the road, which had a fresh covering of mud and a sign warning that parked cars may be damaged by water.

I wondered what the residents of these exclusive riverside terraces thought of Mr Nick living just over the water. The BBC asked two. Both seemed quite happy, one describing him as 'nutty' but adding that he is 'all for nutty people'!

Continuing along the Thames Path I passed few walkers, but a quite remarkable number of fit and occasionally not so fit looking West London runners, each plugged into some kind of miniature music playing device. How different to most of the islands, where I had seen either no one or walkers intent of imbibing every part of the coastal atmosphere. By Chiswick Pier is an RNLI Station, one of four on the tidal Thames, and soon after here the houses ended, the path running alongside sports grounds. My pleasant stroll ended at Barnes Bridge where I caught a train back to Waterloo, crossed one of the Golden Jubilee Bridges to Embankment and picked up the tube home. Today had been my shortest trip, but an enjoyable walk. Every time I walk a bit of the Thames Path I say that soon I shall walk its entire 184 miles. It's on a long list headed 'One Day'!

Before leaving the Thames I should just mention the Kent coast, where the salt marshes of the Thames and Medway estuaries are ideal tidal island territory. Surprisingly however, despite Essex having six, none of Kent's islands met my definition. Several in the Medway are surrounded by mud at low tide, but none can be safely walked to. Perhaps the two of most interest and worthy of inclusion in my 'nearly' list are Hoo Island with its two tiered circular Palmerston Fort and Deadmans Island.

Opposite Queenborough on the Isle of Sheppey and separated from the mainland of Chestney Marshes by a narrow channel, Dead Man's Island as it appears to be called locally (as opposed to the Ordnance Survey spelling I used), has as you might imagine, a rather gruesome history. Like so many island stories, various versions can be found, but all tell us that this small area of salt marsh was used for burying 19th century dead. Hulk ships were kept in the Medway housing prisoners, sufferers of contagious disease, or both, depending on which source you choose to follow. With cholera rife the death rate was high and bodies disposed of either by burial on what became Deadmans Island or burnt on the nearby Burnt Wick Island. With dangerous mudflats Deadmans was not an island I could visit, but photos show it as an eerie place with timber posts marking graves of the poor men who died on the Medway. I was to hear a similar story at Burrow Island, my next port of call, and of course had recently read of the cholera victims buried on St Mary's Island. Whilst most of our tidal islands are serene with beauty and wildlife to the fore, a few I was finding have a somewhat grizzly past.

# CHAPTER TWENTY SIX

# BURROW ISLAND

Most of the tidal islands I found by poring over maps or searching the internet. Burrow Island I spotted from 100 metres up the Spinnaker Tower in Portsmouth, the tallest publicly accessible structure in the UK. Looking down into Portsmouth Harbour, just off Gosport was a small round patch of land, covered with trees, but linked to the shore by a raised strip of mud. An enquiry to one of the tower's staff confirmed that at high tide it is indeed an island, although he was unsure about access and said he'd never seen anyone on it. Research was required.

First port of call was Portsmouth Tourist Information Centre, where Jean, the very helpful lady behind the counter, suggested a harbour boat trip as the island is mentioned in the commentary. An hour later my wife, youngest son and I were on the water, viewing the Navy ships then crossing the harbour towards Gosport and passing Burrow Island, or Rat Island as the captain said it is known locally. His explanation was that there was an abattoir nearby and the rats lived off the blood. Before disembarking I enquired further and was told that the island is MoD property and private, but as you will have realised by now, I don't give up so soon when a tidal island is in sight.

Next enquiries were to Gosport Tourist Information, where Kay Allen was most helpful. Her husband used to play on the island as a child, building dens and such, but he's now 43 so that was a while ago. She gave me a contact email for the MoD, whose response was that on 'Health and Safety Grounds' they could not allow me access to the island. They had 'denied access to others in the past for the same reasons and it would be inappropriate and inconsistent to vary this policy'. Not willing to be fobbed off with this often convenient excuse, I asked for more specific information on the hazards. 'Redundant cabling, rat infestation and debris washed ashore over decades' was the answer, the email adding 'To allow access the MoD would need to prepare a Health & Safety assessment and clear the site which we don't currently have funds for'. Strangely for a tidal island the email ended 'Finally, the MoD have abandoned it operationally and it is inaccessible without a boat.'

A couple of weeks later I spent a lunchtime investigating possible access routes on Google Earth. Confirming what I'd seen from the tower, the island is dry at low tide and it appeared possible to reach it provided I could get onto the harbour foreshore. I wasn't giving up and plans for an illicit visit were being hatched. Then later in the afternoon, out of the blue an email popped up from Kay at Gosport TIC. The news was good. She'd mentioned my quest at a meeting with Explosion! Museum of Naval Firepower and Marc Farrance, Visitor Services Officer, was willing to take me out to the island.

Before returning to Burrow Island I shall however first mention some nearby 'almost tidal islands'. A few miles east of Portsmouth and very different to the busy city, is Langstone Harbour, seven square miles of muddy tidal estuary. Within the harbour are five small islands all of which the map suggests are dry at low tide. John Goodspeed from Havant Nature told me that they are owned by the RSPB, have 'No Access' signs and that I'd get wet and very muddy if I tried to walk to them. He put me in touch with RSPB warden Chris Cockburn and what a helpful man he is. South Binness, Baker's and Round Nap Islands he said cannot be accessed without crossing soft mud and water, however North Binness and Long Island can be reached on foot, but thigh waders are necessary and local knowledge essential. He offered to take me out to these, either on foot or in the reserve's boat and suggested some late August / early September dates, which were the only times that we wouldn't disturb the bird populations. On balance however I decided that if waders were required the islands do not meet my definition and Chris agreed that it wasn't wise to encourage people to venture out onto the mud.

The islands are best viewed from shoreline paths around the harbour, particularly from the seawall that encloses Farlington Marshes, but other than the southern end of Long Island which is a landing area for boat users during daylight hours, public access is not permitted. The restricted access policy has proved to be a great success for conservation. Prior to 1979 when the RSPB bought the area there were no records of successful breeding by terns or gulls. In the first year of wardening to implement the restrictions both started to nest here. Populations grew and by 2009 nest numbers totalled 137 mediterranean gulls, 5,298 black-headed gulls, 153 sandwich terns, 89 common terns and 45 little terns (the island often holds the second largest UK colony). Most of these nest on the higher shingle ridges, but the islands also support breeding populations of shelducks, oystercatchers, redshanks, lapwings, skylarks and meadow pipits, many of which take a chance by breeding on the salt marsh, risking the surging spring tides. What a contrast with Rough Island, where breeding birds are now few, largely a result of human disturbance which the National Trust for Scotland struggle to limit.

And it's not only the birds who benefit from the RSPB's policy here. Much of the vegetation is unique to these coastal habitats and supports rare insects and other invertebrates. Visitors on the islands would not only scare the birds, but trample the fragile life underfoot. Hence the RSPB justify the access restrictions, something which like Worm's Head and Skippers Island, but not St Catherine's and Osea Islands, I was very happy to go along with.

There is much evidence that the Langstone islands were occupied by Bronze Age and Saxon people and like several other tidal islands they played their part in World War Two, acting as a decoy site for Portsmouth Harbour under Operation Starfish.

A few miles east of Langstone Harbour, at the tip of the bridged Thorney Island, is Pilsey Island. A true tidal island as recently as the early 1990s, due to accretion (build up of land mass) this is now only cut off at the highest tides, and is becoming more of a peninsula. Also an RSPB reserve, access is restricted to protect the very fragile habitat, rare lichens and roosting birds.

With no railway to Gosport, on a sunny day I arrived by the busy ferry that leaves from just outside Portsmouth Harbour station. It's about a mile walk from the ferry terminal to Explosion! passing impressive ex military buildings many of which are being converted to private homes, and with occasional glimpses of yachts in the marina. Like Portsmouth, Gosport was once dominated by Navy life, but unlike its larger neighbour most activities have now ceased. No longer are there over a hundred pubs in and around the High Street, although narrow passages and alleys still remind of the days when the unwary might be press ganged.

Burrow Island is opposite the entrance to Forton Lake, a creek off Portsmouth Harbour, which is crossed by an impressive millennium bridge. To the right is Clarence Hard and to the left Priddy's Hard, both of which have a long history of supplying the Navy; food and drink from Clarence and munitions from Priddy's. Some of the old buildings on Priddy's Hard have been taken over by Explosion! which tells the story of the depot that for over 200 years stored and supplied gunpowder, ammunition and mines to the Navy. Here I met Marc Farrance who told me how as the depot wound down from the 1960s a few workers kept items of interest, which formed a private museum after the site closed in 1989. These 2,000 objects were incorporated into the much larger Explosion! which was opened by HRH Duke of York in 2001.

From the museum Marc took me onto the foreshore, under Shell Pier and along the natural causeway that links Burrow Island to Priddy's Hard. At high tide the island is just a small wooded area surrounded by sea, but as the water falls mud and shingle are uncovered and for a few hours a day the causeway appears. Also uncovered are the seaweed covered rails of a narrow gauge railway that used to run to the Burning Point, an area about two thirds of the way to the island where contaminated explosives were taken for disposal. After soaking in diesel to slow the combustion rate they would be set alight, burning with intense bright light, the residues being washed away by the next tide. Years of waves and currents have slowly moved the tracks, so the two rails are no longer parallel, the gap ranging from a few inches to a yard or so. Eventually they will be lost and it's a shame that there appears to be no attempt to preserve or even survey the area.

An archaeology project at Forton Lake found much of interest around the inlet, but a survey of Burrow Island wasn't included, apparently because an unexploded shell was found. Various items of interest have been discovered around the island, including Roman pottery vessels, but it's not known whether these originated here or had been washed up by the sea. It is thought that Romans occupied higher ground around Gosport, but there's no real evidence as to whether they came to Burrow Island.

Although far closer to Gosport, the island is in the Borough of Portsmouth, and it's thought that the name 'Burrow' came from corruption of 'Borough'. I have heard several explanations for the more commonly used local name of Rat Island. The harbour tour boat captain's story of rats feeding on blood from a nearly abattoir has some credence as on Clarence Hard were once a brewery, granary and abattoir, which all helped keep the sailors fed and watered. It's thought that unwanted offal was discharged into the creek and with prevailing westerly winds would have ended up on the island, attracting rats. Mark Bardell's *History and Guide of Portsmouth*, gives another, but perhaps less probable story that returning ships used to open their gun ports and throw offal onto the island, encouraging rats to follow and jump ship. A third explanation is that in the late 1700s and early 1800s moored in Forton Lake and around the island were decaying hulks of old wooden warships that were no longer fit for battle. Stripped of their guns and superstructure, these were used to house French prisoners of war. Rats leaving the hulks would have aimed for the closest landfall which was the island. There seems little doubt that the island attracted a large rat population and hence gained its local name, but as to the precise reason you will have to make your own choice.

Marc took me around the westerly side of the island where there's a raised arc of shingle on which little terns nest. Close to this is an area where French prisoners of war who had died in the unsanitary conditions on the hulks were buried. On both sides of the island large signs warn, 'DANGER HIGH TENSION SUBMARINE CABLES'. These refer not to the many lengths of discarded electrical cabling all along the foreshore, but to cables running on the sea bed to Portsmouth, that can be tightened in order to act as a submarine barrier protecting the dockyard.

On the far side of the island are the remains of a stone jetty that extends towards Portsmouth and of a small fort. Like much of the island these are being gradually being eroded away, a process accelerated by the increased wash from larger boats that use the harbour. The fort was partly demolished in 1827 and although a drawing by William Snape in 1899 shows the walls intact, only part of a stone wall that was once underground now remains. This is covered in vegetation and only visible from the eastern beach.

Known as James Fort and completed in 1679, it was one of three Gosport fortifications designed by Sir Bernard de Gomme in response to Charles

II's concern for the safety of England's dockyards. James Fort would have prevented an enemy from using the island to bombard either the town of Gosport or the dockyards of Portsmouth. It was designed as a smaller version of Fort Charles, the large redoubt on Gosport quay, and consisted of a central square 6 metre high tower containing living quarters and storerooms, above which was a roof for guns and a parapet with sentry boxes at the corners. Outside was a platform with another parapet, and in total up to 20 cannons could be mounted on the tower and outer walls. Several plans of Gosport defences of the 1750s show James Fort with an entirely different shape, but it seems these represented a proposed rebuilding which never took place. There is no evidence for the local legend that King Stephen, the last Norman King of England, built a castle on Burrow Island, and it is certain that the ruins of James Fort date from the 17th not the 12th century.

Surprisingly not mentioned by the MoD in their 'reasons' why I couldn't visit, are ten or so First World War mines on the beach. Submerged by every tide these have probably lain here rusting slowly for almost a century, interesting history but seen by few. It is a shame that access to the island is restricted. Marc told me that youngsters sometimes come out here, using it as a den for bar-b-ques and perhaps a little drinking, but these are unofficial visits and the route they take not easy. I asked if Explosion! had considered running official guided walks or allowing visitors to make their own way across, but this would be difficult. Firstly they are busy opening up more of the Priddy's Hard site so that visitors can walk round the ramparts, but mainly because whilst the occasional visit may not be noticed, to make it regular and official would cause difficulties with the MoD. I wouldn't recommend trying to make your own way to Burrow Island, but Marc suggests that if anyone wishes to visit they contact Explosion! who will do their best to help.

Somewhat in contrast with the MoD's approach, a Gosport councillor recently put forward a proposal to open up the island. He wanted to open a café there and build a platform where people could sit to paint pictures of the harbour and passing boats. The island does have great views across to Portsmouth and its Spinnaker Tower, but the idea seems a little fanciful. Not only would there be the logistical practical problems of access, but currently the island is almost covered with trees, so environmentally there would sure to be objections. I believe his proposal was quietly forgotten.

Burrow Island's flora and fauna don't appear to have been studied, but what is of no doubt is that there are plenty of rats here. Whilst not quite the plague that the MoD implied, Phil Hazell, Explosion! Assistant Manager, told me that he's seen them. He said that foxes cross the causeway and one assumes that small mammals can be found here too. In 1996 local botanist Debbie Allan surveyed the wild flowers of Gosport's beaches and made an interesting find on Burrow Island. Balm-leaved figwort (Scrophularia scorodonia), a perennial with a square stem and small round reddish / purple flowers, is generally found only in the south west of England, and Debbie believed her discovery to be the first natural occurrence of the species in Hampshire. Although Burrow Island is within the political boundary of Portsmouth, as it is only accessible on foot from Gosport she considered it should be an honorary Gosport plant.

Phil Hazell showed me an old map that suggests there was once a causeway to the island from close to Clarence Hard. This would have been shorter than the current route and before the entrance to Fallon Lake was dredged would only have had to cross a narrow strip of water. The island was bigger too then, probably extending to where oak stumps are now on the beach. He thought that these were shuttering and that stone and rock would have been brought from the mainland to extend the island. With no natural rock in the muddy harbour, it's probable that all the stone on Burrow Island was brought here by man, and as the wooden shuttering rotted it spread around the island.

After saying farewell and grateful thanks to Marc and Phil I spent an interesting hour in the museum, which gives an excellent insight into how it must have been to work in this busy, noisy and often dangerous depot. Housed in a group of listed buildings, including the original powder store with walls eight foot thick, it traces development of naval armaments from gunpowder to Exocet missiles. A site where 2,500 women worked in World War Two and which last saw significant naval activity in the Falklands War, is now quiet, and an island where once explosives were burned and cannons trained on the harbour, lies silent.

Unlike many of our tidal islands Burrow Island is neither of remarkable beauty or remoteness, however thanks to its location it has a history and interest far out of proportion to its size. Thousands of people will see it every day as they pass by in boats, walk on the waterfronts, or like me, spot it from high up in the Spinnaker Tower. To those few who do give the island a second glance it will just be a few trees and perhaps a bit of beach. Thanks to Jean, Kay, Marc and Phil, not only had I been one of the privileged few to visit Burrow Island, but what I had learned of its history, with cannons, mines, burning gunpowder and buried Frenchman, had made the island more than a patch of trees on a circle of raised land. Burrow, or shall I say Rat Island, is a small part of the history of a harbour that for many centuries has played a crucial role in the defence of our land.

# CHAPTER TWENTY SEVEN

# **BURGH ISLAND**

Tidal islands are few and far between in the south west of England. After Burrow Island there are none on the south coast until you get almost to Plymouth. None qualify on the north coast, hence my second island visit had been in South Wales, although three come under the heading 'almost tidal'.

The tiny Newquay Island, a 70 foot rocky outcrop on Towan Beach, fails to qualify, being linked to the town by a narrow suspension bridge. When our boys were younger we holidayed at Newquay more years than not and often looked at the island wishing we could visit it. Then it was privately owned by Lord and Lady Long, whose stay here was not always the happiest. Viscount Long, a Tory whip in the Lords throughout the Thatcher and Major years, had bought what is know locally as 'The Island' on a whim, intending to enjoy a quiet retirement here.

Unfortunately many summer visitors to Newquay aren't the quiet type and once the pubs closed hundreds of partygoers descended onto the beach, where marijuana and alcohol were sold openly from wheelbarrows. Naked revellers would run squealing into the surf and couples openly have sex in public. Lady Long threatened to sue the council and Newquay Action Group was formed to clean the place up. This, combined with extended pub opening hours from 2005 put a stop to the beach party, allowing the island's residents a quiet night's sleep. Despite the improvement, the Longs put the island on the market. Interestingly the price of £1.25 million was the same as that asked for the larger but undeveloped Sully Island. Now it is registered with Unique Home Stays, a company arranging Bed & Breakfast at some of the most exclusive properties in the country, so this is another tidal island (albeit bridged) that one can stay on overnight.

A couple of miles further east, Porth Island is separated from the mainland by a narrow gap through which the sea surges at high tide, but a wooden footbridge means it fails to meet my criteria. A shame because this is a beautiful and interesting island, on which can be found Cornwall's finest blowhole.

North Devon's almost tidal island is at Braunton Marshes, between Croyde and Barnstaple. Until 19th century reclamation Horsey Island was an island (and probably tidal), but is now part of the salt marshes, with important bird populations and accessible by footpaths along the embankments.

And so to my final island, probably the third best known of our tidal islands, Burgh Island just off the coast of South Devon by the village of Bigbury-on-Sea.

I did my best to get there by public transport. The nearest railway station is Ivybridge, twelve miles away. There's a bus from Plymouth to Bigbury, but it runs just once a week. Rather inconveniently for the tidal island visitor, it leaves Bigbury-on-Sea at 9.30 every Friday morning, and returns from Plymouth after lunch. There had been many islands that I didn't want to leave, but a week was perhaps a bit too long to stay. There's no bus from Ivybridge, but Devon County Council subsidise an excellent 'Fare Car' scheme, which you have to book a day in advance and runs to a sort of timetable, provided there are passengers. This route is run by Ivy Taxis, but unfortunately the times didn't fit in with my requirements. Twelve miles each way was too far to walk, and although I could have caught a bus for the middle section from Modbury to Aveton Gifford, it wouldn't have allowed me long on the island. A taxi from Ivybridge would have been £25 each way. Hence reluctantly I hired a car, choosing to stay at Torquay rather than Plymouth, partly because the hotels and cars were cheaper, but mainly because I like Torquay. My parents originated from nearby and it's a place that we visited many times to see grandparents and have continued to go back to every year or so.

So 18 months after I'd boarded the sleeper to Penzance I was back at Paddington, this time catching an afternoon train to a rather wet English Riviera. Severe weather warnings had been given for the south west. The train was full, mainly due to a special offer for senior citizens. A slight delay at Taunton caused by 'swans on the line' drew mutterings of 'Reggie

Perrin' from along the carriage, but I caught the connection at Newton Abbot with a few minutes to spare.

Next morning I was a little late picking up the car, mainly due to chatting to Neil and Sally, owners of the Torcroft Hotel, my final hotel and one of the friendliest. Their cat Oscar was both the most friendly and most noisy feline I met on my travels. My route to Bigbury took me on a tidal road alongside the River Avon. A number of places reached by such roads have been suggested to me as tidal islands, notably Sunderland Point in Lancashire, but it isn't an island if one can walk at all state of the tides, even if not by the obvious road route.

I'd visited Burgh Island several times over the last 25 years, but usually in summer and never in weather like this. It was the coldest island since Ardwall and the wettest since Burry Holmes. Surprisingly however there were quite a few cars in the car park, belonging not to island visitors but to intrepid surfers braving the cold November sea.

It was a slightly disappointing approach just parking opposite the island, with only a few hundred yards of hard sand to cross, although with the weather today I was glad not to have walked from Modbury. Half way across the sands a tractor driver pulled up beside me – 'Is that your car in the car park?' If he meant the horrid two door silver Astra with a tiny slit for a back window, yes it was. I thought he was going to mention the note I'd left explaining that the ticket machine had swallowed my four pounds but decided not to bother printing a ticket, however it was more simple – I'd left the car door open. He kindly offered to push it shut when he drove back.

Burgh Island is dominated by its famous art deco hotel on the eastern side of the island. I'd recently read *The Great White Palace* by Tony Porter, who with his wife Beatrice owned the hotel from 1986 to 2001. Of all the island books read over the last year I enjoyed this one the most. At the outset of my island travels the plan had been to end by staying here with my wife, however that was before I knew the cost – £360 to £600 per night for a double room and £280 minimum for a single. I contacted the hotel asking if I could talk to someone and have a look round. Deborah Clark current co-owner kindly sent me some information and said that one of the managers would show me around the public side of the island, although in the end I wasn't able to make contact with him. The hotel and grounds she said are private, so 'I think wouldn't feature in your book'. My reply mentioned that of course they would and hinted at a little disappointment that I couldn't see inside.

Although cut off for six hours in every twelve, Burgh Island is one island that can be visited even at high tide with dry feet and 'no boat required'. Parked by the roadway onto the island was its unique mode of transport – the 'sea tractor'. This strange contraption carries up to 30 passengers (20 after dark) standing on a platform raised above the sea on huge wheels hydraulically driven by a powerful engine. The current vehicle is the third to have ferried hotel guests and the public to the island, and the only one of its kind in the world. It was designed in 1969 by Robert Jackson, a pioneer of the nuclear power industry and cost £9,000 to build. By mutual agreement Mr Jackson's payment for his work was a case of champagne.

To the left of slipway is the big white hotel. Through a gate marked 'Private' steps lead up from the road and close by the main entrance is gated. Another notice advises 'Private Property No Access' and by the main entrance the sign states:

*Burgh Island Hotel and Grounds*

*Strictly Private*

*We are not open to non residents,*
*save for guests and prior reservations in our restaurant*

On the other side of the slipway is the Pilchard Inn, more of which later when I returned for lunch. A footpath leads to the top of the island, which after problems with erosion and damage to wildlife the owners dedicated to public use in 2008, with Devon County Council to be responsible for its upkeep. As I started to climb I saw the tractor driver return, so went back to thank him for shutting the car door. He told me that he was a local farmer bringing bags of sand over to the island and asked what brought me to Burgh Island. He nodded knowingly as I told him about the book and my disappointment at not getting to look around the hotel. Tony Porter would have let me in he said. Seeing that I was taking photos he asked what I'd like drawn for me. It took me a minute to realise that he meant with his tractor in the sand. A flower he decided, on the far side of the beach so I'd see it from the hill. Off he went in his tractor and up the hill I climbed. A few minutes later I was in the unlikely position of standing on the summit of an island in pouring rain, watching a farmer drive his tractor on the beach below – round and round, forward and backwards – all to draw a flower specially for me.

I found a little shelter in the Huer's Hut, a small stone building on top of the hill which was used in the 17th century as a lookout by pilchard fishermen. They would take it in turns to act as watchman, scanning the sea for the silver shoals and the froth they turned up. Once spotted he would hue (as in hue and cry, from the French 'huer' – to shout and raise alarm) to the fishermen on the beach below, who would then launch their boats. It's said that up to a million fish at a time might be landed and sometimes as many as forty horses and carts would be waiting to take away the catch for sale in surrounding towns and villages. Others were sold on the beach, priced at a shilling per hundred.

When the hotel first opened the hut was made into a tearoom for walkers and a camera obscura installed to entertain them. The hut's roof has long since gone and all that remains of its door and windows are wooden frames, but I was glad of at least some protection from the wind and rain. A nice fire in the stone fireplace that once warmed the watchmen would have been even better. As so often there is some dispute about island history, a local guide book of 1874 by a Mr Fox saying that the hut had been built by his grandfather for the added comfort of picnic parties.

On the site of the hut was once a medieval chapel dedicated to St Michael the Archangel, the patron saint of mariners. It's likely that a light was placed in the tower as a beacon and warning to ships. Burgh Island is another with a strong religious past, a monastic community living here in the 14th century, their monastery probably on the most sheltered site of the current hotel.

From the hut I continued my walk along the path that skirts the 'public' side of the island. Far below are tiny rocky coves, mostly inaccessible to all but the island's birds and an occasional seal. In one of the coves there was once a 'Jacob's ladder' leading down to the beach, which was used as the escape route by the murderer in Agatha Christie's *Evil Under the Sun* that was set on Burgh Island. At the outset of war the ladder was removed by the army to prevent secret German landings. Also set on the island was Christie's most successful novel, *And Then There Were None,* which sold over 100 million copies, making it one of the world's best selling novels. The book has had three titles, the original of *Ten Little Niggers* not surprisingly had to be changed, but its replacement of *Ten Little Indians* was soon considered as hardly suitable either.

A tiny and precarious path goes to 'Little Island', which is not actually an island, being linked by a narrow ridge. With almost vertical sides dropping to rocks below there was no way I would be making the crossing. Beyond here is a rocky tidal islet, not named but with some vegetation.

The rocks around the island have brought the end of many a ship, often when seeking shelter in Bigbury Bay but finding their anchors could not hold them. Perhaps the most famous was the *Chanteloupe,* which had just returned from the West Indies when it ran onto the island's rocks. Her crew perished and her cargo fell into the hands of villagers. According to local legend, among the wreckage on the beach a young girl found a wealthy lady still alive and wearing fine jewellery. She ran home to tell her parents who told her to leave the lady to them. A week later the lady was found by walkers, her two ring fingers and ear lobe removed and a knife embedded in her stomach.

Back at the hotel, my island circuit completed, I noticed the electric gates opening. Several workmen were busy in the grounds and whilst it was tempting to slip in for a quick look, I thought better of it. Privacy is clearly guarded but at least unlike Osea Island, the owners allow public access to some of the island. Like Osea however, a helicopter pad indicates the sort of guests who may stay here.

Regrettably therefore my information on the hotel is not first hand, but from that sent to me by Deborah Clark, Tony Porter's book, Burgh Island website, Chips Barber's *Burgh Island and Bigbury-on-Sea* and David St John Thomas's *Remote Britain.* This is an island where information was not hard to find.

The island was once known as St Michael's, after the chapel on its summit. This changed to Chapel of St Michael de la Burgh after the de Burgh family bought it. For a short time it was referred to as Borough Island, but soon reverted to Burgh Island (pronounced 'burr'), although another suggested derivation is from 'burrow' due to the large rabbit population.

In 1895 the island was bought from a local farmer by George Chirgwin the music hall singer known as the 'White-Eyed Kaffir', who built a wooden hotel which still stands today as the staff house. The current hotel was built by the very wealthy Archie Nettleford, who had purchased Burgh Island in 1925 with his fortune partly made from supplying munitions in the First World War. He was the 'N' in the giant firm GKN.

Commissioned to build a palace to suit Archie's theatrical taste, architect Matthew Dawson faced the problem of getting building materials to the island. This was solved by using the trendy new material, concrete, mixed on the spot. Locals were furious. They regarded Burgh Island as theirs and didn't like the idea of the building in the first place, but news of its proposed construction in the new-fangled concrete brought objections and petitions. The building however went ahead, with the design intended to create the appearance of a castle. Work was completed in 1929 and Archie furnished the hotel throughout with fashionable art deco design. Initially just his friends received invites, but after a few years Archie's Great White Palace became a hotel. Guests enjoying the sunshine, sea and 'palm court atmosphere', included Noel Coward, Edward and Mrs Simpson, Agatha Christie, Malcolm Campbell and Amy Johnson.

During World War Two the hotel was requisitioned by the MoD and was reputedly the location for covert meetings between Churchill and Eisenhower. In 1942 however, its north wing was badly damaged by a German bomber which may have been dropping unused bombs on returning from a raid over Plymouth, rendering the hotel unusable. There is a rumour, albeit it unsubstantiated, that Churchill and Eisenhower had been playing cards in one of the destroyed rooms just a week before. As with the Vikings on Northey Island, had circumstances been only slightly different a tidal island might have been at the centre of an event that could have changed the whole course of our nation's history.

After the war the island was bought by Captain Keith Anderson and his wife, the last white Maharaja and Maharani of Sarawak. They repaired the hotel and for a short while it thrived as a beach resort and 'The Best Hotel

West of the Ritz'. After Captain Anderson died in 1955 the hotel became derelict until George Goss, a local businessman, bought the island with plans to market it as 'Ventura – land of adventure and mystery'. His guests self-catered, with small kitchenettes added to the rooms, which the next owners Tom and Sue Waugh continued in the 1970s, the island's only time as a family holiday destination.

The hotel that Tony and Beatrice Porter took over in 1986 was derelict. They had given up their successful careers as London fashion consultants, sold their house and boat, and persuaded the bank to back them as they put all they had into the island. It was hard work and several times almost failed when funds ran out, but over several years the hotel was restored to its 1930s art deco heyday. Once again the ballroom saw dancing, cocktails and fine dining.

Tony Porter tells many of stories of his time on the island and three I shall retell here:

On one occasion *Vogue* magazine held a conference at the hotel, most of the twenty attending being smart young girls. A pianist was employed to play at lunchtime and evening, but he was free to enjoy the island for the rest of the day. One sunny afternoon some of the girls took a walk around the island and returned giggling. Tony asked what was so funny. Apparently one of the girls had strayed from the path into long grass to get a better view with her camera and tripped over a man lying there – and he was wearing just a hat! The pianist was popular that evening and kept a straight face. Only when he took his bow at the end of the evening and as he looked in the direction of one particular young lady, did he allow himself a smile!

Couples often came to the hotel on honeymoon, but one lady wrote to say how Burgh Island had brought her and her husband together. In 1949 she and three friends had been on holiday in Devon and took a boat trip out to sea from the River Dart. Finishing a bottle of lemonade, they decided to write their names and addresses inside and throw it into the sea. A few months later a young serviceman who had broken his ankle, was taken out from hospital to exercise on Bigbury beach. Bobbing in the water by the island he found the bottle and picking one of the names inside wrote to Joyce. They were married five years later and frequently returned to the island that had brought them together.

Burgh Island has its fair share of tide related stories, some near disasters and some amusing. Of the latter Tony tells of an occasion when for a wedding at Bigbury church the whole hotel was booked for the nights before and after the ceremony. Having stayed in separate suites and avoided each other at breakfast, the bride returned to sort out hair, make-up and so forth, while the groom took the guests to the Pilchard Inn for drinks then onto the church. The tide was in when it was time for Sophie the bride to leave, so dressed for the marriage, she and her father carefully climbed into the sea tractor. Halfway across it came to a halt. A hydraulic pipe had burst and there was no way it could be moved. Sophie was told that she had two choices; she could wait an hour for the pipe to be repaired or they could call the safety boat. She chose the latter and as the boat was brought alongside Tony suggested that she should now climb down the steps into the boat. 'Not in this bloody dress I'm not' she retorted. Now Sophie was a stunning bride; six foot tall, blonde and a model, but fortunately she was also great fun. Without hesitating she peeled the dress off over her head and climbed into the boat. The greatest surprise however was that Sophie didn't believe in bras and her wedding day was no exception. To cheers from those gathered on the shore, photographers snapping away and with Tony doing his best to hide her embarrassment behind a towel, Sophie was brought to the mainland holding the dress high above her head. The next day a saucy photo of her rather unconventional arrival was published in one of the tabloids under the headline 'Get Me to the Church on Tide'!

Chips Barber writes of another occasion when the sea tractor broke down. Thirteen passengers were marooned part way to the island and the Bantham lifeboat summoned. With the tractor rocking about in the surf the children and elderly passengers were transferred to the boat and a human chain formed to help the others ashore. On another occasion the sea tractor capsized when a wheel sank in a pothole and the driver, who fortunately was the only person on board, was rescued by canoeists. Like all the tidal islands one can drive to, Burgh Island has its tales of cars lost in the sea. In 1996 the Jones family from London arrived in their brand new Renault Laguna, but with the tide rising got stuck in soft sand. Attempts to reverse failed and when the engine cut out the family quickly scrambled out to safety. Despite a local farmer gallantly driving his tractor into the swirling waves, the tow bar could not be located and in a matter of minutes the car disappeared beneath the sea.

In 2001 Tony and Beatrice decided that it was time to sell the island. Tony Orchard and Deborah Clark had stayed here many times and been married on the island (by now it had a Civil Marriage Licence and Tony Porter had kissed more than 200 brides who'd wedded here). Hearing of their interest the Porters were delighted to sell to the newly married couple, who promised to invest without spoiling what had already been done. When the Porters arrived the hotel was derelict with a couple of unofficial caretakers. Fifteen years later they sold a beautiful hotel – a thriving business with over thirty staff. True to their word Deborah and Tony spent over £3 million in 7 years, upgrading the rooms and increasing their number to 25. The suites as they prefer to call them, are named after local landmarks or characters from the island's history – Eddystone, Avon, Mermaid, Christie, Amy Johnson, Formby and Noel Coward all reflect the setting and ambience of this remarkable art deco hotel.

David St John Thomas and his wife Sheila stayed at many excellent hotels around the UK as they travelled for *Remote Britain* and *Journey Through Britain*, but Burgh Island was their most expensive night ever. David writes that it was undoubtedly worth it and describes the exclusive hotel that many admire from the beach but only a select few will get to see inside:

*'Capitalising on the way it caught the imagination and created a marvellous marketing opportunity, current owners Tony Orchard and Deborah Clark have restored and developed it in its original art deco style. The result is that probably even London's Ritz or Claridges do not have such a pool of would-be British patrons waiting for a special occasion or other excuse to visit, albeit mostly only for a single night.*

*The whole hotel is wonderfully of a piece, consistently art deco, everything with angular and triangular furniture and decorations. The co-ordinated detail is splendid. Our restful bedroom has recessed pelmet lighting, and a dressing table of unimaginable curiosity. The bathroom has an octagonal stepped basin and loo, with period taps. There are many delightful touches throughout the hotel; nothing shoddy or in need of updating from the point of utility. It is wonderfully and consistently off beat art deco.'*

Perhaps it's as well though that we didn't find the funds to stay. To me 'dressing for dinner' means replacing jeans or shorts with casual trousers and putting on a clean T-shirt. The hotel's website advises that on

Wednesday and Saturday nights black tie and evening dress is 'de rigueur'. On other nights, whilst there are no rules, they like guests to wear 'something glamorous'. Perusing the menu I could find not one dish that I would choose; oysters, avocado, venison, chestnut lentils and beetroot puree are not my cup of tea; qunioa lemon, girolle, walnut quince, colcannon and sesame togarishi, I haven't a clue what they are.

Where possible food is sourced locally and meat is free range. Given these commendable ethical and environmental policies, I was somewhat surprised to see foie gras on the menu, which is produced by what most consider the cruel practice of force-feeding geese. I queried this with Deborah who responded;

*'Foie gras – no, of course it's not ethically certified but the production methods are not, I assure you, cruel or as tortuous as you might think. I have a (very small) place in the Dordogne where a large part of the local economy is predicated on the production of foie gras and have taken several inspection tours of the farms and seen the production methods myself. I do not have any ethical issues on the artisan farming of the geese, and I can assure you that they are not cooped up in "battery" type conditions but reared in small units in the open by family-run operations.'*

Compassion in World Farming (www.ciwf.org.uk) state that the consensus of expert opinion considers that force-feeding for foie gras, which is banned in many countries including the UK, is a serious welfare problem. Intensive production involves battery caged ducks or geese having a tube inserted into the gullet with a mechanised system delivering a mixture of boiled maize and fat so fast that one person can force-feed up to 500 birds an hour. The bird is slaughtered after 2 to 3 weeks and its liver, which has enlarged by up to ten times normal size so that its ability to walk may be severely impaired, is then consumed as this 'luxury food'. I don't doubt Deborah's assurance that the foie gras served on Burgh Island is not produced in the worst conditions, but there's no way that I would eat it, or indeed patronise a restaurant where it is served.

Lunch at the Pilchard Inn proved to be rather a disappointment – an expensive bowl of a rather strange apple and celery soup, with a meagre portion of French bread. The East European barman was polite enough but hardly the genial host one might expect in such a location. Two other couples ate in silence. Background music of *Alexander's Ragtime Band* would have been more suited to the art deco hotel than the tiny 14th century pub; (the sign which was repainted by Beatrice Porter – and could do with another coat now – says 1336, however Tony recalls seeing a photo with another sign stating 1395). It was however warm and dry inside, and maybe I'd not come at the best time as a certificate on the wall listed it as one of the top 50 in the *Rough Pub Guide 2008*:

> '*A roaring log fire, foaming nut-brown ale, tales of resident ghosts and smugglers and a brimy moat between you and civilisation. Certainly beats your local harvester.*'

Lunch completed, I found that the rain had stopped, so in slightly better light repeated my walk around the island and re-took another set of photos. My flower in the sand was still there on the beach, and in the other direction Eddystone Lighthouse could be seen far away across the sea.

With time to spare I walked along the beach towards the River Avon, first scrambling over rocks by the island to see if I could get a look at the Mermaid Pool. This tidal pool is available only for the use of hotel guests. A wall holds back the water and walking round the island below the low cliff I wondered if it might be possible to climb the rocks and get a quick look. The climb however wouldn't be easy and another of the island's 'Private' signs kept me off.

Although the rain had stopped the strong wind remained, whipping up foaming breakers. I counted more than fifty wetsuit clad surfers enjoying their sport, with the English Channel waves rivalling those on the more famous north coast surfing beaches. Two gentlemen in waders stood more sedately fishing in the River Avon. The river can be waded at low tide and there are superb coastal walks on this part of the South Devon coast, but with a train booked back to London my time was limited. I turned back at the river, walking along the beach enjoying the famous view of Burgh Island.

Back on the mainland I stopped to admire my flower in the sand and noticed that the Venus beach café was open. Still hungry after my disappointing lunch, a bacon roll seemed an entirely suitable way to end my visit. Finding that they open every day of the year and that I could have had an entire breakfast in a bun, plus chips, I wished I'd eaten here rather than the Pilchard Inn. Standing on the cliff in gentle rain I looked back across to the island and reflected.

My island odyssey was over. I'd made it to all 43 tidal islands and whilst each one had been enjoyable and special in its own way, now I felt a sense of disappointment. It wasn't just that the travels were over, but that Burgh Island hadn't quite been the high point on which I'd hoped to end. The weather hadn't helped, but I think it was more than this. Maybe as I'd been here before in sunshine, it didn't seem so special on a wet November day. Parking opposite the island, so arriving with no sense of journey was perhaps a factor. The main reason however was probably one of disappointment that whilst I'd seen the cliffs and coves of one side of Burgh Island, something was missing – the real story of the island, the hotel, its grounds and mermaid pool were out of bounds. I had looked from outside, read what others had written, but unlike most of the islands, I hadn't really got to know it. Perhaps one day we will come back and stay here and perhaps then I'll rewrite this final chapter.

As the train took me back to London I thought of all the islands I'd visited and started to compose thoughts for my final chapter of reflections. One thing was sure though. When I finished my Essex Coast Walk the first thing I wrote was that I'd like to turn round and do it all over again. As we pulled into Paddington on a damp winter evening I'd only too gladly have waited on Platform One, caught the sleeper back to Cornwall, and started once more at St Michael's Mount. One day!

# REFLECTIONS

I've already lost count of the number of times people have asked me which was my favourite island. It's a question I just can't answer. There were 43 islands, but all so different. Never did I visit an island and think that it resembled another one. And of course I saw each island only once, a snapshot in time of a very long history. The time of year, weather and even my mood will have affected my views of each island. What I shall do however is pick out ten highlights:

The semi-tropical gardens nestled under the castle on St Michael's Mount.

The expanse of Rhossili Bay with tidal islands at each end.

The spectacular cliffs of West Wales and Ynys Lochtyn (but not climbing down them!).

The guided walk across Morecambe Bay to Chapel Island.

Eating a bacon roll cooked by the King of Piel as I watched the little ferry boats ply back and forward.

Ardwall Island at minus ten degrees in the January snow, with the sun shining over Fleet Bay and surrounding snow clad hills.

The painting of Christ's crucifixion in a Davaar Island cave.

The stunningly beautiful Loch Moidart, sheltering the castle of Eilean Tioram and lovely Shona Beag with its own tree covered tidal islets.

The walk across Morrich Mhor and the secret beach beyond Innis Mhor.

Walking around Mersea Island – a microcosm of my much loved Essex coast.

How can I pick a favourite?

Our coast is never still. Wind, waves and currents are constantly changing the coastline and our tidal islands, which with their delicate balance between sea and land are particularly vulnerable. Sandy islands like Innis Mhor and Scolt Head are gradually moving. The salt marshes of Essex's islands are a dynamic feature, slowly eating into the land, sometimes with human help to provide sustainable barriers to the sea. The soft rock of Hilbre and Piel islands is eroding and the mud of Chiswick Eyot would have been washed away had a wall not been built around it. Mankind is working to protect islands, but globally it is our actions that are changing climate, raising sea levels and causing more storms that eat away at the coast.

It's not just our islands that are threatened, but also the creatures and plants that live on them. As we continue to use the Earth's precious resources without thought to what will happen when they are gone, and to release carbon at a rate the planet cannot sustain, we threaten the very existence of so many species. It is not just the iconic creatures – the polar bear or the whale who will be lost – but a whole host of seemingly insignificant but interdependent species. On Skippers Island it's not only the sea hogs fennel that will die out if it cannot be established away from rising sea water, but the dependant fisher's estuarine moth which will disappear with it. How many more examples are threatened around our coast and islands?

Perhaps greater than the physical changes to the islands are the human changes. Islands that were once isolated settlements or farms have reverted to nature. Some have been left to run wild as nature chooses, others are carefully managed promoting biodiversity and wildlife, and a few now cater mainly for tourists. A dozen or so are still inhabited, but most are now home to just the diverse and often plentiful wildlife that lives around our coast.

It has been interesting to compare the way our attitudes to wildlife have changed. No longer do we shoot seals for fear they spoil the salmon fishing, slay otters lest they compete for fish, take pot shots at porpoises, or put a lost deer in a zoo. Sadly however some people still pursue wildlife for 'sport', taking perverse pleasure in the slaughter of noble beasts.

Mostly we have learned that for wildlife to thrive it needs to be free from human disturbance. Few now expect to walk amongst brooding terns and our tidal islands provide many protected areas where birds may breed. Restriction of access to Skippers, Scolt Head, Foulney and the Langstone Harbour islands has allowed bird numbers to rise, but ironically at Rough Island, supposedly a bird sanctuary, human disturbance means that they choose to breed elsewhere. Our islands provide peaceful refuges for wildlife, often making them places that birds will choose above the busier mainland coast.

I was always happy to keep off islands or specific areas if those entrusted with managing them for nature conservation believed that this was necessary for the sake of wildlife. As you will have gathered, I was less happy to be barred from islands where the owners simply wished to keep them private for themselves or their guests. Our islands are a national treasure and should be accessible to all. Does having enough money to buy an island give the owners of Osea and St Catherine's the moral right to stop the general public from enjoying these historic and beautiful islands? Burgh Island shows that there is room for compromise, an exclusive hotel but access for all on the rest of the island.

Burgh Island hotel was beyond my means, but it was interesting to stay at a variety of hotels, guest houses and B&Bs around our coast. Almost without exception their owners and staff were friendly and most passed my very simple quality test – would I return there if staying in the area again? Often I found that the facilities in a small guest house or B&B were at least equivalent to larger hotels, but with a more friendly and personal touch, and a considerably lower price. It is rarely easy to choose accommodation. Sometimes the establishment's website requires a degree of interpretation – I've learned through experience that when a large city centre hotel is described as 'Victorian' this might mean that was the last time it was painted, that there is invariably a good reason if the only photos are of the interior, and that 'convenient location' often equates to noisy. Rarely is there a place where all the internet reviews are positive (although I found one in Dumfries) and again interpretation is required to determine whether guests are unreasonably picky or if the faults are real. Personal recommendation is generally the best guide, so I hope the various comments I've included may be of assistance to anyone wishing to follow my footsteps to tidal islands – but please don't blame me if you don't agree!

I'd hoped that my travels would show that much of our coast and most of our tidal islands can be visited by public transport – train, bus and walking being far less environmentally damaging than the private car. On occasions I did have to hire cars, although in most cases walking or buses could have got me to the islands had I been able to spare the time. Public transport rarely let me down. Rural buses proved to be an extremely reliable and friendly way to travel. I caught 23 buses and only once was one late – and that when the driver got lost! Trains too served me well, just 7 of 174 arriving late and with many spectacular routes that made the journey a true travel experience. I must add a word about the overnight sleepers. What a superb way this is to travel to Cornwall and Scotland. Go to sleep in London and wake up by mountains, loch or sea. Leave home in the evening and arrive next morning – it is almost as if one has travelled without taking any time. And of course walking, which was the most satisfying way to arrive by an island. To travel slowly, appreciating the gradually changing views, then suddenly get a first glimpse of a much anticipated island; to appreciate the near view, the flower, the bird or the butterfly, to breathe the fresh air and feel breeze on your face. Only on foot does one really get close to nature.

Many of the islands have religious connections with monasteries or chapels built in years gone by. Holy Island is closely linked to the history of Christianity in Britain and is still a place of pilgrimage, but other islands have a spiritual presence and almost all a sense of peace. Davaar Island is a fitting setting for Archibald MacKinnon's painting of Christ's crucifixion, its remoteness adding to the aura of the cave. One can see why medieval hermits chose tidal islands as places of refuge from the stresses of life, just as Mr Nick has found his freedom on Chiswick Eyot.

A few of the islands are well known nationally, some just locally, but others hardly seem to be noticed by anyone. Many people will see Burrow Island in Portsmouth harbour and Fort William's islands, but few realise that they are tidal islands or give them more than a second glance. Others like Eileanan nan Gad in Kentra Bay, Eilean Mor on Loch Sunart and Innis Mhor in the Dornoch Firth are isolated from population and even fewer will know they exist. It took many hours of poring over maps to find all these islands. When I mentioned my quest to islanders, wardens or locals none knew of anyone else who had visited them all. There seems to be no other book and the longest list I've found totalled no more than a dozen islands. Had someone beaten me to it I'm sure I would have found out somewhere along the way, so yes I think it is reasonable for me to claim to be the first person to visit the 43 tidal islands that can be walked to from the UK mainland.

One of the aims of my travels was to decide whether tidal islands have the character of true islands, or if their part-time status makes them in some way inferior. Those I spoke to on the likes of Mersea, Lindisfarne and Piel Islands were very clear that they consider their homes to be on islands. Talk of raising the causeways to Mersea and Holy Island elicits strong feelings from locals who remain fiercely protective of their island status. They may be regularly accessible on foot, but to those living here these are true islands. Talk is of island life and that there is a dry connection to the mainland often seems irrelevant.

Most of my visits were over one low tide, but as soon as I arrived on an island it seemed apart from the rest of the world. The feelings of remoteness, of being a special place and occasionally of a unique community, transcend the tides. Even when connected all 43 islands were not simply extensions of the mainland, but a separate and often very different place. Only on St Michael's Mount, Skippers and Holy Island did I stay over while the tide was high, but here I felt even more remote. Being used to the convenience and flexibility of town life it was a strange feeling on Holy Island to know that whatever my needs, there was no way I could get to a late night shop or travel home until the tide fell. When the causeway was covered Holy Island became a quieter and even more tranquil island, but with its flotilla of little ferry boats it was the view rather than the people that changed on St Michael's Mount. On Skippers Island I was truly cut off, reliant on Ray Marsh to ferry me back or to guide me over the mud.

With such varied islands it's hard to generalise, but yes I conclude there are differences between tidal and true islands, but often these are quite small. A tidal island is far more akin to a true island than it is to an area of mainland, even a remote peninsular. Tidal islands though are very special places – each one of them different. Many with remarkable history, interesting and amusing human stories and abundant wildlife. All beautiful in their different ways. Each one I would like to walk to again. And for those of us wary of the 'Farne Island bucket', each can be visited with 'no boat required'.

# APPENDIX 1

# LIST OF TIDAL ISLANDS

The following islands meet my definition of tidal and were all visited, although for one I was only able to climb onto the edge of the island.

| | | |
|---|---|---|
| An Caol | Loch Linnhe (Fort William) | Chapter 14 |
| Ardwall Isle | Fleet Bay (Dumfries & Galloway) | Chapter 12 |
| Barlocco Isle | Fleet Bay (Dumfries & Galloway) | Chapter 12 |
| Burgh Island | Bigbury, South Devon | Chapter 27 |
| Burrow Island (Rat Island) | Portsmouth Harbour (Hants) | Chapter 26 |
| Burry Holmes | Rhossili Bay (South West Wales) | Chapter 3 |
| St Catherine's Island | Tenby (South West Wales) | Chapter 4 |
| Cei Ballast (Ballast Island) | Porthmadog (North Wales) | Chapter 6 |
| Chiswick Eyot | River Thames, London | Chapter 25 |
| Cramond Island | Firth of Forth (Edinburgh) | Chapter 17 |
| Chapel Island | Ulverston (Morecambe Bay) | Chapter 8 |
| Davaar Island | Campbeltown (Kintyre) | Chapter 13 |
| Foulney Island | Barrow-in-Furness (Cumbria) | Chapter 9 |
| Eileanan nan Gad | Kentra Bay (Ardnamurchan) | Chapter 14 |
| Ynys Gifftan | Talsarnau (North Wales) | Chapter 6 |
| Hestan Island | Dumfries & Galloway | Chapter 11 |
| Hilbre Island | Dee Estuary (Wirral) | Chapter 7 |
| Horsey Island | Hamford Water (Essex) | Chapter 20 |
| Eilean Ighe | Arisaig (West Highlands) | Chapter 14 |
| Innis Mhor | Dornoch Firth (NE Scotland) | Chapter 16 |
| Holy Island of Lindisfarne | Beal (Northumberland) | Chapter 18 |
| Little Eye | Dee Estuary (Wirral) | Chapter 7 |
| Ynys Lochtyn | Cardigan Bay (West Wales) | Chapter 5 |
| St Mary's Island | Whitley Bay (Northumberland) | Chapter 19 |

# APPENDIX 2

# SOME 'NEARLY TIDAL ISLANDS'

The following 'islands' failed to meet my definition for various reasons. Some were visited, some not, but are all mentioned in the chapters shown.

| | | |
|---|---|---|
| Eilean Buidhe | Craobh Haven, NW Scotland | Chapter 13 |
| Canvey Island | Thames Estuary, Essex | Chapter 20 |
| Cat Craig | Fleet Bay, Dumfries & Galloway | Chapter 12 |
| Ceann na Creig | West Loch Tarbert, W Scotland | Chapter 13 |
| Crain y Gwbert | Cardigan, West Wales | Chapter 5 |
| Eilean na Craoibhe | Fort William, NW Scotland | Chapter 14 |
| Danna Island | Tayvallich Peninsula, W Scotland | Chapter 13 |
| Deadmans Island | Medway Estuary, Kent | Chapter 26 |
| Eilean Donan | Loch Alsh, NW Scotland | Chapter 15 |
| Dova Haw | Barrow-in-Furness, Morecambe Bay | Chapter 9 |
| Eilean nan Gamhainn | Plockton, NW Scotland | Chapter 15 |
| Foulness | Thames Estuary, Essex | Chapter 20 |
| Garvellan Rocks | Fleet Bay, Dumfries & Galloway | Chapter 12 |
| Glen Isle | Kippford, Dumfries & Galloway | Chapter 11 |
| Headin Haw | Barrow-in-Furness, Morecambe Bay | Chapter 9 |
| Hogmarsh Island | Stour Estuary, Essex | Chapter 20 |
| Holme Island | Grange-over-Sands, Morecambe Bay | Chapter 10 |
| Hoo Island | Medway Estuary, Kent | Chapter 26 |
| Horsey Island | North Devon | Chapter 27 |
| Long Island | Langstone Harbour, Hampshire | Chapter 26 |
| The Murray Isles | Fleet Bay, Dumfries & Galloway | Chapter 12 |
| Newquay Island | Newquay, Cornwall | Chapter 27 |
| North Binness | Langstone Harbour, Hampshire | Chapter 26 |
| Oldany Isle | Assynt, NW Scotland | Chapter 16 |
| Pilsey Island | Langstone Harbour, Hampshire | Chapter 26 |
| Porth Island | Newquay, Cornwall | Chapter 27 |

# APPENDIX 3

# BOOKS FROM WHICH INFORMATION SOURCED

The following books and booklets all provided information on the islands and nearby coast. A few other books which I did not purchase also provided information, and these are credited in the text.

*137 Steps The Story of St Mary's Lighthouse*, North Tyneside Council, 1998

*A Short History of Mersea*, Elsie M. Karbacz, Mersea Island Museum Trust, 1980

*After All*, Norman Angell, Farrar, Straus & Young (USA), 1951

*Burgh Island and Bigbury-on-Sea*, Chips Barber, Obelisk Publications, 1998

*Castle Tioram in Moidart*, Christian Aikman, Booklet reprinted 1999

*Cramond Island*, John Dods, Cramond Heritage Trust

*Davaar Island*, James P. Hynes, J.P. Hynes, 2000

*Hilbre The Cheshire Island*, J.D. Craggs, Liverpool University Press, 1982

*Islands of Essex*, Ian Yearsley, Ian Henry Publications, 1994

*Island of Terns*, Bob Chestney, Quiller Press, 1993

*Journey Through Britain*, David St John Thomas, Frances Lincoln, 2004

*Lindisfarne Castle*, The National Trust, 1999

*Lindisfarne Priory*, Joanna Story, English Heritage, 2005

*Nature Conservation in Hounslow*, David Pape, London Ecology Unit

*On a Galloway Island*, Revd. Beryl M. Scott, 2003

*Remote Britain*, David St John Thomas, Frances Lincoln, 2010

*Shell Guide to Scotland*, Moray McLaren, Ebury Press, 1965

*St Michael's Mount*, John St. Aubyn, John St. Aubyn, 2004

*Tales of Piel Island*, Jack Nicholson, Jack Nicholson, 2004

*The Scottish Islands*, Hamish Haswell-Smith, Canongate Books Ltd, 1996

*The Great White Palace*, Tony Porter, Transworld Publishers, 2002

*The Solway Firth*, Brian Blake, Robert Hale Ltd, 1955

*Walks on Holy Island*, Chrissie Anderson, Rural Arts, 2009

# ALSO BY THE AUTHOR

## ESSEX COAST WALK

When Peter Caton set out to walk the Essex coast he had no idea of the beauty, wildlife and stories that he would find on the way. He takes the reader up and down the many creeks and estuaries of the longest coastline of any English county, through nature reserves, seaside resorts, unspoilt villages, sailing centres and alongside industry past and present. On the way we read of tales of witchcraft, ghosts, smuggling, bigamy and incest. We learn of the county's varied history – stories of battles with Vikings, of invading Romans bringing elephants, a fort where the only casualty occurred in a cricket match, burning Zeppelins and of Jack the Ripper.

Whilst an entertaining narrative, not a guidebook, *Essex Coast Walk* contains a wealth of information, including many little-known facts and stories. With gentle humour to match the coastline's gentle beauty, and illustrated with photographs and maps, the book makes for easy reading. It tells of the solitude of the most remote coastal areas in England and of the huge range of wildlife to be found here. In contrast we read of the docks and industry of the Thames, but find that even here there is beauty for those willing to look.

The book highlights how climate change may alter our coast and looks at new methods of coping with rising sea levels. It tells us how tiny settlements grew into large holiday resorts and how other villages have remained as unspoilt and isolated communities.

The author's thought provoking final reflections consider how the coast has changed over the centuries and what its future may be.

Written in an accessible style, *Essex Coast Walk* has been enjoyed not only by those living in the county, but by others who have been surprised to read of the beauty and history of this little known part of our coast.

£9.99 376 PAGES  ISBN 9781848761162  Published by Matador